Architectures of Emergency in Turkey

Architectures of Emergency in Turkey

Heritage, Displacement and Catastrophe

Edited by
Eray Çaylı, Pınar Aykaç, and Sevcan Ercan

I.B. TAURIS
LONDON • NEW YORK • OXFORD • NEW DELHI • SYDNEY

I.B. TAURIS
Bloomsbury Publishing Plc
50 Bedford Square, London, WC1B 3DP, UK
1385 Broadway, New York, NY 10018, USA
29 Earlsfort Terrace, Dublin 2, Ireland

BLOOMSBURY, I.B. TAURIS and the I.B. Tauris logo are trademarks of Bloomsbury Publishing Plc

First published in Great Britain 2022
This paperback edition published 2023

Copyright © Eray Çaylı, Pınar Aykaç, Sevcan Ercan, 2022

Eray Çaylı, Pınar Aykaç, Sevcan Ercan and contributors have asserted their right under the Copyright, Designs and Patents Act, 1988, to be identified as Authors of this work.

Copyright Individual Chapters © 2021 Eray Çaylı, Pınar Aykaç, Sevcan Ercan, Murray Fraser, Banu Pekol, Herdem Doğrul, Emre Özyetiş, Merve Bedir, Mesut Dinler, Jane Rendell

For legal purposes the Acknowledgements on p. xiv constitute an extension of this copyright page.

Series design by Adriana Brioso
Cover image: Sulukule, Istanbul, Turkey, 2014. (© Kate Geraghty/The Sydney Morning Herald/Fairfax Media/Getty Images)

All rights reserved. No part of this publication may be reproduced or transmitted in any form or by any means, electronic or mechanical, including photocopying, recording, or any information storage or retrieval system, without prior permission in writing from the publishers.

Bloomsbury Publishing Plc does not have any control over, or responsibility for, any third-party websites referred to or in this book. All internet addresses given in this book were correct at the time of going to press. The author and publisher regret any inconvenience caused if addresses have changed or sites have ceased to exist, but can accept no responsibility for any such changes.

A catalogue record for this book is available from the British Library.

A catalog record for this book is available from the Library of Congress.

ISBN: HB: 978-1-7883-1989-8
PB: 978-0-7556-4532-9
ePDF: 978-1-7883-1990-4
ePub: 978-1-7883-1991-1

Typeset by Deanta Global Publishing Services, Chennai, India

To find out more about our authors and books visit www.bloomsbury.com and sign up for our newsletters.

Contents

List of Figures	vi
List of Contributors	vii
Foreword *Murray Fraser*	xi
Acknowledgements	xiv

1 Introduction: The material and spatial politics of emergency
   Eray Çaylı 1

2 The mutual construction of heritage and emergency: Neo-Ottomanist heritage policies in 2010s Turkey *Pınar Aykaç* ... 21

3 Destabilizing national heritage: Preserving Turkey's non-Muslim architectural heritage *Banu Pekol* 43

4 Emergency as normalcy in mid-2010s Amed/Diyarbakır
   Eray Çaylı and Herdem Doğrul 69

5 *Forum* in relation to the polis: The case of I.39 and Turkey
   Emre Özyetiş 89

6 Between the guests and the hosts: Spaces of illegalized migration in Turkey *Merve Bedir* 113

7 The politics of normalcy: Examining the festival on the island of Imbros/Gökçeada *Sevcan Ercan* 137

8 Coda: Establishing authority over historic areas under emergency *Mesut Dinler* 159

After the emergency? *Jane Rendell* 189

Bibliography 201
Index 223

Figures

3.1	Church at Ambar, Mardin, 2018	48
3.2	Church at Ambar, Mardin, 2018	49
3.3	Agia Paraskevi Church, Bursa, 2016	50
3.4	Agia Paraskevi Church, Bursa, 2016	51
3.5	Church of Surp Stephanos, Kayseri, 2015	53
3.6	Saint Garabed Monastery, pre-1915	54
3.7	Portugal Synagogue, 2016	56
3.8	Signage at the church at Ferhatlı, Adana, 2015	57
3.9	Signage at the Church of the Holy Trinity, Kayseri, 2015	58
3.10	Church from Varagavank monastery complex, Van, 2012	60
6.1	Berlin–Baghdad Railway, c. 1850	120
6.2	Nusaybin Tent City, June 2013. Capacity: 2,000 tents and 6,000 people	122
6.3	Harran Container City, January 2013. Capacity: 2,000 container units and 13,540 people	123
6.4	Nizip Hospitality Centre ID Card	123
6.5	Drawings of a container unit, 2013. Karmod technical catalogue	125
6.6	Photo of Nizip Hospitality Centre from the nearby hill	126
6.7	Plan of The Kitchen, 2014	129
6.8	Logo of The Kitchen, 2014	130
8.1	Spatial distribution of the renewal sites	166
8.2	Fener and Balat	167
8.3	Helmuth von Moltke's 1837 Istanbul map	168
8.4	Fener and Balat in Helmuth von Moltke's 1837 Istanbul map	169
8.5	Masonry houses in Balat District	170
8.6	The visual mapping of 'the firm behind plans to demolish historic Tarlabaşı and Fener-Balat neighbourhoods', created by *Networks of Dispossession* initiative	175

Contributors

Murray Fraser is Professor of Architecture and Global Culture in the Bartlett School of Architecture at University College London, UK. Trained both as an architect and architectural historian, in 2018 he received the RIBA Annie Spink Award for Excellence in Architectural Education. He is General Editor of Sir Banister Fletcher's *Global History of Architecture* (21st Edition), published by Bloomsbury in 2020, and is currently also Chair of the Society of Architectural Historians of Great Britain.

Eray Çaylı, PhD (University College London, 2015), studies the spatial and visual politics of violence in Turkey, currently through their urban ecological implications. Çaylı is Leverhulme Early Career Fellow (2018–22) at London School of Economics and Political Science, where he also teaches at postgraduate level. He is the author of *Victims of Commemoration: The Architecture and Violence of Confronting the Past in Turkey* (Syracuse University Press, 2021), and guest-editor of special issues for the *International Journal of Islamic Architecture* (themed 'Field as Archive/Archive as Field') and for the *Journal of Visual Culture* (themed 'Testimony as Environment: Violence, Aesthetics, Agency'). Çaylı's articles have appeared in *Antipode*, *Environment and Planning D: Society and Space*, *International Journal of Urban and Regional Research*, and *Transactions of the Institute of British Geographers*, among other journals. In Turkey's largest predominantly Kurdish-inhabited city Amed/Diyarbakır, he has collaborated with the local Chamber of Architects and with the independent artist-run space loading to coordinate free-of-charge research workshops on urban political ecology. Çaylı's first book in Turkish, *İklimin Estetiği: Antroposen Sanatı ve Mimarlığı Üzerine Denemeler* [Climate Aesthetics: Essays on Anthropocene Art and Architecture], was published in 2020 by Everest.

Pınar Aykaç, PhD (University College London, 2017), is a conservation architect with an MSc in the Conservation of Cultural Heritage from the

Middle East Technical University. Her PhD thesis is titled 'Musealisation as an Urban Process: The Transformation of Sultanahmet District in Istanbul's Historic Peninsula' from the Bartlett School of Architecture. Aykaç was involved in various conservation projects in Turkey, including the Presidential Ataturk Museum Pavilion Conservation Project and the Commagene Nemrut Conservation and Development Programme. Her research interest is museums' role in urban regeneration and heritage politics. Aykaç was a Weinberg fellow at Columbia University's Italian Academy for Advanced Studies in America during the fall semester of 2017–18. She is currently an assistant professor at the Middle East Technical University's Department of Architecture.

Banu Pekol, PhD, works on peacebuilding and conflict transformation in relation to contested cultural heritage. Her research spans cultural heritage entailing difficult pasts and projects that develop creative and research-based results, specializing in cultural diplomacy, contested heritage interpretation and management. She has worked as a full-time assistant professor and has over a decade of experience with different cultures at numerous heritage sites. She currently works at the Berghof Foundation, on intercultural and interreligious conflict transformation and peace education. She was previously a Historical Dialogue and Accountability fellow at the Institute for the Study of Human Rights at Columbia University. Banu is a co-founder of the Association for the Protection of Cultural Heritage (KMKD), a trainer in the 2020 European Diplomatic Programme, an elected member on the Advisory Council of the Global Diplomacy Lab (2019-2021) and is a BMW Responsible Leader.'

Herdem Doğrul was born and raised in Amed (in Turkish: Diyarbakır). He is a qualified architect with a degree from Amed's Dicle University. During his undergraduate studies, Doğrul began volunteering at the local chapter of Turkey's Chamber of Architects, where he contributed to work on the *Glossary of Kurdish Architecture and Engineering Terms*. Soon after obtaining his undergraduate degree in 2013, Doğrul became a board member of the Chamber of Architects' local chapter and served as a branch secretary for two years. He spent 2016 in Kobane, participating in the effort to rebuild the city following its liberation from the Islamic State of Iraq and the Levant. Doğrul continued serving on the board of the Chamber of Architects' Amed chapter until 2020. Between June 2019 and March 2020, he worked as the director of urban planning and public works at the municipality of Silvan, a district of Diyarbakır province. He currently continues to work as a self-employed architect.

Emre Özyetiş graduated from the Middle East Technical University with degrees in architecture and philosophy in 2009 and 2010, respectively. He started doing a postgraduate degree with the RMIT University under the SIAL in 2011, which he completed in 2013 with his thesis on Manfredo Tafuri and the critique of architectural ideology. Özyetiş continues his research activities as a PhD candidate at the Middle East Technical University, working on destruction, memory and codes.

Merve Bedir is an architect based in Hong Kong/Shenzhen. Her previous research explored the relationship between urban transformation and public space, connecting architectural technologies, law and urban politics. Her current research focuses on infrastructures of hospitality and mobility and, most recently, on human and non-human relationships in the context of ecology and cybernetics. Bedir is an adjunct assistant professor in Hong Kong University's Department of Architecture, Division of Landscape Architecture, and a founding partner of Land and Civilization Compositions. She is also a co-founder of Aformal Academy (focused on experimental pedagogies in Pearl River Delta region), a founding member of Mutfak خبطم Workshop (focused on migration and kitchen as cultural space in Gaziantep), and a founding member of Center for Spatial Justice in Istanbul. Bedir holds a PhD from the Architectural Engineering Department in Delft University of Technology, and a BArch from Middle East Technical University in Ankara.

Sevcan Ercan, PhD (University College London, 2020), is a lecturer in the Faculty of Art, Design and Architecture, Istanbul Medeniyet University. She trained as an architect, receiving her BArch from Middle East Technical University, before moving further into the field of architectural history. After working on several archaeological sites and conservation projects across Turkey, Ercan relocated to London in order to pursue her MA in Architectural History followed by a PhD in Architectural History and Theory at the Bartlett School of Architecture. Her doctoral research examined the spatial histories of displacement and emplacement in relation to communities on the island of Imbros/Gökçeada in the north Aegean.

Mesut Dinler is an assistant professor at the Inter-university Department of Regional & Urban Studies and Planning in Politecnico di Torino, where he received his PhD in Architectural and Landscape Heritage Programme. He was involved in various international conservation projects including those managed by Historic Charleston Foundation with US/ICOMOS, the Getty Conservation Institute and the Association for the Protection of Cultural Heritage. Currently he is involved in the management of heritage-related research projects funded by the European Commission under its Horizon programme. His research interests include heritage-related activist movements, politics of heritage, urban history and digital humanities.

Jane Rendell (BSc, DipArch, MSc, PhD) is Professor of Critical Spatial Practice at the Bartlett School of Architecture, University College London, where she co-initiated the MA Situated Practice and supervises MA and PhD projects. Rendell has introduced concepts of 'critical spatial practice' and 'site-writing' through her authored books *The Architecture of Psychoanalysis* (2017), *Silver* (2016), *Site-Writing* (2010), *Art and Architecture* (2006), and *The Pursuit of Pleasure* (2002). With Dr David Roberts, she leads the Bartlett's Ethics Commission; and with Dr Yael Padan, 'The Ethics of Research Practice', for KNOW (Knowledge in Action for Urban Equality).

Foreword

Murray Fraser

I think that it can never be inherent in the structure of things to guarantee the exercise of freedom. The guarantee of freedom is freedom.[1]

Michel Foucault expressed these words when quizzed by an interviewer about the architectural and urban projects of Le Corbusier. Should Corbusier's work be regarded as a form of liberation or of oppression? Foucault replied by observing that Corbusier had good intentions, yet in practice his projects were not nearly as liberating as their designer might have hoped. Nor could they be, for the reason that Foucault gave.

It is a brilliant quote. Hence, just as one cannot simply enact legal structures to ensure that a condition of freedom exists, so too only the continuous open-ended observance and pursuit of architectural creativity can guarantee the required conditions for those wishing to tackle issues such as inclusion/exclusion through their designs. Intellectual and material endeavours in architecture need to be shaped in such a manner as to make this possible. Nothing can be prefigured. Everything has to be questioned. Yet what cultural practices like architecture can undoubtedly do is to examine and experiment with the conditions under which its ideas and forms are conceived and produced, which thus makes it a very real task for architecture to act also as a self-reflexive mechanism that is able to critique its own discourses and practices.

With Foucault's vivid phrase in mind – 'the guarantee of freedom is freedom', echoed by another quote from the same interview, 'liberty is a practice' – it is worth mentioning how and why this edited book of essays emerged. Its genesis came from the 'state of emergency' imposed by the president of Turkey, Recep Tayyıp Erdoğan, on 21 July 2016. Initially supposed to be for three months, it lasted until 19 July 2018, and during that time there was in parallel a brutal clampdown on academic freedoms in Turkish universities.

Greatly alarmed by this assault upon intellectual knowledge and free speech, I suggested to others that we ought to organize a symposium at the Bartlett School of Architecture, University College London. It was duly held on 19 May 2017. We titled the event 'Field as Archive/Archive as Field' and issued this following call for contributions: 'The symposium aims to create a platform for architectural researchers to reflect upon the methodological and ethical implications of conducting research in particular fields and/or archives.' We deliberately caged the description in this generic manner because we knew that any Turkish academics who might wish to take part in the symposium would find it impossible to do so if our aims were stated too openly. But in actuality we meant something very different, which was to use this event as an opportunity to examine academic repression, focusing upon Turkey but very much with the idea that this issue is deeply relevant to other countries too.

It is thus important to stress that Turkey is not being presented as sui generis: indeed, every nation in the world suffers to some degree under the kind of ideological and power distortions discussed in the essays in this book. Our decision to highlight Turkey was based on two factors: firstly, the apparent willingness of Erdoğan to act as the reckless trailblazer for the 'big bad boy' populist politics followed by the likes of Donald Trump (USA), Vladimir Putin (Russia), Jair Bolsonaro (Brazil), Narendra Modi (India) and others; and secondly, the fortunate presence at that time in the Bartlett School of Architecture of a group of exceptionally bright and committed younger scholars from Turkey, who were there either as early career academics or as PhD students. This group, spearheaded by Eray Çaylı as the most senior among them, working alongside Pınar Aykaç and Sevcan Ercan, took over the task of organizing the Bartlett symposium and then assembling the book you are about to read. They were, both then and now, more than ably assisted by some truly excellent Turkish architects and scholars living in their home country or else working abroad.

Despite our attempts to set up the symposium as carefully and subtly as we could, numerous difficulties emerged. We were very keen to include architects practising in Turkey, and one of those that we invited (Dr Senem Doyduk) was denied – twice in the same day – her legally documented right to board a plane in Istanbul to attend, clearly as part of ongoing persecution by Turkish authorities due to her involvement in community projects supporting many of the poorest and most marginalized residents of Istanbul. Instead, she joined us by online video-link – a medium now ubiquitous in the current Covid-19 pandemic, but back then symptomatic of the abrogation of legal powers by the ultra-right-wing government in Turkey.

Eray Çaylı gives a superb overview of the themes and contents of this book in his introductory chapter, discussing inter alia vital questions about cultural heritage, war-torn damage and social displacement, so I will just stress one important general point here. All of the chapters in their own differing ways talk about an epochal transformation in Turkey's recent history, one which is now very much affecting its urban and architectural practices. This change is from a situation of a laissez-faire economic boom based on runaway construction in Istanbul and other cities, as part of a surreptitious attempt by the Erdoğan faction from the early 2000s to pursue an agenda of Muslimification-cum-private-profiteering – to a new situation in which, following the 2008 global financial crash, Erdoğan's strategy has effectively collapsed and, instead, the Turkish government is retreating into a policy of dominance and violence towards the country's populace.

Those like myself who always wish to see glimmers of positivity can point to some very recent developments in Turkey that show citizens fighting back against the terrible crudity of state power, but to a very large extent the structural repressions are still in place. I cannot think of any book other than this one that holds the recent architectural and urban debates in Turkey up to the magnifying glass in such a lucid and insightful manner. We therefore need to read this book not only to find out more about Turkish conditions but also to realize how our own architectural and urban freedoms are being steadily chipped away by the socioeconomic tendency generally labelled as neoliberalism.[2] To be able to counter such forces in whatever ways we can, we clearly need to better understand what is happening on the ground. This book is a valuable contribution to that aim.

Notes

1 'An interview with Paul Rabinow', *Skyline*, March 1982 (trans. Christian Hubert), in Michel Foucault, *Power/Knowledge: Selected Interviews and Other Writings, 1972-77* (New York: Pantheon, 1980), viewable online at The Funambulist: Architectural Narratives, accessed 10 March 2013, http://thefunambulist.net/2012/06/20/foucault-episode-1-michel-foucaults-architectural-underestimation/.

2 Douglas Spencer, *The Architecture of Neoliberalism: How Contemporary Architecture Became an Instrument of Control and Compliance* (London: Bloomsbury, 2016).

Acknowledgements

The idea behind this edited volume originated in May 2017, when the co-editors organized a symposium titled 'Field as Archive/Archive as Field: Architectural Insights from Contemporary Turkey', held at the Bartlett School of Architecture, University College London. In addition to those whose contributions are published in this book, we would also like to thank Senem Doyduk and Göksun Akyürek, who presented their work at that same symposium, and Zeynep Kezer, Davide Deriu and Peg Rawes, who participated as lively and informed discussants. We are grateful to Murray Fraser for his help in securing institutional support from the Bartlett for this symposium, and for agreeing to write a Foreword for the book. We would like to also express our sincere gratitude to Jane Rendell for her Afterword. The opportunity to rethink the volume through these scholars' respective fields of expertise – heritage and globalization, particularly those within conflict-ridden contexts such as Palestine (Murray Fraser), and the interdisciplinary approach to 'critical spatial practice' and 'site-writing' (Jane Rendell) – has immeasurably enriched the contributions to this book. Eray Çaylı's work on this volume took place during a Leverhulme Trust Early Career Fellowship (ECF-2017-529).

Introduction

The material and spatial politics of emergency

Eray Çaylı

As I type this introduction, the novel coronavirus – or, officially, Covid-19 – is raging across the globe, prompting numerous governments of various persuasions to implement measures in the name of 'emergency'. Many countries are under one form of curfew or another. Where there is incompliance, the police are given powers to chase the incompliant ones back home and to fine or even detain them. Therefore, even the slightest possibility of appearing and encountering others in public space, which many theorists of democracy have considered the precondition of politics, is foreclosed. Globally, the authorities speak of staying at home as key to saving lives, obscuring the fact that domesticity, for many women and children suffering from patriarchal violence, means the exact opposite of safety and security. Whether due to their implications for domesticity or for publicness, these developments are united in reiterating the marked materiality and spatiality of the politics of emergency. They throw into sharp relief the role that the built environment plays in the politics of emergency as the latter's primary medium, rather than an auxiliary instrument that merely gives it material and spatial form.

The topic of this book is, of course, not Covid-19. Yet, its critical and analytical objectives are rendered all the timelier by current developments around the coronavirus, particularly those that highlight architecture's centrality to the politics of emergency. *Architectures of Emergency in Turkey* takes up the scholarly imperative to attend to this centrality. It, moreover, does so in an empirically grounded and context-specific manner; as the title indicates, the book focuses on contemporary Turkey. This is a particularly compelling context through which to explore the material and spatial politics of emergency. Between 2016 and 2018, Turkey was subjected to countrywide emergency rule. Throughout the same period, the country saw unprecedented levels of construction activity. Contributions to the book proceed from this combination of a full-blown emergency rule coinciding with a construction boom to ask what a focus on architecture might mean for critical analyses of the politics of emergency – a methodological question that remains underexplored in related scholarship. Based on research carried out in the mid- to-late 2010s, the contributors identify three phenomena through which to explore this question: heritage, displacement and catastrophe. Taken together, they argue that states of emergency are not merely predetermined by policy and legislation but are produced, regulated, distributed and contested through the built environment in both embodied and symbolic ways.

Emergency and normalcy in Turkey

A major body of scholarship that considers critically the relationship between emergency and normalcy revolves around the notion of exception. This critical scholarship has shown that the relationship between the exception and the rule as modes of governmentality has, throughout modern history, been one of interdependence and entanglement rather than antitheticality. Within that scholarship, a strand most pertinent to the built environment disciplines has revolved around biopolitics. This introduction evidently does not lend itself to a comprehensive survey of this strand of scholarship. But suffice it to say here that, more than any other scholar of biopolitics, it has been Agamben's notion of exception that has influenced contemporary architectural theory.[1] Following on from Foucault's theory of biopower as 'making live and letting die' (and thus, as opposed to sovereign power's focus on making die and letting live), Agamben's theory of biopolitics reconceptualized modern governmentality as the power to make live to let die meaninglessly, such that the distinction between life and death itself becomes meaningless.[2] Agamben traced this modern mode of biopolitical governmentality back to the ancient Roman figure of *homo sacer*, or sacred man, who was abandoned to oblivion, and whose murder was treated as a normalized exception as the constitution classed it neither as sacrifice nor as crime. The murder of *homo sacer* was a normalized exception in at least two ways, both because it was exceptionally devoid of legislative meaning, and because this meaninglessness was never truly an exception, given that it was constitutionally prescribed and thus always already part of the rule. Agamben's history of modern biopolitics culminated in the twentieth-century concentration camp. For Agamben, the history stretching from ancient Rome and the Holocaust saw the sort of normalized exception that characterized the treatment of *homo sacer* become increasingly prevalent. So prevalent did this normalization become as to render 'the camp' central to 'the models by which social sciences, sociology, urban studies, and architecture today are trying to conceive and organize the public space of the world's cities'.[3]

Agamben is criticizable for disregarding that the normalized-exceptional-meaningless death his history charted is, in fact, not so socially sweeping an experience as he considered it – that its workings shape and are shaped by a number of sociopolitical forces absent from his analysis, including patriarchy, racism and poverty.[4] But his architecturally resonant conclusions of the sort cited earlier might help address this very absence. In arcing from the *homo sacer* through the concentration camp to conventional models of public space, Agamben's history indicated that the normalization of the meaninglessness of the life-cum-death he charted has come to increasingly depend on material-spatial arrangements as well as legislative ones.[5] Put differently, no longer are bodies abandoned *to* meaningless life-cum-death merely by law, while still being allowed to remain within the city – within spaces paradigmatic of dominant architecture and urbanism. They are now abandoned *by* and *from* the city. A most pertinent and contemporary case in point is homelessness in the neoliberal city. Not only are the homeless excluded by law from, for instance, public space; that very spatial category has itself become conducive to rendering exclusive the fundamental practice of inhabiting the city by transforming inhabitation from the stuff of human rights or freedoms into that of commodity possession, accumulation and speculation.[6] If the normalized exceptions constituting modern biopolitics do not affect everyone equally, then physical space is not only the scene where these socially uneven effects play out. Instead, they have by now also become constitutive of the unevenness in question.

It is particularly this constitutive significance that *Architectures of Emergency in Turkey* aims to explore – an aim that responds directly to the book's empirical context. Spanning mid-to-late 2010s Turkey, this context has two defining features. The next section of this chapter will detail these features. But suffice it to introduce them here in the following way. The first feature concerns intense demolition and construction activity. While this activity gradually increased throughout the late 2000s and early 2010s, it entered a new phase in mid-2012, during the aftermath of which it reached new heights. Mid-2012 was when a piece of legislation known popularly as the Disaster Act, whose avowed aim is to disaster-proof the country, was issued. The second context-specific feature relevant to our analysis is the increasing visibility of political tension and acceleration of violence, which followed a period of purported democratization and peace in the late 2000s and the early 2010s. Here the adjective 'purported' is used advisedly; the mainstream approach to political periodization that has been at work in the case of Turkey, and that is premised on the binarisms of peace versus violence and democracy versus authoritarianism is, as detailed later, itself worthy of critical reconsideration in such a debate on emergency as that pursued in this edited volume.

Working from these two features that frame the empirical context of our study, we ask the following questions: Precisely what is architecture's role in the politics of the entanglement between normalcy and emergency? How might this politics be understood not only as operative through or aided by architecture but also as produced by it in ways that otherwise would have been unproducible or not producible with the same political effects? In exploring these questions, we take our cue not only from the larger literature on the politics of emergency but also from the more specific scholarship on related developments in contemporary Turkey. While scholarly accounts of Turkey's recent state of emergency are manifold, here I would like to focus on one by Saygun Gökarıksel and Umut Türem that I suggest is most insightful and relevant to this book's critical analytical purposes. Gökarıksel and Türem problematize the prevalent scholarly tendency to understand such states of emergency as a '"backsliding" or "retreat" from democratic gains'.[7] The authors find this tendency problematic for overlooking the ways in which liberal and illiberal methods of governance are entangled in, rather than antithetical to, one another, and for focusing narrowly on political ruptures at the expense of historical continuities that, indeed, evidence such an entanglement. Gökarıksel and Türem's alternative, as relevant particularly to the case of Turkey, is to focus on how seemingly 'exceptional' states of emergency, in fact, build on purportedly 'ordinary' precedents that have been implemented in different parts of the nation state's geography, and at different times in its history.⁸ Turkey is known to have experienced successive periods of emergency rule in one way or another since 1940; the military interventions in politics that took place in 1960, 1971, 1980 and 1997 have figured particularly prominently in relevant scholarship.⁹ But such a focus as Gökarıksel and Türem's draws attention to the various episodes of emergency rule that have taken place often outside of these periods in the predominantly Kurdish-inhabited eastern and south-eastern region of Turkey (also known unofficially as northern Kurdistan). '[S]ince the foundation of the Republic', observe Gökarıksel and Türem, these episodes of emergency rule not only have 'been more frequent, intensive, and enduring' in the region, but also have become particularly 'immobilizing and destructive' following the end in 2015 of the de facto peace talks that had been underway since the late 2000s.¹⁰

Gökarıksel and Türem's attention to the geographically and historically uneven ways in which states of emergency have been implemented in Turkey is relevant to this book for both contextual and methodological reasons. The contextual relevance is evident in the geographical and historical span of our case studies. Geographically, cases discussed in this book range from Gökçeada/Imbros and Istanbul in western Turkey, through Ankara, Niğde and Kayseri in the Anatolian heartland, to Gaziantep and Diyarbakır/Amed in the country's southeast, the very region that Gökarıksel and Türem consider most disadvantaged by the uneven distribution of emergency rule. The demographic make-up of these regions is, or has historically been, much more varied than that which is assimilable into the marker of Turk (the ethnicity of Turkey's citizens as per its constitution), including Orthodox Greeks, Armenians and Kurds. This difference has been formed by, and formative of, numerous measures implemented in the name of emergency in those regions and elsewhere in modern Turkey. To address this differential distribution of emergency, the book adopts an approach that is as cross-historical as it is geographically comprehensive. While the research and practice that constitute the empirical material of each chapter date mainly from the 2010s, the political periods and events they feature criss-cross the history of modern Turkey. The aim in so doing is to navigate those episodes of emergency that have been constituted by, and constitutive of, the marking of particular demographics as being different from Turkey's officially avowed ethnic identity.

Architectures of emergency in Turkey: Heritage, displacement and catastrophe

Two interrelated features shaped Turkey's urban and architectural affairs throughout the 2010s, the empirical context explored in this book: first, a so-called 'construction boom', and secondly, the increasing visibility of political tension and acceleration of violence. The latter feature operated against the backdrop of government-endorsed discourses and practices of democratization that had been in circulation since the mid-to-late 2000s. It was then that a project of Europeanization and democratization was instituted by the ruling AKP (Adalet ve Kalkınma Partisi; literally: Justice and Development Party) led by Recep Tayyip Erdoğan. AKP first rose to power in late 2002 and have since ruled Turkey in what has become the country's longest-ever series of consecutive majority governments by a single party since its transition to multi-party democracy in 1946. The AKP government's project of Europeanization and democratization promised to confront the troubles of the twentieth century throughout which various episodes of state-endorsed violence had targeted demographically minor or politically dissentient groups, including Kurds and Alevis.[11] This promise did initially materialize as a series of culturally oriented reforms geared towards historically marginalized populations like Kurds and Alevis, and constitutional minorities such as non-Muslims. The period, moreover, saw the government carry out what were in effect peace talks (although not formally named as such) with the Kurdistan Workers' Party (in Kurdish: *Partiya Karkerên Kurdistan*, or PKK) guerrillas, who since the 1980s have led an insurgency against the state. While limited in scope, the reforms still had wide popular appeal as they pledged to resolve some of Turkey's longest-standing sociopolitical problems.

The government instrumentalized the resulting boost in its political legitimacy for the purpose of consolidating its social and economic grip.[12] This instrumentalization manifested itself in the built environment, whether directly or indirectly.[13] Among the direct manifestations was the revamping of urban areas deemed 'historical' and 'cultural', where the history and culture in question concerned Turkey's Ottoman past, including those parts that involved the country's once-sizeable non-Muslim populations.[14] Mid-2005 saw the issuing of a new piece of legislation called Act (no. 5366) for the Protection of Dilapidated Historical and Cultural Real Estate through Protection by Renewal. The adjectives featuring in this legislation, 'dilapidated historical and cultural', in effect concealed two histories of dispossession, the first of which was triggered by nation state-building in the first half of the twentieth century, and the second, by Turkey's integration into the post-war global capitalist economy. The first history of dispossession affected non-Muslims, who had once constituted a significant part of the urban population until their being targeted through various measures geared towards their eradication from Turkey, ranging from population exchange, forced labour and unfair taxation to pogroms, massacres and genocide.[15] The second history of dispossession targeted rural populations throughout the second half of the twentieth century who – whether due to war in Kurdistan or to capitalist agriculture policies – moved to cities to become the urban poor. This latter situation occurred especially due to the lack of a social housing policy, filling in many cases the spatial vacuum left behind by the non-Muslim populations dispossessed earlier on in the century.

Therefore, what the mid-2005 legislation referred to as dilapidation was, in fact, both the product of non-Muslim dispossession and the abode of dispossessed rural-to-urban migrants, and the histories it referenced included violence, marginalization, impoverishment and lack of housing provision. As indicated in these erasures, underpinning the legislation passed in mid-2005 was a notion of 'culture' that comprised a past obscured and made distant, including that of a now-nearly-extinct non-Muslim population. This notion helped prop up the image of a Turkey democratizing and respectful of multiculturalism, while also nullifying contemporary ways of inhabiting the city such as those found among populations with a domestic migration background, excluding them from what urban culture might entail. The practical implications were drastic: inhabitants of neighbourhoods deemed 'historical and cultural', albeit 'dilapidated', were expelled in the name of the protection of such urban areas, two most notorious examples being Istanbul's Sulukule and Tarlabaşı.[16] The state's housing development agency TOKİ (Toplu Konut İdaresi; literally: Mass Housing Administration), founded in 1984 to address the earlier-mentioned and long-standing lack of a comprehensive social housing policy, was refashioned in the 2000s to facilitate this expulsion. In such places as Sulukule and Tarlabaşı as well as in many others that gradually throughout the late twentieth century had become home to the urban poor, residents were forced to relocate to settlements built by TOKİ on the peripheries of cities and were thus deprived of the livelihood they had developed in such neighbourhoods even if they managed to gain a new roof over their heads in the barest sense of the word.[17]

These developments facilitated by the 2005 legislation foreshadowed the first contextual feature I would like to unpack – Turkey's so-called 'construction boom' – and the architectonic role ascribed to historical temporality therein. A series of economic policies that sought to mitigate the negative impact which Asia's rise as the global factory made on Turkish businesses – by directing capitalist-accumulationist activities of industrially driven corporations to construction and real estate – transformed the construction sector into the foremost driver of Turkey's alleged 'economic miracle'.[18] The government aided this transformation in two ways: through publicly funded large-scale infrastructural projects such as bridges and rail transport networks, which catalysed land speculation and privatization of publicly owned lands, and by launching a comprehensive and legally stipulated episode of physical transformation across urban Turkey through a specific piece of legislation passed in May 2012: Act (no. 6306) on the Transformation of Areas under Disaster Risk, known popularly as 'the Disaster Act'.[19]

According to the government, the Disaster Act was aimed at disaster-proofing the country's building stock, following on from the experience of the violent earthquakes which devastated parts of Turkey's tectonically active northwest in 1999 and which killed nearly 20,000 and destroyed more than 150,000 buildings.[20] But its purview has not been limited to vulnerable regions or buildings. Areas redeveloped under this legislation include not just buildings and areas designated as 'risky', but also zones identified as 'safe' for new settlement.[21] This renders its scope so expansive as to make the entire country susceptible to redevelopment. Indeed, over the past five years, the authorities have declared numerous neighbourhoods in their entirety as 'urban transformation' areas to be redeveloped, often by pro-government contractors. The Disaster Act has therefore been criticized for serving 'ideological, political and economic interests' in line with the government's agenda, such as power centralization, population redistribution, conflict management and the reorganization of land-based interest groups.[22] Moreover, it has implications for the everyday lives of millions, as flat owners whose property is located in a building or area subject to redevelopment under the Disaster Act are left with two choices: either to have their property expropriated if they refuse to agree with fellow residents on the terms of their building's transformation or to engage in intense deliberation, survey and market study to try and stretch those terms as much as possible.²³ The 2005 legislation had seized control over the present by conjuring up a multicultural past whose remnants were posited as being in need of protection. The 2012 Disaster Act achieved this by invoking the threat of a catastrophic future as an imperative to replace the existing building stock with a new one whose promise was architectonic strength. This invocation has therefore misappropriated disasters' ability to overlap 'deep time' with the temporality of the the everyday – an overlap that relevant scholarship has considered capable of politicizing the everyday by transforming it into a realm where ordinary people grapple with urban and environmental injustices.²⁴ The misappropriation is that the Disaster Act's overlapping of 'deep time' with the everyday has rendered the latter not a realm of progressive socio-political transformation, but, rather, one of land speculation, dispossession and repossession.²⁵

The second feature characterizing the empirical context explored in this book is the increasing visibility of political tension and acceleration of violence. In 2011, civil war broke out in Syria, the country with which Turkey shares its longest border. Turkey's government took a side in the war in late 2011 as Erdoğan, then prime minister, called on Bashar al-Assad to quit, and soon moved from rhetoric to practice by working to facilitate his downfall: at first, this occurred indirectly through proxy forces, and then directly through Turkey's own army. By 2012, the two governments were engaging in open combat and by 2014 the number of Syrian refugees in Turkey had surpassed one million. In mid-2013 Turkey's government staged its own violent response to a wave of anti-government protests taking place in the country, which erupted in Istanbul's Gezi Park and Taksim Square and then rapidly spread across all its cities barring one. In late 2015 and early 2016, war flared up between the PKK and the state's forces in Turkey's southeast, bringing immense destruction to urban centres across the region and causing hundreds of deaths. A coup attempt took place in July 2016, ultimately failing but causing more than three hundred deaths in the process. The government followed by unleashing a witch-hunt through which it targeted not only the network led by Fethullah Gülen, the US-based cleric with whom it was on friendly terms until the coup and whom it saw as the conspiracy's plotter but also members and supporters of various political movements left of the centre, ranging from the main opposition party to the pro-Kurdish movement. It was amid these developments in 2015 and 2016 that Turkey began to witness successive periods of emergency rule proper, first in urban centres across its southeast and then, following the coup attempt, across the entire country. Countrywide emergency rule was lifted in July 2018, whereas the southeast-specific one continues in a de facto fashion, due to a blockade that remains in parts of Turkey's largest predominantly Kurdish-inhabited city.

It is this latest wave of states of emergency proper that has caused, alongside the loss of lives, thousands to be imprisoned and/or to lose their jobs and has engendered numerous critical analyses from scholars working on Turkey.[26] These analyses have been astute in identifying the geographically and historically uneven distribution of emergency measures, coupled with the longer-standing histories of marginalization targeting specific demographics that condition such unevenness. But relatively underexplored is how the states of emergency proper implemented between 2015 and 2018 may have shaped (and have been shaped by) the markedly architectural emergencies the government invoked throughout the late 2000s into the 2010s by appropriating such imperatives as preserving heritage, disaster-proofing the building stock or sheltering refugees. In using a material and spatial focus to contextualize contemporary politics of emergency in longer-standing histories of marginalization and dispossession, including those where architecture has been given a prominent role, this book aims to make a methodological contribution to recent spatially focused scholarship on Turkey. Throughout the past decade, a growing part of this scholarship has attended to how historic sites, the urban poor, and informal settlements have all been affected by neoliberal governmentality, focusing particularly on the related role of political rhetoric, ideology, collaborative relationships, local actors and agencies.[27] That is, the methodological focus has largely been on discourse, legislation and policy,[28] indicating the need for further empirical research on the material and embodied ways in which neoliberal governmentality takes effect spatially and is challenged as such.[29] To date, works that offer this sort of empirical research have remained oriented towards practice rather than critical analysis. Surveys of the practical underpinnings and consequences of urban warfare enabled by the declaration of states of emergency in Turkey's south-eastern cities between 2016 and 2018, and of socio-spatial practices of refugees and calls for their incorporation into professional architectural and urban responses to displacement, are cases in point.[30] This volume aims to contribute to these works not only by examining such practical examples critically but also by developing a unified approach to the issues around heritage, displacement and disasters they tackle separately.

Through the particular way in which it brings developments around the Disaster Act into the debates surrounding emergency rule in Turkey, *Architectures of Emergency in Turkey* aims to facilitate a twofold methodological contribution. First, it aims to problematize the avowed universalism of emergency measures, including those of an architectural character such as heritage protection and disaster-proofing thrusts, and to draw attention to their socio-politically differential effects. Secondly, situating the question of emergency in a context framed by intense destruction and construction activity enabled by the Disaster Act promises to complement existing analyses of such questions. Notwithstanding the numerous differences that set various analyses of emergency in contemporary Turkey apart from one another in terms of rhetoric and/or argumentation, the majority have tended to share a focus on legislation and policy. This sort of focus presumes the dynamics between emergency and normalcy as having already been determined prior to their being produced in ways that are bodily, interpersonal and tangible. As such, it overlooks the ways in which emergency is not only imposed on but also challenged by the populations it is said to affect. A methodological prioritization of the built environment – and thus of the embodied and materially symbolic (rather than merely discursive or legislative) ways in which normalcy and emergency are produced, regulated, distributed and contested – helps address this oversight.

Outline of the book

Contributions to this book address the oversight in question by discussing critical-spatial research in and on Turkey carried out over the past decade – the same period that has seen emergency become a major talking point in mainstream politics and the media as well as in academia, on both national and international levels. They offer insights on urban and architectural affairs which have played a structural role in Turkey throughout this period, but which have also remained absent from analyses of the country's state of emergency. These affairs include large-scale construction and infrastructural projects driving Turkey's alleged 'economic boom', urban warfare in its southeast, the implications of the influx of Syrian refugees for life in its cities and the spatial impact of populist politics on its historical minorities.

Alongside this introduction, the volume consists of six core chapters and a coda. The three themes of heritage, displacement and catastrophe that subtitle this book undoubtedly permeate all these chapters. Nevertheless, each theme figures more prominently than the other two in particular core chapters, and this prominence informs book's structure. The two chapters that follow this introduction prioritize heritage. In Chapter 2, Pınar Aykaç explores how heritage has shaped and has been shaped by the emergency footing on which the government put the country, first through the Disaster Act and then through the full-blown states of emergency declared in 2016 and 2018. She does so through the cases of the Hagia Sophia Museum and Atatürk Cultural Centre in Istanbul, and the Saraçoğlu district in Ankara. While each of these cases has its particularities – the former being a Byzantine church turned into a museum in the early Republican era, whereas the latter is a 1940s modernist housing estate – Aykaç suggests that the authorities' attitude towards both these sites shows how the focus of their neo-Ottomanist ambitions shifted amid discourses and practices associated with emergency. The shift, reveals the author, was from multiculturalism to Turkish-Islamism. Aykaç argues that this shift bolstered the emergency paradigm by exacerbating future uncertainty, but importantly, she also details how this played out differently in particular sites, the difference having much to do with longer-standing histories of nation state-building and rebuilding. In Chapter 3, Banu Pekol reflects on her recent extensive experience in the conservation of non-Muslim heritage across Turkey. Pekol reconceptualizes the notions of risk and emergency that have loomed large in Turkey's urban and architectural affairs since the early 2010s, rendering them as more than the mere technical problem to which resilience or security policies reduce them. For Pekol, such heritage sites excluded by and from nation state-building and rebuilding processes, such as those she has sought to conserve, are at risk precisely because of such policies and the technicalist approach that underpins them. Specifically, such sites, argues the author, are deprived of their authors and users through a prolonged and near-permanent state of emergency that has affected these demographics since the late nineteenth century. Taken together, chapters 2 and 3 demonstrate how heritage's significance to the politics of emergency in mid-to-late 2010s Turkey has involved not only historical representation, on which its architectural critique often focuses, but also a material register, affecting the social life and physical make-up of urban contexts in which relevant sites are located in more-than-symbolic ways.

Chapters 4 and 5 prioritize the theme of 'catastrophe' and concern Turkey's now predominantly Kurdish-inhabited southeast. Chapter 4, co-authored by Herdem Doğrul and myself, discusses the entanglement between normalcy and emergency as it has unfolded in this region's unofficial capital, the city of Diyarbakır (or, in Kurdish: Amed). The chapter focuses in particular on the wave of intense demolition and construction activity which has been taking place in the city's historic centre since the late 2000s, and which took a new turn in the early-to-mid-2010s, due both to the Disaster Act and to urban warfare that flared up between the PKK and Turkey's counter-insurgency forces. Doğrul and I argue that, whether carried out in the name of disaster resilience or that of national security, emergency policies implemented in the region ought to be contextualized within a history that is much more expansive than just the mid-2010s, meaning one that stretches back to the early twentieth-century dispossession and violence suffered by Turkey's non-Muslim populations who, in the case of Diyarbakır, constituted half of the city's population prior to their eradication in the early twentieth century and many of whom still remember this violent episode as a 'catastrophe' visited upon them. It is with such a longer-standing context in mind that we conceptualize the region's experience of emergency as a case of intra-colonization, albeit without subscribing to a hierarchy between centre and periphery that informs Foucauldian understandings of such colonization. Chapter 5 is by Emre Özyetiş. It contextualizes the recent flare-up of war between the PKK and Turkey's counter-insurgency forces in a 35-year-long history of emergency rule in the country's predominantly Kurdish-inhabited southeast, navigating towns most affected by this war such as Nusaybin, İdil, Cizre and Şemdinli. This contextualization allows Özyetiş not only to conceptualize the impact of emergency rule in the region through the democracy-related notions of forum, polis, agora and *parrhesia* (free speech), all of which have recently come to feature prominently in the spatially focused scholarship on political violence but also to rethink those very concepts through the context his chapter explores. Having done so, Özyetiş finds that the region's recent history of catastrophe throws into disarray the emphasis on speaking truth to power in and through an idealized public space that, he suggests, characterizes much of the relevant scholarship. This history, he argues, is one where catastrophe was visited on the polis, forum and agora by the emergency: not only in a political-discursive sense but also in a physical, architectural and environmental one, reshaping truth itself rather than the freedom to speak it and doing so in markedly material and spatial ways. Working in tandem, the two chapters demonstrate the analytical and political potential of rethinking policies that purport to prepare for so-called natural disasters and those that have been involved in building and maintaining ethnically based nation states through one another. It is this act of rethinking that helps grasp the interdependence between the various registers in which the violence of nation state-building operates, including epistemic, economic and urban ones, coupled with the importance of understanding what makes catastrophe catastrophic as a feature of the violent political projects within which it is wreaked or forecast.

Chapters 6 and 7 prioritize the theme of displacement. In chapter 6, Merve Bedir discusses displacement caused by the war in Syria and the waves of illegalized migration that have ensued from it. The discussion draws on Bedir's research-led architectural practice in the city of Gaziantep, which is situated near Turkey's border with Syria, and which since the mid-2010s has become a major hub for displaced peoples from the latter country. She contextualizes the emergency, which has been woven in Turkey around the displaced, within the insufficiency or lack of relevant legislation on both national and international levels. Bedir then reflects on her practice which has aimed to shift the public's gaze away from the body of the migrant towards the materialities and spatialities that condition the precarious existence of migrants. The reflection takes her readers not only through spaces commonly associated with the plight of the displaced, such as the refugee camps but also through sites of agency and solidarity, such as a kitchen set up jointly by women from Syria and Turkey. Bedir argues that the acts of solidarity unfolding in such sites reshape and even reverse the hierarchies between host and guest, both of which feature prominently in mainstream discourses and practices of refuge, rendering them conducive to the upending of the uncertainty that surrounds displacement and its treatment by authorities. In chapter 7, Sevcan Ercan explores histories of displacement and minoritization on the island of Gökçeada (or, in Greek: Imbros), the westernmost point in today's Turkey and one of its two Aegean islands historically inhabited by a predominantly Greek population, also known as the Rum. She focuses particularly on a major community festival held on the island by its Rums and attended by members of the wider Rum diaspora. Ercan charts a process in the mid-2010s whereby the festival first enjoyed unprecedented popularity and surging attendance numbers and concomitantly became the subject of emergency controls imposed by the state authorities. The chapter works from the latter set of controls to rethink the purported normalcy which preceded them, and under which the festival became more popular than ever. Festivals are by definition exceptional occasions, the author reminds us, but in the case of Gökçeada/Imbros they have also been particularly significant due to their role in constructing – materially and spatially, rather than simply through rhetoric – everyday life on the island as the normal, and continually reconstructing it as such. Ercan argues that the normalcy of the everyday in question itself was the product of a problematic exceptionalism that legitimized the hierarchies between the sociopolitical categories of minority and majority, and in so doing masked histories of marginalization involved in nation state-building in the Aegean.

Finally, a coda authored by Mesut Dinler wraps up the volume's core chapters, serving as something of a mirror image for this introduction, given that it interweaves all three themes subtitling the book. Dinler discusses the case of Fener and Balat, two of Istanbul's oldest neighbourhoods situated along the Golden Horn and within the city's historic centre. Once the epicentre of Istanbul's Jewish and Greek Orthodox communities, these neighbourhoods underwent a demographic overhaul between the late nineteenth and mid-twentieth centuries throughout which Turkey reinstituted itself as an ethnically based nation state. More recently, that is, from the 1980s onwards, a series of projects some of which had international backing, intervened in Fener and Balat in the name of protecting heritage and the environment. The two neighbourhoods were gradually transformed into one of the foremost targets of Istanbul's investors and speculators in tourism and real estate, and this transformation was given legislative impetus through the aforementioned pieces of legislation passed in 2005 (i.e., for the 'renewal' of 'dilapidated historical and cultural' areas) and in 2012 (i.e., the Disaster Act). A new wave of displacement thus began in the two neighbourhoods, one which confronted the populations that had replaced the non-Muslim communities expelled by nation state-building. The threat was partly averted by way of neighbourhood-level organizing against gentrification. Dinler asks if, and to what extent, the historical processes of displacement that took place in Fener and Balat might help us understand the threat of new ones, while also attending to the resistance that formed against the latter. In so doing, he argues that the way in which international and national approaches to historic urban environments relate to one another involves a greater degree of continuity than is often acknowledged.

In sum, although the period covered in this edited volume culminated in a state of emergency proper introduced in mid-2016, the book's contributors identify emergency as the stuff of a much longer-term spatial production and contestation, in evidence through armed conflict in and around Turkey's southeast, urban renewal schemes proclaiming to disaster-proof the country's building stock and large-scale infrastructural projects impinging on heritage sites. The chapters that follow show not only that the normalcy alleged by certain commentators to have recently plummeted in Turkey was never available to all in equal measure in the first place. They also show that emergency, seen in the context of real estate speculation catalysed by the Disaster Act, and in the new waves of displacement caused by urban warfare, is – contrary to received wisdom – rarely the ineluctable destiny predetermined by actors and factors above and beyond the populations it affects. The sort of attention that this edited volume seeks to dedicate to the material, spatial and bodily ways in which states of emergency are not only produced, but also challenged in everyday life, and by ordinary citizens, we argue, is imperative not just for students of Turkey, of architecture, and/or of the architecture of Turkey. It is also imperative for those in academia and beyond who are interested in better understanding the historical and geographical contexts subject to similar debates centring on emergency and normalcy that have recently become all the more heightened due to the various ecological, epidemiological, financial and political crises that have been unfolding across the world.

Notes

1 For a survey of architectural theories influenced by Agamben's notion of exception, see Camillo Boano, *The Ethics of a Potential Urbanism: Critical Encounters Between Giorgio Agamben and Architecture* (New York: Routledge, 2017), 28–39.

2 Michel Foucault, *Society Must Be Defended* (London: Penguin, 2003), 247; Giorgio Agamben, *Homo Sacer: Sovereign Power and Bare Life* (Stanford: Stanford University Press, 1998), 52–3.
3 Agamben, *Homo Sacer*, 181.
4 Judith Butler, *Precarious Life: The Powers of Mourning and Violence* (London: Verso, 2004), 68.
5 Eray Çaylı, 'Making Violence Public: Spatializing (Counter)publicness through the 1993 Sivas Arson Attack, Turkey', *International Journal of Urban and Regional Research* 43, no. 6 (2019): 1107–8.
6 Leonard C. Feldman, *Citizens without Shelter: Homelessness, Democracy, and Political Exclusion* (Ithaca: Cornell University Press, 2018), 38–44.
7 Saygun Gökarıksel and Z. Umut Türem, 'The Banality of Exception? Law and Politics in "Post-Coup" Turkey', *The South Atlantic Quarterly* 118, no. 1 (2019): 177.
8 Ibid., 179.
9 Gizem Tuğba Özkut and Jülide Aşçı, 'Long-Lasting State of Emergency: Use of (In)security for Consolidation of Power in Turkey', *Democracy and Security* 16, no. 3 (2020): 193. As Özkut and Aşçı explain, until 2002 when the AKP rose to power, it was the top leadership of the Turkish Armed Forces, the Republic's self-proclaimed "guardians," who had a strong influence on governmental affairs often by implementing extraordinary measures such as emergency rule and regardless of the reintroduction of democratically elected governments after each coup. The main instrument through which the generals exercised this influence was the so-called National Security Council established as a result of the first coup (1961) in the country's modern history. Both the National Security Council and the state of emergency declared following the July 2016 coup attempt were abolished in July 2018 when Turkey transitioned into an executive presidential system that replaced its parliamentary one. The coups but especially the 1980 coup are relevant to this book also in a methodological respect, as state archives "underwent a major cleanup" in its aftermath and were cleansed of their documents that the authorities saw as potential "threats" to official historiography; see Taner Akçam, *The Young Turks' Crime against Humanity: The Armenian Genocide and Ethnic Cleansing in the Ottoman Empire* (Princeton: Princeton University Press, 2012), 24. This methodological relevance reverberates across our edited volume, particularly through the fact that many contributors, including historians employing archival research, have introduced fieldwork-based methods into their research rather than relying solely on archives.

10 Gökarıksel and Türem, 'The Banality of Exception', 180. The most recent region-wide emergency rule that affected Turkey's predominantly Kurdish inhabited east and southeast started with a piece of legislation on July 19, 1987 to then be extended (and in some cases geographically expanded) 46 times for four months each until November 30, 2002, when it was shelved. The years between these two dates witnessed vast human rights violations across the region under emergency rule. The official number of deaths resulting from it have been recorded as the following. A total of 5105 civilians, 3541 security personnel, and 25344 guerrilla fighters died. 371 members of the armed forces and 572 civilians lost their lives due to mine or bomb explosions, and 1248 activists or politicians were extrajudicially killed. Perpetrators of 421 of the latter remain unidentified. 18 lives were lost under custody and 194 were disappeared. Some of the latter were found in prison, either still serving their time or having lost their lives therein, but 132 are still missing. 1275 complaints of torture were recorded, 1177 of which were investigated. 296 cases against civil servants were brought to court. Although 60 of these court cases resulted in convictions, only 4 sentences have been carried out while the rest have been suspended. See Türkiye İnsan Hakları Vakfı, *2003 Türkiye İnsan Hakları Raporu* (Ankara: Buluş, 2004), 30–2. Importantly, the emergency rule in question had reverberations that exceeded these regional confines, due particularly to the numerous anti-terror laws issued alogside it. These laws have led since the 1990s to the marginalization of Kurdish, Alevi and socialist populations in Turkey's major metropolises outside of its predominantly Kurdish-inhabited southeast, such as Istanbul. See Deniz Yonucu, 'The Absent Present Law: An Ethnographic Study of Legal Violence in Turkey', *Social & Legal Studies* 27, no. 6 (2018): 728–9; Deniz Yonucu, 'Urban Vigilantism: A Study of Anti-Terror Law, Politics and Policing in Istanbul', *International Journal of Urban and Regional Research* 42, no. 3 (2018): 419–20.

11 Emiliano Alessandri, 'Democratization and Europeanization in Turkey after the September 12 Referendum', *Insight Turkey* 12, no. 4 (2010): 23.

12 Joost Jongerden, 'Conquering the State and Subordinating Society under AKP Rule: A Kurdish Perspective on the Development of a New Autocracy in Turkey', *Journal of Balkan and Near Eastern Studies* 21, no. 3 (2019): 269–70.

13 Indirect manifestations included the increasing emphasis that municipalities held by the governing party placed on the construction of new parks and squares or the revamping of existing ones, so as to give the idea of democratization a certain material and spatial form; see Eray Çaylı, 'Democracy Under Construction, Construction as Regime: Design, Time and Imaginaries of Publicness in Mid-2010s' Turkey', in *Design, and Democracy: New Critical Perspectives*, eds. Michael Erlhoff and Maziar Rezai (Basel: Birkhäuser, 2020).

14 Another direct albeit spatially less expansive manifestation concerned projects regarding the commemorative transformation of sites of state-endorsed violence; see Eray Çaylı, *Victims of Commemoration: The Architecture and Violence of Confronting the Past in Turkey* (Syracuse: Syracuse University Press, 2021).
15 Marc David Baer, *Sultanic Saviors and Tolerant Turks: Writing Ottoman Jewish History, Denying the Armenian Genocide* (Bloomington: Indiana University Press, 2020), 156.
16 Özlem Ünsal, 'Inner City Regeneration and the Politics of Resistance in Istanbul: A Comparative Analysis of Sulukule and Tarlabaşı' (PhD diss., City University London, 2013), 2.
17 Cihan Tuğal, 'Urban Symbolic Violence Re-Made: Religion, Politics and Spatial Struggles in Istanbul', *International Journal of Urban and Regional Research* 45, no. 1 (2021): 161–2.
18 Eray Çaylı, '"Make it too public and the riot police will arrive": Turkey's Construction Boom as Opportunity and Publicness as Medium of Subversion', *Archfondas* 4 (2015): 2, http://www.archfondas.lt/leidiniu/node/175.
19 Evinç Doğan and Aleksandra Stupar, 'The Limits of Growth: A Case Study of Three Mega-Projects in Istanbul', *Cities* 60, part A (2017): 281–2.
20 Özlem Güzel, 'The Last Round in Restructuring the City: Urban Regeneration Becomes a State Policy of Disaster Prevention in Turkey', *Cities* 50 (2016): 43.
21 The Disaster Act defines three urban-architectural categories as its purview: (1) 'risky areas', i.e., zones identified as at risk of causing damage to lives and property due to their soil composition or the characteristics of the buildings they host; (2) 'risky buildings', i.e., buildings which, while not necessarily located within risky areas, have 'completed their economic lifespan' or have been 'scientifically proven' to be at risk of falling down or receiving severe damage in case of disaster; (3) 'reserve building areas', i.e., zones identified as safe for new settlement. See Eray Çaylı, 'Inheriting Dispossession, Mobilizing Vulnerability: Heritage amid Protest in Contemporary Turkey', *International Journal of Islamic Architecture* 5, no. 2 (2016): 365.
22 Miray Özkan Eren and Özlem Özçevik, 'Institutionalization of Disaster Risk Discourse in Reproducing Urban Space in Istanbul', *ITU A|Z* 12, no. 1 (2015): 236.
23 Elizabeth Angell, 'Assembling Disaster: Earthquakes and Urban Politics in Istanbul', *City* 18, no. 6 (2014): 675.
24 Donna Houston, 'Crisis Is Where We Live: Environmental Justice for the Anthropocene', *Globalizations* 10, no. 3 (2013): 441.
25 Yıldız Atasoy, 'Repossession, Re-informalization and Dispossession: The "Muddy Terrain" of Land Commodification in Turkey', *Journal of Agrarian Change* 17, no. 4 (2017): 659.

26 Zerrin Özlem Biner, 'Precarious Solidarities: "Poisonous Knowledge" and the Academics for Peace in Times of Authoritarianism', *Social Anthropology* 27, no. S2 (2019): 18.

27 Asuman Türkün, 'Urban Regeneration and Hegemonic Power Relationships', *International Planning Studies* 16, no. 1 (2011): 70–1; Tolga İslam, 'Current Urban Discourse, Urban Transformation and Gentrification in Istanbul', *Architectural Design* 80, no. 1 (2010): 63; Mehmet Penpecioğlu, 'Urban Development Projects and the Construction of Neo-Liberal Urban Hegemony: The Case of Izmir', *METU Journal of the Faculty of Architecture* 30, no. 1 (2013): 176; Tuna Kuyucu, 'Politics of Urban Regeneration in Turkey: Possibilities and Limits of Municipal Regeneration Initiatives in a Highly Centralized Country', *Urban Geography* 39, no. 8 (2018): 1168–72; Bülent Batuman, *New Islamist Architecture and Urbanism: Negotiating Nation and Islam through Built Environment in Turkey* (London: Routledge, 2017), 61–107. For an excellent ethnography of how some of the multiple types and histories of dispossession mentioned above have intersected in the city of Mardin in southeastern Turkey or northern Kurdistan, see Zerrin Özlem Biner, *States of Dispossession: Violence and Precarious Coexistence in Southeast Turkey* (Philadelphia: University of Pennsylvania Press, 2020).

28 Ozan Karaman, 'Urban Neoliberalism with Islamic Characteristics', *Urban Studies* 50, no. 16 (2013): 3412.

29 Tuna Kuyucu and Didem Danış, 'Similar Processes, Divergent Outcomes: A Comparative Analysis of Urban Redevelopment Projects in Three Turkish Cities', *Urban Affairs Review* 51, no. 3 (2015): 402; Mehmet Barış Kuymulu, 'Reclaiming the Right to the City: Reflections on the Urban Uprisings in Turkey', *City* 17, no. 3 (2013): 275.

30 Olgu Çalışkan, ed., *Conflict, Planning and Design* (Ankara: METU Faculty of Architecture Press, 2018); Neslihan Dostoğlu et al., eds., *Architecture in Emergency: Rethinking the Refugee Crisis* (Istanbul: Istanbul Kültür University Press, 2016).

2

The mutual construction of heritage and emergency

Neo-Ottomanist heritage policies in 2010s Turkey

Pınar Aykaç

Preface

In June 2013, Turkey witnessed a series of massive public demonstrations as part of an attempt to stop the reconstruction of a nineteenth-century Ottoman military barracks on the site of Gezi Park, situated at the edge of Taksim Square in Istanbul.[1] While the protests were sparked by the uprooting of trees in the park, they soon evolved into a rejection of the government's neo-Ottomanist policies, affecting not only the urban space and heritage-making apparatus but also the social life of the people.[2] In an interview during the first day of the public demonstrations, then prime minister Recep Tayyip Erdoğan stressed that a 'historic' barracks would be built on the site of Gezi Park, and that the Atatürk Cultural Centre (AKM), again facing Taksim Square, would also be demolished to make way for a new opera house.[3] This statement was not simply coincidental but, rather, part of a shifting set of heritage policies. Soon after the Justice and Development Party (AKP) took over the reins of government, the administration attempted to mobilize the legacy of the Ottoman past to place Istanbul, as the former capital of the Ottoman Empire, in the global network of metropolises.[4] Initially, AKP's neo-Ottomanist policies had reframed Turkey's Ottoman past as a multicultural heritage, in line with Turkey's attempts to enter the European Union (EU).[5] This state-driven discourse of multiculturalism was initially adopted to contest the early Republican heritage discourse, which isolated Istanbul from its Imperial and religious associations.⁶ Starting from the 2010s, however, this narrative of multicultural heritage was gradually replaced with Turkish and Islamic heritage, homogenizing and even silencing alternative narratives.⁷ This shift in neo-Ottomanist heritage policies concurrently invoked particular states of emergencies for heritage places through the creation of an uncertainty about their official status as such, in an attempt to 'normalize' otherwise questionable conversions or demolitions.⁸ These particular states of emergency, however, have not affected all heritage places equally, but, rather, targeted sites associated with the modern Republic of Turkey that do not fit comfortably into emergent official narratives of heritage.

This chapter explores how neo-Ottomanist heritage policies transform the urban form of cities along Turkish and Islamic lines, and how such policies concurrently create certain states of emergency especially for heritage places, which are seen as symbols of the modern Republic in Turkey. By engaging with recent discussions regarding the Hagia Sophia Museum and Atatürk Cultural Centre in Istanbul, plus the Saraçoğlu quarter in Ankara, this chapter discusses how official practices of heritage create a state of emergency for heritage places that do not fit within the authorized heritage discourse,⁹ given the fact that heritage is produced, challenged and contested according to its contemporary societal and political context.¹⁰

Heritage and uncertainty as states of emergency

The notion of uncertainty has always been a significant component of heritage debates. Rodney Harrison links the rise of the concept of heritage with modernity's response to time and uncertainty.¹¹ In fact, heritage as a discipline has largely developed as a response to a rapidly changing traditional world and the fear of its disappearance, which can be considered as a perceived emergency.¹² The possible loss of heritage places triggered inventory and the listing works, and heritage as a concept has broadened its concern from historic monuments to rural and urban areas, cultural landscapes and cultural habitats. Similarly, intangible aspects of heritage became a concern only after the recognition of the uncertain future of specific cultural practices or groups.¹³ Earlier attempts at heritage conservation were initiated from an impulse to salvage the imprints of the past that were under threat of either demolition or transformation, given as a perceived emergency. Pierre Nora elaborates this impulse when he suggests, 'no one knows what the past will be made of next, anxiety turns everything into a trace, a possible indication, a hint of history'.[14] Although they first arose as a response to uncertainties of the future, these attempts at heritage conservation, which might be called 'official practices of heritage',[15] leave other practices of heritage unrecognized, unofficial or, sometimes, marginalized. In his book *The Rule of Experts*, Timothy Mitchell suggests that official practices of heritage of nation states include certain groups by first excluding them, demolishing their heritage and then declaring their pasts as lost only to be recovered later.[16] In this way, official practices of heritage make the futures of specific groups and the heritage places associated with them uncertain, putting them in a continuous state of emergency, or in a 'zone of uncertainty', as suggested by Giorgio Agamben.[17]

The official practices of heritage and their relationship with the past began to be challenged as early as the 1980s.[18] Questioning the accuracy and universality of both the past and history in terms of being an objective and scientific discipline resulted in discussions of a variety of pasts, sometimes conflicting, for different groups.[19] Consequently, unified narratives became the locus of debates concerning dominant and powerful groups who had been privileged in telling the past.[20] As Elizabeth Pye describes it, 'while accepting that it is never possible to know the past it will always be uncertain and open to different interpretations which are affected by the context (cultural and political) in which they take place'.[21] Therefore, the questioning of official heritage practices also involves the notion of uncertainty, although this time the uncertainty in question was not the future but the past in relation to the present. More specifically, it derived from how former authorized heritage discourses were made to saturate the present as the products of a 'zone of uncertainty' that is unplaceable as per present-day laws.[22] Parallel to these debates, the relevance of the present within the heritage-making process became widely embraced, and heritage as a concept was reconceptualized as a present-day construct, given in relation to current cultural and ideological politics rather than as the evidence of an accurate and universal past.[23]

In recent years, the notion of uncertainty has once again become central to contemporary heritage studies, appearing this time in the context of humanitarian emergencies due to environmental, economic and/or political conflicts.[24] Consequently, heritage sites have received both scholarly and professional attention, after facing sudden loss or the probability of such loss. The current practices of heritage conservation are again being questioned, based upon their adequacy to respond to humanitarian emergencies. Risk preparedness, emergency measures and developing resilience are among the many themes dominating current practices.[25] The notion of uncertainty is once again central to these discussions. Zeidermann et al. evaluate these attempts as representing the uncertain future's saturation with the present.[26] In this way, the invocation of future emergencies affects the destiny of heritage places in the present. Hence, heritage practices are not only evaluated based on their response to a probable near future, but also according to their present state of alertness towards future emergencies. The notion of emergency preparedness, however, became a useful tool for governing bodies seeking to intervene in those sites which do not fit the official narratives of heritage. Such heritage sites are selectively identified as under threat of being lost, thereby legitimizing interventions or even destructions. As DeSilvey and Harrison suggest, the question is now reversed, with heritage sites selected not to be conserved but to be lost.[27]

The official practices of heritage have always been related to the notion of uncertainty at different levels. Although it initially emerged as a response to uncertainty of the future as a perceived emergency, the practice of heritage-making itself is also the manufacturer of further states of emergency. By recognizing specific groups and their associated sites as heritage, official practices of heritage-making leave other heritage sites in a continuous state of emergency. Therefore, heritage sites are constantly produced with, against and through emergencies, whether perceived or actualized. The following section introduces the current neo-Ottomanist heritage policies adopted by the Turkish government, discussing how these policies simultaneously create different states of emergency for heritage places associated with the Turkish Republic, and those which run counter to the emerging official narratives.

Neo-Ottomanist heritage policies and invented states of emergency

AKP's initial emphasis on multiculturalism aimed to challenge the early Republican heritage policies, melding the multicultural and multinational legacy of the Ottoman Empire into the formation of a collective national heritage.[28] Early Republican attitudes towards the Ottoman legacy they inherited integrated heritage places into the official narrative in different ways. One strategy was their conversion of sites into museums, as in the cases of Hagia Sophia in Istanbul, or Rumi's Tomb in Konya. In other cases however, these heritage sites were left to their own fate, leaving them in a state of uncertainty. The multiculturalist discourse of the Ottoman past also had physical implications, including the state-sponsored restoration of important heritage places of politically under-represented groups, such as the Armenian Church of Surp Khach (the Holy Cross) on an island in Lake Van, the Bulgarian Orthodox Sveti Stefan Church in Istanbul or the Grand Synagogue of Edirne. Recep Tayyip Erdoğan publicly announced the government to be responsible for the conservation of every heritage place in the country, since discrimination in historical monuments is the denial of inheritance.[29]

However, this multiculturalist approach towards neo-Ottomanist heritage policies has progressively been replaced with Islamic and Turkish overtones. As neo-Ottomanist heritage policies became increasingly hegemonic, the symbols of the Republican nation state were left in a state of uncertainty concerning their official status as heritage places through the creation of particular states of emergency. Thus, official practices of heritage-making are first challenged and soon deemed unofficial with the changing of ideologies and urban politics. In this way, as Gregory Ashworth suggests, heritage sites of certain groups associated with certain ideologies are demolished, while the people associated with these sites are left in situ with the intention that they will eventually have to adapt and become associated with the remaining official heritage sites.[30] The following section discusses how neo-Ottomanist heritage policies first challenged early Republican heritage policies – those which had distanced the nascent nation state from its imperial and religious past – and second, how this gradually put the future of the modern nation state's symbols into a state of uncertainty.

Istanbul's Hagia Sophia and uncertainty about its future as a Museum

We could even name it as the Hagia Sophia Mosque instead of a museum so that everybody can visit it without charge. . . . Its status of museum could be stripped off. Actually, that status was given by a step taken with the mentality of the CHP [Republican People's Party that founded the Republic of Turkey in 1923]. We can take back the step taken by the CHP mentality.[31]

In a live interview given in 2019, President Recep Tayyip Erdoğan mentioned that Istanbul's Hagia Sophia could be reopened as a mosque. As one of the most significant Byzantine churches converted into a mosque after the Ottoman conquest of Constantinople, Hagia Sophia has remained the focus of debates following its conversion into a museum in 1935. Using Hagia Sophia as an example, Gregory Ashworth evaluates the conversion of iconic monuments into museums as a process of neutralizing the contemporary meaning of symbols by interpreting them as objects possessing only historic artistic value, and changing the message to one with less contemporary social or political relevance.[32] By converting Hagia Sophia into a museum, Turkish authorities neutralized the contemporary associations of the monument as the symbol of the Ottoman conquest of Constantinople, and transformed it into the symbol of the secular Turkish Republic.[33]

After AKP came to power, Istanbul's Hagia Sophia once again entered the spotlight. Encouraged by AKP governance, an NGO named the Association of Service to Foundations, Historic Monuments and Environment requested the Prime Ministry in 2004 that it revoke the 1934 decision of the Council of Ministers which officially declared Hagia Sophia as a museum. When the Prime Ministry did not respond, the association, founded that same year, appealed in 2005 to the Council of State for the cancellation of the 1934 decision. The Council of State rejected the association's appeal.[34] The same year, Istanbul's historic peninsula conservation master plan was prepared by the Istanbul Metropolitan Municipality, and they identified Hagia Sophia as 'Ayasofya Mosque (Museum)'. The Istanbul Directorate of Pious Foundations, together with the association, objected to the master plan and requested that the naming of the monument appear only as 'Ayasofya Mosque', in line with its title deed.[35] The Istanbul Directorate was referring to the ownership status of converted Byzantine churches. When these churches were converted into mosques during the Ottoman period, they were integrated with the waqf system.[36] After the foundation of the Turkish Republic, the General Directorate took over the management of pious and charitable foundations. The 1934 decree of the Council of Ministers not only declared the monument to be a museum but also transferred its ownership to the Ministry of Education, which was then the body responsible for state museums.[37] The request of the Istanbul Directorate was not well received by the government, since turning Hagia Sophia into a functioning mosque would not only conflict with the neo-Ottomanist heritage discourse emphasizing multiculturality but also jeopardize Turkey's attempts to enter the EU.[38] The General Directorate of Pious Foundations opened an investigation targeting Istanbul's regional director about his request to name Hagia Sophia solely as a mosque.[39]

With the shift in neo-Ottomanist heritage policies, two other Hagia Sophias in İznik and Trabzon, which were also functioning as museums, were converted back into mosques in 2012 and 2013, respectively. The Hagia Sophia in İznik started functioning as a museum as early as the 1940s, whereas Trabzon's Hagia Sophia opened as a museum during the 1960s, after significant frescoes were unearthed.[40] The Directorate of Pious Foundations, which is responsible for the management of pious or charitable foundations, opened a lawsuit against the Ministry of Culture and Tourism, claiming that the museum function of these two Hagia Sophias was illicit since these monuments had become part of a pious endowment after their initial conversions into mosques during the Ottoman period.[41] Hence, the early Republican practice of converting former Byzantine churches into museums, which had already been pointed out by those demanding that they reopen as mosques, was now recognized as extrajudicial.[42]

The reopening of the Hagia Sophias in İznik and Trabzon as mosques put Istanbul's Hagia Sophia's future as a museum into a state of uncertainty. In 2013, Yusuf Halaçoğlu, deputy chairperson of the Nationalist Movement Party, submitted a draft law to the parliament to restore Hagia Sophia's status as a mosque. One of Halaçoğlu's major arguments concerned the inauthenticity of the signature of President Mustafa Kemal in the decree of the Council of Ministers, which declared the opening of Hagia Sophia Museum in 1934.[43] In fact, the discussions on the authenticity of the signature had already been exploited by different groups who wished to see the monument as a functioning mosque.[44] With the invention of uncertainty about the past, these groups wanted to revoke the decree of the Council of Ministers. Along with the signature, Halaçoğlu also added that the monument was registered to the Foundation of Mehmed the Conqueror as a mosque in its title deed dating back to 1936, and therefore it was against the law to use Hagia Sophia as a museum.[45] In this way, Halaçoğlu considered the decree of the Council of Ministers issued in the ethos of the early Republican period as unlawful, given that some regarded this as a period of prolonged state of emergency due to the exceptional measures taken against pious foundations (*vakıf*).[46]

While this draft law was not approved, the Association of Service to Foundations, Historic Monuments and Environment applied to the Constitutional Court in 2015, claiming that the current status of the Hagia Sophia serving as a museum is a violation of the freedom of religion and belief. The Constitutional Court called the opening of the Hagia Sophia to worship as 'inadmissible', on the grounds that there was not a 'violation of religious freedom' affecting the association specifically.[47] Despite the court decision, however, the debates regarding Hagia Sophia became heated once again after the Council of State ruled that Chora Museum, another converted Byzantine church, 'cannot be used except for its essential function', which was as a mosque.[48] The decision of the Council of State regarding the Chora Museum is particularly important since the monument, which was functioning as a mosque from the Ottoman period onwards, was reopened as a museum by a decree of the Council of Ministers in 1945. According to the ruling of the Council of State, the 1945 decree was recognised as unlawful and could set a precedent for Istanbul's Hagia Sophia, which was also opened as a museum by a decree of the Council of Ministers.

The reopening of the Hagia Sophias in İznik and Trabzon as mosques, and the ruling of the Council of State for the Chora Museum, can both be evaluated as part of neo-Ottomanist heritage policies, challenging the heritage practices of the early- Republican period. The Hagia Sophias in İznik and Trabzon had been functioning as museums for decades and were converted into mosques by claiming that their museum function was almost illicit. In the case of the Chora Museum, an uncertainty about its past was recreated by a court decision claiming that the official decree of the Council of Ministers was, in fact, unlawful, since it was issued during a period of exceptional measures affecting its future as a museum. The ruling of the Council of State put not only the Chora Museum into a state of uncertainty, thus providing a useful leverage for Turkey's domestic and international politics, but also Istanbul's Hagia Sophia and its function as a museum, itself regarded as one of the most prominent symbols of the secular Republic.

Atatürk Cultural Centre: Conservation uncertainty and demolition

Atatürk Cultural Centre (AKM) was one of the first cultural centre complexes in Turkey. The idea to construct a new public square for the Republic was started by French urbanist Henri Prost's master plan and was approved in 1939. Prost suggested the demolition of the Ottoman military barracks for the rearrangement of the area as today's Gezi Park, coupled with a theatre building framing Taksim Square.[49] The Istanbul Municipality changed the function of the theatre building into one of an opera house. A preliminary design was prepared by French architect Auguste Perret, and was later revised by Turkish architects Rüknettin Güney and Feridun Kip.[50] Although the construction of the opera house began in 1946, it was never finalized due to both the economic difficulties during the Second World War and the negligence of the newly elected conservative Democrat Party in 1950.[51] After long years of neglect, the project was handed over to Hayati Tabanlıoğlu and the building was finally opened in 1969 as Istanbul Cultural Centre, with the revision of function from an opera house to a multipurpose cultural centre. The building received its new name, Atatürk Cultural Centre, following its reopening in 1977 after it was destroyed by a fire in 1970.[52]

In time, the building became an emblem associated with modern Turkey in Taksim Square and a 'hostile symbol in Islamic imaginary'.[53] As the largest public square of Istanbul, Taksim Square gradually evolved into a locus of public demonstrations, while AKM's facade was the backstage of these demonstrations. The Labour Day celebrations in 1977, also known today as Bloody May 1, was a turning point for the square and its place in collective memory. The celebrations tragically ended in pandemonium after unknown assailants opened fire on the demonstrators, assassinating thirty-seven and wounding hundreds. After 1977, Taksim Square was declared off-limits to mass demonstrations, and this marked the beginning of the struggle among left-wing groups to regain access to the square.[54]

Although the centre was registered as cultural heritage in 1999, AKM's future became uncertain as early as 2005, when the then Minister of Culture and Tourism publicly announced that they would demolish the building and construct a new complex.[55] Following this announcement, the ministry applied to the Istanbul Second Regional Conservation Council for the deregistration of AKM to pave the way for its demolition. As a response, the Regional Council classified the building's status as a first group cultural heritage, meaning that even if the building is demolished, it needs to be rebuilt in its original form.[56] Despite the decision of the Council, the construction of a new Atatürk Cultural Centre was included in the law issued for the preparations of Istanbul as the 2010 European Capital of Culture.[57] Considering public opposition and criticism from several NGOs, the Ministry of Culture and Tourism (coupled with the Istanbul 2010 European Capital of Culture Agency) signed a protocol for the renewal of the existing building, and Murat Tabanlıoğlu, the original architect's son, was commissioned for the renewal project. After the renewal project's concept was approved by the Istanbul Second Regional Conservation Council, the Culture and Arts Union opened a lawsuit against the conceptual project that would significantly alter the building. With the court decision, a new renewal project was prepared, which mainly aimed to conserve the existing building as much as possible with structural consolidation.[58]

In the wake of discussions regarding AKM's renewal, the struggle to regain access to Taksim Square for Labour Day celebrations was intensified for the thirtieth anniversary of the deadly demonstrations.[59] As a result of the persistent struggle, Labour Day was restored as an official holiday and Taksim Square was opened to celebrations in 2010. This achievement, however, did not last long. The Gezi protests in 2013 not only banned mass demonstrations in Taksim Square for good but also affected the destiny of AKM. During the protests, the facade of the building (which had been shut down in 2008) was used for anti-government propaganda, calling to mind earlier public demonstrations of the 1970s. The Gezi protests added a further dimension to AKM, rendering it the symbol of sociopolitical opposition against the government's urban and cultural policies, and a security threat in the eyes of the authorities. It was in this context that then Prime Minister Erdoğan publicly announced that they would not only reconstruct the demolished Ottoman barracks but also demolish AKM for a new cultural centre and a mosque at Taksim Square.[60] During the Gezi protests, police entered Taksim Square to remove banners on AKM's facade, and hung two Turkish flags and a poster of Atatürk, marking the beginning of the building's use as a temporary police checkpoint in line with the government's securitization policies in the square.[61] This transformed AKM from an important symbol for the opposition into an instrument of exceptional security measures put forward in response to a perceived emergency. These exceptional security measures continued even after the Gezi protests had ended, and the building continued to function as a de facto 'police station' for a long time. During this period, *We're at AKM Initiative* filed a criminal complaint on 27 May 2015 (World Theatre Day) on the grounds that the building was occupied illegally by the police forces and purposefully left to demolition.[62] In line with the continuing security measures, the initiative was banned from issuing a press briefing in front of AKM. Meanwhile, a completely new project was under preparation, again by Tabanlıoğlu, behind closed doors. In 2018, soon after the project was publicized, AKM was demolished, while a new mosque across from the building was under construction, as the new symbol of Taksim Square.

The Gezi protests not only marked a shift in the politics of the AKP government but also provided a breaking point for AKM. First, the earlier statements of the government put the building, officially recognized as heritage due to being an important representative of modernist architecture, into a state of uncertainty. After the building regained its symbolic value associated with anti-government propaganda, AKM was first deregistered from being cultural heritage by the Regional Conservation Council, then became an instrument of exceptional security measures, and eventually bulldozed from Istanbul's urban scenery forever. During the ground-breaking ceremony of the new AKM Building, President Erdoğan clearly identified the reason behind AKM's demolition in claiming that it was seen by certain groups as 'the symbol of their marginal ideology'.[63] The construction of the new AKM today proceeds under COVID-19 lockdown, implying that this health crisis is being used as an opportunity for the government to intervene in heritage places to avoid public opposition.

Saraçoğlu quarter and the legitimization of its demolition

As the capital of the Turkish Republic, Ankara has also been on the agenda of neo-Ottomanist urban politics. Early Republican architecture has gradually become the symbol of the modern Turkish nation state, and thus has been the target of urban renewal projects.[64] Under the AKP mayor, significant buildings from the early Republican period were demolished, such as the Maltepe

Electric and Gas Factory (1928–30), Marmara Kiosk (1928), May 19 Stadium (1930), Etibank Building (1935–6) and the Municipalities Bank (1937).[65] While some of these buildings were not registered as cultural heritage, Maltepe Electric and Gas Factory and the Municipalities Bank were, in fact, protected by law. The tragic end of the Municipalities Bank is an important example for revealing how neo-Ottomanist urban policies have gradually replaced the symbols of modern Turkey with Islamic symbols. The Municipalities Bank was one of the earliest examples of modernist architecture, designed by the famous Turkish architect Seyfi Arkan.[66] After a new mosque was constructed within close vicinity, the Ankara Second Regional Conservation Council decided to reconstruct the building – officially registered as cultural heritage as early as 1980 – in a neighbouring lot. The reason behind the building's reconstruction decision was stated by the council as being due to the fact that it 'did not meet the requirements of earthquake regulations'.[67] In this way, the demolition of the existing building was legitimized through the creation of the uncertainty of a future emergency, in this case an earthquake – even though the earthquake regulations are not valid for registered historic buildings.[68] While the Municipalities Bank was demolished in 2017 following the council's decision, there have not to date been any attempts to reconstruct the building. After the Ankara Chamber of Architects opened a lawsuit against the demolition of the building, the court cancelled the council's decision in 2019.[69]

Parallel to the demolition of significant early Republican buildings, large-scale urban areas of modern Ankara were also under the risk of being lost. One such area was found in the Saraçoğlu quarter, which was constructed as one of the first mass housing projects of the Republic between 1945 and 1946.[70] Designed by German architect Paul Bonatz, the housing complex is regarded as an important representative of modern national architecture, inspired by traditional residential architecture.[71] From its establishment onwards, the quarter served as the boarding house of public employees in the capital. Saraçoğlu quarter was designated as an urban site in 1979, although the boundaries of the urban site were identified only in 1993.[72]

After the enactment of the Act on the Regeneration of Areas Under Disaster Risk (no.6306, d.16.05 2012), the Saraçoğlu quarter was designated as an area under disaster risk. The reason given for this designation was that the quarter posed 'the risk of causing loss of life and property' due to dilapidation.[73] The controversial disaster act gave the Ministry of Environment and Urbanism the right to declare any area, regardless of whether they are designated urban sites, as a disaster risk area.[74] Although the act aimed at rehabilitation, resettlement and renewal, the regulation for the act's implementation contains clauses only about how demolition will be made, indicating that the major approach in the designated risk areas is the demolition of existing structures.[75] The act also paves the way for the transfer of properties within the disaster risk area to the Ministry of Governmental Mass Housing Administration (TOKİ) through allotment or expropriation.[76] With this act, the notion of risk becomes a useful tool not only for the demolition of designated heritage sites but also for their privatization.

After the Saraçoğlu quarter was declared a disaster risk area, there was no comprehensive investigation of the buildings' structural integrity.[77] Hence, the Ankara Chamber of City Planners and Chamber of Architects jointly opened a lawsuit to cancel the quarter's declaration as a risk area. While this lawsuit was ongoing, the allocation of the properties to different ministries was cancelled due to their 'contribution to the economy'.[78] This decision paved the way for opening up the quarter for urban rent. In 2015, the Council of State cancelled the Saraçoğlu quarter's declaration as a disaster risk area on the grounds that the declaration was based only on reports of three buildings within the quarter, and lacked any evaluation of the ways in which the structures posed a risk of loss of life or property.[79] Despite the court decision, the residents were forcefully evacuated, and the entire quarter was allocated to Emlak Konut Real Estate Investment Company, belonging to TOKİ.[80] In this way, Saraçoğlu quarter's future as a designated heritage site for public use was jeopardized on the basis of a potential future emergency.

Following its allocation, a conservation master plan was prepared for the quarter. While this master plan proposed commercial and touristic functions for the area with a small percentage for residential use, it also proposed considerable new construction areas and an underground car park, both of which would significantly alter the character of the quarter.[81] This plan was also cancelled by a court decision on the grounds that it went against the principles of urban planning and public interest.[82]

Saraçoğlu quarter's declaration as a disaster risk area can be evaluated as part of neo-Ottomanist heritage politics with a neoliberal agenda, aiming not only to demolish an early Republican heritage site but also to open the entire quarter to private investment. Unlike the previously demolished early

Republican buildings, the quarter is a very large settlement, composed of registered buildings and green areas with registered monumental trees. Since the cancellation of the registration decision would have attracted serious opposition, the Ministry of Environment and Urbanism exploited the Act of the Regeneration of Areas Under Disaster Risk for the quarter's demolition. Thus, the uncertainty of the quarter's future was invented in relation to a future, imagined emergency. As Trinidad Rico argues, 'heritage at risk' can be an instrument for rationalizing the dominant politics of heritage construction.[83] In the case of Saraçoğlu, the perceived likelihood of a future emergency was employed to declare it 'heritage at risk' and rationalize the demolition of the entire quarter.

Concluding remarks: Dealing with emergencies

Since all heritage is produced completely in the present, our relationship with the past is understood in relation to our present temporal and spatial experience.[84]

Heritage as a concept is not static, but, rather, constitutes a dynamic process, being continually produced in the present. In some ways, heritage is more closely linked to the present than the past or the future, as heritage-making is inevitably negotiated in a cultural, political, social or economic context directly related to the needs of the present.[85] The present, however, cannot be separated from the past or the future, and thus the temporality of the present has been saturated with the anxieties of the past and the future.[86] Therefore, heritage can be defined as 'the conservation or preservation of objects, places and practices from the past, in the present, for the future'.[87]

Along with many other factors, the relationship between heritage and temporality is associated with the notion of uncertainty. Through the lens of uncertainty, heritage is made in the present as a response to contemporary uncertainties. However, heritage-making also generates further uncertainties by invoking particular states of emergency, especially for sites or groups that do not fit authorized heritage discourses which might normalize their suppression or eradication. This chapter argues that after neo-Ottomanist heritage policies have become the authorized heritage discourse in Turkey, heritage sites that are associated with the early Republican heritage discourse are put in a state of uncertainty through the invention of past, present or future emergencies.

Gezi protests were an important turning point for neo-Ottomanist heritage policies in Turkey. After AKP came to power in 2002, multicultural and multi-ethnic aspects of the Ottoman past were emphasized in heritage discourses, adopted by the government in an attempt to challenge the early Republican heritage practices. In time, however, this emphasis gradually disappeared, and the Turkish and Islamic character of Ottoman heritage became dominant in the official narratives, especially after the Gezi protests. While neo-Ottomanist heritage policies have created their own authorized heritage discourse, heritage places that are not in line with this discourse, especially those regarded as symbols of the modern Republic, have been put into a state of uncertainty. The reopening of Istanbul's Hagia Sophia as a museum was probably one of the most symbolic acts of the early Republican authorities. By reframing the early Republican period as an era of exceptional measures, the future of Hagia Sophia as a museum, associated with the secularist heritage practices of the early Republic, became uncertain. AKM, an important example of modernist architecture at Taksim Square, initially had its official status as cultural heritage revoked. Consequently, uncertainty was created surrounding the building's official recognition as cultural heritage. After gaining further symbolic value associated with anti-government propaganda during the Gezi protests, the AKP government quickly integrated the building into its securitization policies as an instrument of exceptional security measures. In this way, AKM became the symbol of a perceived emergency that would legitimize its destruction, despite the lawsuits filed for its conservation. In the case of the Saraçoğlu quarter in Ankara, the government exploited the disaster act, meaning the quarter was declared as a disaster risk area in order to avoid potential criticism and lawsuits regarding the demolition of such a large-scale, officially designated heritage site. Consequently, the act of (almost) inventing a future emergency created a sense of uncertainty for the future of Saraçoğlu quarter in order to legitimize the destruction of this early Republican heritage site.

The recent histories of these three heritage sites in Turkey reveal that official heritage practices utilize alternative narratives and approach heritage sites with the aim of creating uncertainties through the invocation of past, present or future emergencies alongside other tools. In fact, the notion of emergency is embedded in the heritage-making process, and cannot simply be delineated as a recent phenomenon reduced to a specific era, commonly referred to as 'a state of exception'.[88] Therefore, grasping the heritage-making process requires one to work with, against and through the various invocations of emergency central to it.

Notes

1. Eray Çaylı, 'Inheriting Dispossession, Mobilizing Vulnerability: Heritage amid Protest in Contemporary Turkey', *International Journal of Islamic Architecture* 5, no. 2 (2016): 360–3.
2. Can Bilsel, 'The Crisis in Conservation: Istanbul's Gezi Park between Restoration and Resistance', *Journal of the Society of Architectural Historians* 76, no. 2 (2017): 141.
3. 'Başbakan'dan Gezi Parkı açıklaması', *Hürriyet*, 1 June 2013, https://www.sabah.com.tr/gundem/2013/06/01/basbakan-erdogan-konusuyor.
4. For further information, see Çağlar Keyder, 'Imperial, National, and Global Istanbul: Three Istanbul "Moments" from the Nineteenth to Twenty-First Centuries', in *Istanbul: Living with Difference in a Global City*, eds. N. Fisher-Onar, S. C. Pearce and E. F. Keyman (New Brunswick: Rutgers University Press, 2018), 25–37.
5. Deniz İkiz Kaya and Mehmet Çalhan, 'Impediment or Resource? Contextualisation of the Shared Built Heritage in Turkey', in *Cultural Contestation. Palgrave Studies in Cultural Heritage and Conflict*, eds. J. Rodenberg and P. Wagenaar (Cham: Palgrave Macmillan, 2018), 87.
6. Ayşe Öncü, 'The Politics of İstanbul's Ottoman Heritage in the Era of Globalism: Refractions through the Prism of a Theme Park', in *Cities of the South: Citizenship and Exclusion in the 21st Century*, ed. B. Mermier, F. Drieskens and H. Wimmen (Beirut: Saqi Books, 2007), 236.
7. Courtney Michelle Dorroll, 'The Spatial Politics of Turkey's Justice and Development Party (AK Party): On Erdoğanian Neo-Ottomanism' (PhD diss., University of Arizona, 2015), 16.
8. Ülke Evrim Uysal, 'An Urban Social Movement Challenging Urban Regeneration: The Case of Sulukule, Istanbul', *Cities* 29, no. 1 (2012): 15.
9. Laurajane Smith defines authorized heritage discourse as the discourse privileging the experts, which not only attempts to construct the official practices

of heritage but also excludes competing discourses, *Uses of Heritage* (Oxon: Routledge, 2006), 31, 48.

10 David C. Harvey, 'Heritage Pasts and Heritage Presents: Temporality, Meaning and the Scope of Heritage Studies', *International Journal of Heritage Studies* 7, no. 4 (2001): 320.

11 Rodney Harrison, *Heritage: Critical Approaches* (Milton Park, Abingdon and New York: Routledge, 2013), 3, 11.

12 Adèle Esposito and Inès Gaulis, *The Cultural Heritages of Asia and Europe: Global Challenges and Local Initiatives* (Leiden and Amsterdam: International Institute for Asian Studies and the Asia-Europe Foundation: 2010), 14.

13 Harrison, *Heritage: Critical Approaches*, 18.

14 Pierre Nora, 'Between Memory and History: Les Lieux de Mémoire', *Representations* 26, Special Issue: Memory and Counter-Memory (1989): 17.

15 For further information on the official practices of heritage, see Smith, *The Uses of Heritage*; Harrison, *Heritage: Critical Approaches*.

16 Timothy Mitchell, *Rule of Experts: Egypt, Techno-Politics, Modernity* (Berkeley and Los Angeles; London: University of California Press, 2002), 191.

17 In his well-known book State of Exception, Giorgio Agamben evaluates the state of emergency as an 'uncertain zone', which cannot be defined either within or outside the law. For further information, see Giorgio Agamben, *State of Exception*, trans. Kevin Attell (Chicago: The University of Chicago Press, 2005), 29.

18 One of the earliest publications on the relationship of heritage with the present, see David Lowenthal, *The Past Is a Foreign Country* (Cambridge: Cambridge University Press, 1985).

19 Andreas Huyssen, *Present Pasts: Urban Palimpsests and the Politics of Memory* (Stanford: Stanford University Press, 2003), 2.

20 Smith, *Uses of Heritage*, 41.

21 Elizabeth Pye, *Caring for the Past: Issues in Conservation for Archaeology and Museums* (London: James & James, 2000), 11.

22 Agamben, *State of Exception*, 29.

23 See Smith, *The Uses of Heritage*; Harrison, *Heritage: Critical Approaches*.

24 Harrison, *Heritage: Critical Approaches*, 3.

25 See Herb Stovel, *Risk Preparedness: A Management Manual for World Cultural Heritage* (Rome: ICCROM, 1998); Nancy E. Gwinn and Johanna G. Wellheiser, *Preparing for the Worst, Planning for the Best: Protecting our Cultural Heritage from Disaster: Proceedings of a Special IFLA Conference Held in Berlin in July 2003* (München: K. G. Saur, 2005); Chiara Bertolin,

Preservation of Cultural Heritage and Resources Threatened by Climate Change (Basel: MDPI, 2019).

26 Austin Zeiderman, Sobia Ahmad Kaker, Jonathan Silver and Astrid Wood, 'Uncertainty and Urban Life', *Public Culture* 27, no. 2 (2015): 284.

27 Caitlin DeSilvey and Rodney Harrison, 'Anticipating Loss: Rethinking Endangerment in Heritage Futures', *International Journal of Heritage Studies* 26, no. 1 (2020): 3.

28 Yılmaz Çolak, 'Ottomanism vs. Kemalism: Collective Memory and Cultural Pluralism in 1990s Turkey', *Middle Eastern Studies* 42, no. 4 (2006): 591.

29 'Erdoğan: Tarihi Eserlerde Ayrımcılık Reddi Mirastır', *Milliyet*, 2 February 2009, http://www.milliyet.com.tr/siyaset/erdogan-tarihi-eserlerde-ayrimcilik-reddi-m irastir-1057732.

30 Gregory J. Ashworth, et al. *Pluralising Pasts: Heritage, Identity and Place in Multicultural Societies* (London: Pluto Press, 2007), 110.

31 'Hagia Sophia Can Be Reverted to a Mosque: Erdoğan', *Hürriyet Daily News*, 25 March 2019, http://www.hurriyetdailynews.com/hagia-sophia-can-be-reverted -to-a-mosque-erdogan-142153.

32 Gregory Ashworth, 'The Conserved European City as Cultural Symbol: The Meaning of the Text', in *Modern Europe: Place, Culture, Identity*, ed. B. Graham (London: Arnold, 1998), 268.

33 Pınar Aykaç, 'Musealisation as an Urban Process: The Transformation of the Sultanahmet District in Istanbul's Historic Peninsula' (PhD diss., University College London, 2017), 290.

34 'Danıştay, Ayasofya'nın ibadete açılması talebini reddetti', *Hürriyet,* 24 June 2005, http://www.hurriyet.com.tr/gundem/danistay-ayasofyanin-ibadete-acilmasi-tal ebini-reddetti-329832.

35 'Ayasofya cami olarak anılsın' talebine soruşturma', *Birgün*, 06 November 2005, Available online: https://www.birgun.net/haber/ayasofya-cami-olarak-anilsin-ta lebine-sorusturma-24867.

36 For further information on the early waqf system in Istanbul, see Halil İnalcık, 'Istanbul: An Islamic City', *Journal of Islamic Studies* 1 (1990): 1–23.

37 Decree of Council of Ministers, Presidential Ottoman Archives, Document no: 4979.06./30.18.1.2., 24 November 1934.

38 The same year a group of Swiss scholars petitioned the European Parliament demanding the reopening of Hagia Sophia as a church before Turkey joins the European Union. For further information, see Jonathan Luxmoore, 'Swiss Scholars Want Famous Church Returned before Turkey Joins EU', *Catholic News Service*, 25 September 2005, http://www.orthodoxytoday.org/articles5/Luxmo oreHagiaSophia.php.

39 '"Ayasofya cami olarak anılsın" talebine soruşturma', *Birgün*, 6 November 2005, https://www.birgun.net/haber/ayasofya-cami-olarak-anilsin-talebine-sorusturma-24867.

40 For further information, see Pınar Aykaç, 'Contesting the Byzantine Past: Four Hagia Sophias as Ideological Battlegrounds of Architectural Conservation in Turkey', *Heritage & Society* 11, no. 2 (2018): 151–78.

41 Yakup Emre Çoruhlu and Osman Demir, 'Trabzon Ayasofya Camii'nin "Mülkiyet Hakkı" Üzerine Bir İnceleme', *Vakıflar Dergisi* 42 (2014): 93–4.

42 Ahmet Akgündüz, Said Öztürk and Yaşar Baş, *Üç Devirde bir Mabed: Ayasofya* (İstanbul: Osmanlı Araştırmaları Vakfı, 2005), 724–40.

43 'Ayasofya sahte Atatürk imzasıyla müzeye çevrildi', *Milliyet*, 24 November 2013, http://www.milliyet.com.tr/gundem/ayasofya-sahte-ataturk-imzasiyla-muzeye-c evrildi-1796961.

44 'Ayasofya'yı sahte imzayla müze yaptılar', *Yeni Şafak*, 01 June 2012, https://www.yenisafak.com/gundem/ayasofyayi-sahte-imzayla-muze-yaptilar-386368.

45 'Ayasofya sahte Atatürk imzasıyla müzeye çevrildi', *Milliyet*, 24 November 2013.

46 Gizem Zencirci, 'Civil Society's History: New Constructions of Ottoman Heritage by the Justice and Development Party in Turkey', *European Journal of Turkish Studies* (2014): 4–5, http://ejts.revues.org/5076; Murat Çızakca, *A History of Philanthrophic Foundations: The Islamic World from the Seventh Century to the Present* (Istanbul: Boğaziçi University Press, 2000), 55–6.

47 'Demand for Hagia Sophia to be opened for prayer "inadmissible", says top court', *Hürriyet Daily News*, 13 September 2018, http://www.hurriyetdailynews.com/de mand-for-hagia-sophia-to-be-opened-for-prayer-inadmissible-says-top-court-1 36815.

48 Ayla Jean Yackley, 'Court Ruling Converting Turkish Museum to Mosque Could Set Precedent for Hagia Sophia', *The Art Newspaper*, 3 December 2019, https://www.theartnewspaper.com/news/court-ruling-converting-turkish-museum-to -mosque-could-set-precedent-for-hagia-sophia.

49 Henri Prost, *Taksim Amenagement Des Terrains de la Caserne*, File no: 40 Hrt_Gec_002057, Atatürk Library Archives.

50 Esra Akcan, 'How Does Architecture Heal?: The AKM as Palimpsest and Ghost', *South Atlantic Quarterly* 118, no. 1 (2019): 84.

51 Zafer Akay, 'İstanbul'un Cumhuriyet Dönemi Simgesi: AKM', *Mimarlık Dergisi* 392 (2016), accessed 23 January 2020, http://www.mimarlikdergisi.com/index .cfm?sayfa=mimarlik&DergiSayi=406&RecID=4050.

52 Akcan, 'How Does Architecture Heal?', 84.

53 Bülent Batuman, '"Everywhere Is Taksim": The Politics of Public Space from Nation-Building to Neoliberal Islamism and Beyond', *Journal of Urban History* 41, no. 5 (2015): 897.

54 Aysegul Baykan and Tali Hatuka, 'Politics and Culture in the Making of Public Space: Taksim Square, 1 May 1977, Istanbul', *Planning Perspectives* 25, no. 1 (2010): 63.
55 'Atatürk Kültür Merkezi', accessed 23 January 2020, http://www.mimarist.org/calisma_raporlari/39Donem/html/6.15.htm.
56 Ibid.
57 Ayça İnce, 'Converted Spaces, Converted Meanings: Looking at New Cultural Spaces in Istanbul through a Cultural Policy Lens', in *Turkish Cultural Policies in a Global World*, eds. M. Girard, J. Polo and C. Scalbert-Yücel (Cam: Springer International Publishing, 2018), 105–25, 117.
58 Istanbul Chamber of Architects, 'Basına ve Kamuoyuna: Atatürk Kültür Merkezi 9 yıldır kapalı!', 28 June 2017, http://www.mimarist.org/basina-ve-kamuoyuna-ataturk-kultur-merkezi-9-yildir-kapali/.
59 Baykan and Hatuka, 'Politics and Culture', 65.
60 'Erdoğan: AKM yıkılacak, Taksim'e cami de yapılacak', *Radikal*, 02 June 2013, http://www.radikal.com.tr/politika/erdogan-akm-yikilacak-taksime-cami-de-yapilacak-1135947/.
61 Stephen Lewis, 'Gezi Park/Taksim Square: A Change of Banners on the Atatürk Cultural Center + A Few Words on the Iconography of Public Space', 24 June 2013, https://bubkes.org/2013/06/24/gezi-parktaksim-square-ataturk-cultural-center-during-and-after-occupation-plus-a-word-on-the-iconography-of-public-space/.
62 'Dünya Tiyatro Günü'nde suç duyurusu: "AKM'yi kapattınız, işgal ettiniz, talan ettiniz!"', 27 March 2015, https://sendika63.org/2015/03/dunya-tiyatro-gununde-suc-duyurusu-akmyi-kapattiniz-isgal-ettiniz-talan-ettiniz-253994/#more.
63 'Cumhurbaşkanı Erdoğan: İstanbul Atatürk Kültür Merkezi bir zafer anıtı olacaktır', *Anadolu Agency*, 10 February 2019, https://www.cnnturk.com/turkiye/son-dakika-yeni-akmnin-temeli-atiliyor-binali-yildirim-torende-konusuyor.
64 Bülent Batuman, '"Early Republican Ankara": Struggle over Historical Representation and the Politics of Urban Historiography', *Journal of Urban History* 37, no. 5 (2011): 662.
65 'Ankara'da Gökçek döneminde yıkılan cumhuriyet mirası yapılar', *İleri Haber*, accessed 23 January 2020, https://ilerihaber.org/icerik/ankarada-gokcek-doneminde-yikilan-cumhuriyet-mirasi-yapilar-78223.html.
66 Esra Akcan, *Architecture in Translation: Germany, Turkey, and the Modern House* (Durham: Duke University Press, 2012), 67.
67 Ankara Second Regional Conservation Council Decision, date: 16 June 2017, see http://www.mimarlarodasiankara.org/index.php?Did=8901.
68 Turkish Building Earthquake Code, Official Gazette, date: 18 March 2018.

69 Ankara Chamber of Architects, 'Yargıdan ders veren İller Bankası kararı', accessed 23 January 2020, http://www.mimarlarodasiankara.org/index.php?Did=10400.
70 Zeynep Günay, T. Kerem Koramaz and A. Şule Özüekren, A. Ş. 'From Squatter Upgrading to Large-Scale Renewal Programmes: Housing Renewal in Turkey', in *Renewing Europe's Housing*, eds. R. Turkington and C. Watson (Bristol: Policy Press), 217.
71 Akcan, *Architecture in Translation*, 244.
72 Demet Erol and Kaan Sakaklı, 'Saraçoğlu Mahallesi'nin Değerinin Değişimi', in *Gazi Üniversitesi Şehir ve Bölge Planlama Bölümü 30. Kuruluş Yılı Anısına Seksen Sonrasi Mekan ve Planlama,* eds. Aysu Uğurlar et al. (Ankara: Gazi Üniversitesi, 2016), 393.
73 Ibid., 396.
74 Özgün Özçakır, Güliz Bilgin Altınöz and Anna Mignosa, 'Political Economy of Renewal of Heritage Places in Turkey', *METU Journal of Faculty of Architecture* 23, no. 2 (2018): 231.
75 Erol and Sakaklı, 'Saraçoğlu Mahallesi', 395.
76 6306 Act on the Regeneration of Areas Under Disaster Risk, date: 16 May 2012, no. 6306. https://www.mevzuat.gov.tr/MevzuatMetin/1.5.6306.pdf.
77 'Saraçoğlu Yerleşkesi, '"Ekonomiye Kazandırmak"(!) Amacıyla Yok Edilemez', accessed 24 January 2020, http://www.spo.org.tr/resimler/ekler/826a13a53ad67 67_ek.pdf?tipi=3&turu=X&sube=1.
78 'Regulation Amending the Regulation on Public Housing', *Official gazette*, date: 5 August 2014. Decision no: 2014/6643.
79 'Saraçoğlu Mahallesi için Danıştay kararı', accessed 24 January 2020, http://mul kiyehaber.net/saracoglu-mahallesi-icin-danistay-karari/.
80 Nuray Bayraktar, 'Ankara Kent Merkezinde Bir Mücadele Alanı: Saraçoğlu Mahallesi', *Betonart* 56 (2018): 46.
81 Ibid., 47.
82 'Mimarlar Odası'ndan Mansur Yavaş'a 'Saraçoğlu Mahallesi' çağrısı: Koruma Amaçlı İmar Planını katılımcı bir yöntemle birlikte yapalım', accessed 24 January 2020, https://www.istanbulgercegi.com/mimarlar-odasindan-mansur-yavasa-saracoglu-mahallesi-cagrisi-koruma-amacli-imar-planini-katilimci-bir-yontemle-birlikte-yapalim_201138.html.
83 Trinidad Rico, 'Heritage at Risk: The Authority and Autonomy of a Dominant Preservation Framework', in *Heritage Keywords: Rhetoric and Redescription in Cultural Heritage*, eds. K. L. Samuels and T. Rico (Boulder: University Press of Colorado, 2015), 158.
84 Harvey, 'Heritage Pasts and Heritage Presents', 325.

85 Laurajane Smith, 'Discussion', in *Heritage Regimes and The State,* eds. R. F. Bendix, A. Eggert and A. Peselmann (Göttüngen: Universitätsverlag Göttingen, 2013), 391.
86 Huyssen, *Present Pasts,* 11–29.
87 Rodney Harrison, 'Heritage Ontologies: Understanding Heritage as Future-Making Practices', *Heritage Futures / Utopian Currents,* June 4, 2019, https://sites.grenadine.co/sites/patrimoine/en/ACHS2016/items/733.
88 Agamben, *State of Exception,* 29.

3

Destabilizing national heritage

Preserving Turkey's non-Muslim architectural heritage

Banu Pekol

Introduction

A historic building can be at risk if it is in an earthquake zone or in a war zone. However, the historic buildings my work focuses on are at risk because they are left unmaintained and their original architects, owners and/or users are no longer present to look after them. Further, they have been appropriated as building stock without consideration given to their religious, historical or architectural value. These buildings are of non-Muslim heritage, and Turkey has not been accommodative towards its non-Muslim history. The Armenian and Syriac genocides, the forced population exchange and the expulsion of Rums, the anti-Jewish pogrom in Eastern Thrace in 1934, the vandalization and unlawful possession of non-Muslim homes, shops and religious sites are all fresh in the memories of these communities. With this in mind, the Turkish state has dealt with its non-Muslim heritage through emergency measures, not only in times of political conflicts, but also as part of a prolonged and permanent state of emergency, challenging the dichotomy of emergency and normalcy. Such heritage sites have been lawfully (such as Law 5366 Law on Renovating, Conserving and Actively Using Dilapidated Historical and Cultural Immovable Assets which resulted in the destruction of many historic houses built by non-Muslims), unlawfully and systematically dealt with throughout the history of the Turkish Republic. This continuous degradation of the non-Muslim built heritage constitutes a state of ongoing emergency, placing buildings in a state of risk and uncertainty. In this chapter, the concept of emergency is examined through the history of non-Muslims in Turkey, underlining how the process described previously resulted in this particular heritage embodying the concept of emergency in both spatial and material ways.

This research draws on fieldwork conducted between 2015 and 2019 in eight regions of contemporary Turkey. The eight regions are Adana, Artvin, Bursa, Elazığ, Izmir, Kayseri, Niğde and Tur Abdin, all of which housed large concentrations of non-Muslim populations in the past.[1] This research documented the state of non-Muslim buildings which have been stripped of their original community and left to the mercy of those living in their vicinity. It involved visiting sites, documenting and reporting on their current state, conducting detailed historical background research and preparing risk assessment and recommendation reports.[2] The findings of this fieldwork – in terms of both the physical condition of the buildings and the approach of current inhabitants towards them – reveal the way in which the Turkish state, as well as the locals, appropriates or rejects these heritage sites. The devaluation of these sites is visible through the assessment of their extremely poor physical condition, which is continuously deteriorating due to deliberate damage and squalor. This chapter discusses the current state of non-Muslim heritage at risk across contemporary Turkey, demonstrating how it is entangled in diaspora discourses, traumascapes[3] and more generally within geographies of power. It argues that the Turkish state has utilized Muslim heritage to help make sense of dominant or authorized nationalistic cultural claims, subjecting it to a politics of (dis)recognition, resulting in a substantial loss of these cultural assets. When heritage conservation is approached as the intangible process of negotiating cultural identities and meanings, the reasons behind the destruction of such heritage become clear.

Hall writes that 'heritage . . . is one of the ways in which the nation slowly constructs for itself a sort of collective social memory'.[4] As with all nation states, this interpretation is valid for the role which heritage politics plays in the construction of Turkish national identity. Heritage is entangled with the management of public affairs and how the state wants to construct or reconfigure its collective identity. With the establishment of the Republic of Turkey, nationalistic historiography and discourse dominated all forms of historical knowledge production. Sunni Islam in particular has been functional in the nation-building process in Turkey, and is crafted by the state as a factor that unites the majority of the population. Microhistory studies developed relatively late in Turkey, with scholarly research on these subjects only recently proliferating. Even though local histories have been gradually studied, attention to the historical presence of non-Muslim communities in these studies remains insufficient. There is still a tendency to consider non-Muslims as exceptions to Turkey's history, rather than an integral part of it.

The buildings of non-Muslim heritage studied in this chapter are abandoned to dilapidation since their historical memory value – as defined by Riegl – is high.[5] Their historical memory value makes them a bold, physical proof of a particular history, one which the Turkish state prefers not to be represented or documented. The higher this value is in a building, the more it forms a bridge between an 'unwanted' past and the present, and the more it becomes susceptible to swifter demolition. To rewrite history, it is necessary to eliminate physical evidence. This is because the physical evidence such as a city with six churches of varied denominations (Armenian Gregorian, Armenian Catholic, Latin Catholic, Protestant and Anglican)[6] and numerous ancillary buildings (schools, hospitals) will openly contest the official narratives and statements that this is a historic Muslim city. This was the case for Antep, where many such churches were demolished within the first ten years of the Turkish Republic, or else repurposed. This attitude of erasing or appropriating is seen in every city with a non-Muslim heritage within Turkey. This is precisely because buildings speak of the past, they are narratives of social engineering, and the larger their size and importance, the louder they speak of what was and is no longer.[7]

This situation gives symbolic significance not only to the act of saving this heritage but also to that of its restoration and maintenance. As Cosgrove argues, 'it is the act of conservation itself that makes an object part of the cultural heritage, not the cultural heritage that demands conservation' and that the ultimate goal of conservation is not to conserve buildings, but to retain their meaning for collective memory.[8] Heritage provides a physical representation and reality to the ephemeral and slippery concept of 'identity'.[9] By allowing the total annihilation of these buildings, not only is a tangible cultural asset reflecting the identity of non-Muslims erased but their role as a vessel of memory is also terminated. Heritage links the past to the present.[10] It reflects the presence of communities who have lived in Anatolia in the past, and are now spread across the Middle East, Europe, United States and other countries. As Harrison observes, architectural heritage is something that also binds diaspora communities to their homeland and to the new places in which they settle.[11] The state of many non-Muslim historical buildings in Turkey makes it impossible for the grandchildren of those who lived in these cities to go back and find physical traces of the homeland where their roots lie.

As manifested through both the state of the surviving buildings and the attitude of preservation towards them, they embody a state of ongoing emergency. This state is defined by Schmitt as the sovereign powers suspending or fundamentally halting the ordinary legal order through unconventional rules, institutions and suchlike, and declaring this to be for the public good.[12] The phenomenon of emergency becoming permanent, or as Agamben states 'the state of exception has by now become the rule', has been studied extensively.[13] Hardt and Negri claim that 'the state of exception has become permanent and general; the exception has become the rule'.[14] Ackerman also recognizes that 'emergency measures have a habit of continuing well beyond their time of necessity'.[15] Emergency is usually defined as being the exception to normalcy, with these two states being mutually exclusive. A normalcy which may be seen to be dominant in the Muslim communities was never available to the non-Muslim demographics and their architecture in equal measures. Emergency and normalcy have a blended or intertwined relationship when studied through the lens of non-Muslim built heritage. This mixed state is a result of a national narrative told through architecture appropriated in various ways (legal or illegal, depending on the political climate) throughout the history of the Turkish Republic. Whether lawful or not, this destruction has been systematic and enduring, causing irreparable damage to the buildings and the memory they embody.

As will be seen in the case studies that follow, emergency became a convenient framework to deal with problematic situations and lasted for centuries. Conventionally designed to be limited to a certain time period, states of emergency in this context become a tactically used constant, enabling the heritage of non-Muslims to be eroded and left at risk. In the case of the non-Muslim built heritage within Turkey, states of emergency are not predetermined by legislation within a certain limited time frame but are repeatedly produced and distributed in both physical and symbolic ways. Such sites are deprived of their original owners and users through a prolonged and near-permanent state of emergency that can be traced back to the late nineteenth century. These heritage sites were excluded by and from nation state-building and rebuilding (including conservation) processes. The appropriation of non-Muslim properties into the hands of Muslims was framed within the shadow of emergency politics, and this gave new owners the opportunity to accept a situation that they may have normally opposed.

Church of Ambar in Mardin

Focusing on structures built by communities that no longer remain in Anatolia, the fieldwork that informed this chapter scientifically documented the present conditions of these buildings under risk. Along with the physical destruction these structures have suffered, the loss of material (including vital historical information such as inscriptions) also constitutes a significant threat. It is essential to document this inheritance properly so that future generations maintain its value. These buildings reflect the multiple and ever-changing stories which they have become home to over the years, taking shape accordingly throughout the multilayered history of Turkey. I have therefore considered them within their own context and in light of information on historical processes in the region.[16]

This historical process is strikingly exemplified by the sixth-century church complex in the village of Ambar in the predominantly Syriac, historic Tur Abdin region. This region is in southeast Turkey, and includes the eastern half of Mardin province, plus certain districts within Batman and Şırnak provinces. This colossal complex covering an area of nearly 350 square metres consists of a combination of churches of different sizes. Its dominance in the landscape and the fact that many structures of this complex are still mostly standing makes it unique. Currently, there is no Christian population left in the village.[17] Like the Armenians in Asia Minor, Syriacs too were victims of genocide in 1915 which they call *Seyfo*.[18] Some who managed to survive escaped to Syria, leaving their architectural heritage behind.

The village was called 'Ambar'[19] after a family who settled there started to use the church as a barn/warehouse. Three houses were built directly on it in the twentieth century. Although these houses were unauthorized when they were constructed, they were given private ownership in 1973, which legalized them and their location. The church complex itself now belongs to the State Treasury. Moreover, two buildings and garden walls were constructed adjacent

Figure 3.1 Church at Ambar, Mardin, 2018. Courtesy of KMKD.

to the church. The spaces have been partitioned inside, and are used as stables and haylofts by the villagers. In certain sections, the stone walls have been drilled into in order to add storage levels. The niches are used as mangers and the ground is filled with debris, soil and animal faeces. This filling level sometimes reaches up to 1.5 metres, making it difficult to comprehend the building's architecture. The entire complex is dilapidated and its current use as a barn/warehouse/haystack, as well as the houses constructed on top of it, has accelerated the deterioration of the building. Although an official decision to remove the buildings constructed on top of the church was taken after the church was registered as a cultural asset in 2007, these buildings were still inhabited during the field survey in November 2018 (Figures 3.1 and 3.2).

This approach taken towards property rights – exemplified in Ambar Church's ownership being transferred to the state – continued well into the twentieth century. A decision taken in 1974 by the Joint Civil Chambers of the Court of Cassation reads:

> It is forbidden for non-Turkish legal entities to acquire immovable property. This is because, as legal entities are stronger compared to natural entities,

Figure 3.2 Church at Ambar, Mardin, 2018. Courtesy of KMKD.

if acquisition of immovable properties by them is not restricted, the state could face various dangers and diverse inconveniences may arise.[20]

The term 'non-Turkish' was a reference to the Rum trustees (all of whom were citizens of Turkey) of the Balıklı Rum Hospital Foundation.[21] This demonstrated how the Turkish state refused to include these minorities in a national discourse, even regarding them as a threat to its integrity.[22]

Church of Agia Paraskevi in Bursa

Rums are ethnically Greek populations of the former Ottoman Empire and citizens of modern Turkey. After the fall of the Ottoman Empire, in 1923 the Rums were subjected to a population exchange agreement between Turkey and Greece which forcibly exchanged around 1.5 million Rum Orthodox Christians in Anatolia with a lower number of Muslims in Greece. In the following years, the *Varlık Vergisi Kanunu* (Capital Tax Law) which came into effect on 11 November 1942 resulted in many non-Muslim merchants and industrialists going bankrupt and their wealth usurped by Muslim families, who gradually replaced them.

The pogrom of 6–7 September 1955 was mainly directed towards Rum houses, shops, offices, schools and churches. After the 1974 and 1980 military tensions many Rums left Turkey. Many properties of the Rums who departed in these multiple waves were abandoned to the mercy of the state.[23]

One example of these properties is the Church of Agia Paraskevi in the village of Dereköy in Bursa. It served the Rum population of Mudanya and was converted into a mosque after the population exchange of 1923. It was used as a mosque until 1972, and then abandoned.[24] The lowest floor of the church was used as a stable in the 1980s with annexes added.[25] The church, which now belongs to the local municipality, is significant as a mid-nineteenth-century monument with its unique architecture and decorative, liturgical elements. It is also significant for the high-quality stone, wood and plaster work within. As well as these unique interior and exterior characteristics, Agia Paraskevi has cultural heritage value, given as a result of its place within the history of the region. According to what the *mukhtar* (village headman) said in 1986, tourists dismantled and took away much of it, and the remainder was destroyed. Photographs taken in 1986 show that the liturgical elements and fabric of the church were in much better condition back then, compared to now.[26] Today, it is found to be in a structurally poor condition and open

Figure 3.3 Agia Paraskevi Church, Bursa, 2016. Courtesy of KMKD.

Figure 3.4 Agia Paraskevi Church, Bursa, 2016. Courtesy of KMKD.

to human depredation. It is unmaintained and at serious risk of being lost. The extremely rich interior decoration is vandalized and stolen. Only a very small amount of the iconostasis remains. The vault and roof have completely collapsed, and the collapsed material has been stolen. The major part of the flooring is lost due to vandalism, with plant roots and pits dug by treasure hunters. Currently there is no lock on the door, and graffiti is both painted and incised on the façades (Figures 3.3 and 3.4).

Churches of Surp Stephanos and Surp Tanyel Monastery in Kayseri

Similar to the Rums, Armenians are also indigenous to Anatolia, and lived primarily in the south Caucausus and in eastern Anatolia. After the Hamidian and Adana massacres in 1894–6 and 1909, respectively, the main blow inflicted on Armenians was the 1915 genocide.[27] On 27 May 1915, the Ottoman Empire passed the *Tehcir Yasası* (Deportation Law),[28] especially aimed at the Armenian population but also with effect on the Syriacs in southeast Turkey. This resulted in thousands of Armenians being deported and never again returning to their homelands, with the future of their properties left in the hands of the Ottomans and, later, Turkey.

In 2015, I surveyed Surp Stephanos, a mid-sized, nineteenth-century Armenian church in Efkere, Kayseri. It was striking in its sophisticated architecture and detailing, lying off to the side of a narrow village road, with yellowish-green central Anatolian scrub growing around it. The church had been out of use for a long period of time after being abandoned. Armenians who returned to the village in 1919 reported that the dome and altar were missing. The church was purchased from the Treasury by an individual in 1957 and was used residentially for twenty-five years.[29] When it was used as a house, several additions and alterations were made to the building, including opening new windows/doors, bricking in old ones and installing extra storeys and walls inside. It is still a private property but is now abandoned. Today, the interior and exterior of the church lie severely damaged by vandalism and treasure hunters. The galleries and bell tower are also destroyed.

This church provides an explicit example of study for fieldwork, given that what *does not* remain tells more than what does. There were four Armenian and one Turkish neighbourhood in Efkere in the early nineteenth century. When studying historical travelogues mentioning the Church of Surp Stephanos, you read about the presence of two other churches in the same neighbourhood. However, the main point of interest in these accounts is not either of these churches. The massive St. Garabed Monastery (Surp Garabed Vank), established in the fourth century, used to sprawl out across the western face of the valley in Efkere. This significant pilgrimage site hosted the relics of Saint John the Baptist and attracted many believers. The wealthy monastery complex was popular for Armenian pilgrimage in Anatolia, with its ninety-three rooms for pilgrims. Efkere became affluent enough to build not only sizeable schools but also sophisticated churches such as Surp Stephanos, which closely resembles Armenian churches in Istanbul. This points to the presence of an expensive commission, probably involving architects from the capital. In short, this village did not contain only 500 Armenian households served by three churches (in 1914), but it was also home to a great pilgrimage monastery.³⁰ British geographer and traveller Tozer who visited the monastery in 1879, described it as follows:

> The gate of the entrance stands in the middle of the front, where a long terrace overlooks the steep slopes below . . . we were conducted to the guest chamber, a good-sized room with a divan running around three sides of it, and a large airy window occupying the whole of the front, and commanding a superb view . . . it is a very important society, and in Armenia we heard it spoken of as ranking probably third among the conventional establishments of the Armenian Church, those of Etchmiadzin in Russian Armenia and of Jerusalem being the two first.³¹

Although I had visited Surp Stephanos for a risk assessment, when writing my report, I found myself staring at photos of the current empty village and comparing them to historic images. I then tried to imagine how a semanthron or a religious chant would have rung out in the valley during the nineteenth century.³² Near to nothing of the massive sprawl of the monastery survives today, except some foundations which fall within the military zone. Neither do the schools nor most of the homes which had housed 500 families at one point in time remain.³³ The destruction of such a massive building stock in such a short time cannot have been through natural causes (Figures 3.5 and 3.6).

Figure 3.5 Church of Surp Stephanos, Kayseri, 2015. Courtesy of KMKD.

Figure 3.6 Saint Garabed Monastery, pre-1915. Courtesy of Jonathan Varjabedian.

Not all the buildings and their furnishings are lost because of disrepair and abandonment. Koymjian writes of nine demolition strategies, among which is wilful destruction carried out during the genocide, similar to what happened to the eleventh-century Surp Tanyel (St. Daniel) Monastery in Balagesi, Kayseri, right after the Armenians left the village in 1917.[34] One account states that between 1915 and 1922, 1,036 Armenian churches or monasteries were completely destroyed, while 691 were partially (but always wilfully) destroyed. The other demolition strategies include destruction by dynamite or artillery, wilful neglect, encouragement of trespassing, adaptive reuse, destruction for public works, neutralization by effacing of inscriptions and attribution to other cultures.[35] From a twenty-first-century perspective, all these are active agents in manipulating the past to serve a nationalistic discourse.

The Portuguese Synagogue in Güzelyurt

The fourth main non-Muslim community in Turkey are Jews, known as one of the first settlers in Asia Minor. They grew in size significantly when they fled from Portugal and Spain to the Ottoman Empire in the late fifteenth century. As a group which largely migrated into Anatolia, they have always strived to be in 'harmony' with the state.[36] The final example studied in this chapter demonstrates the result of this compromise that affected a Jewish historic property.

The Portuguese Synagogue in Güzelyurt neighbourhood of Izmir was established by the Portuguese Marranos who migrated from North Africa and Venice. The synagogue is of importance in terms of marking the origin of Jewish migration (continuing through the sixteenth, seventeenth and eighteenth centuries) to Izmir. It was also the centre of the seventeenth-century Sabbatian movement, of which vast groups of Izmir Jews were a part. The Rothschild family donated 3000 francs to the synagogue in 1903 and the current structure dates to 1909, as can be read from the inscription above its exterior door. After a fire in 1976, the Portuguese Synagogue was rented out as a depot and later used as a clothes workshop.[37] It remains vacant and unmaintained since 2005.

Today the plan layout of the synagogue is altered, as the building has lost its original function. Due to various interventions, the structure has lost its authentic characteristics, with only the original façade overlooking the road and courtyard entrance being discernible. The structural stability is weak, making it susceptible to earthquakes, and rain and damp have deteriorated the walls. The most striking difference of this building compared to all others analysed in this chapter, is that ownership of it still belongs to its original community: the Izmir Jewish Community Foundation. After the fire in the synagogue, there was no sufficient funding from the community to restore the building. Furthermore, the dwindling number of Jews in Izmir means that active need for synagogues is a fraction of what it used to be. Despite still belonging to the Jewish Foundation, the building is neither repurposed as a cultural space nor simply rented out for profit by the community. This reluctance is visible in other Jewish architectural heritage sites (such as the Rabbinate or cortijos of Izmir), which similarly still belong to the Jewish community but are abandoned and at risk of being lost completely.

Restoration of properties that still belong to these communities has never been easy. As the Council of Europe reported in 2011, 'even minor maintenance work on buildings owned by non-Muslim foundations could not be carried out without a decision of the Directorate General for Foundations', and as these decisions were rarely given on time, 'numerous properties fell into a state of disrepair' (Figure 3.7).[38]

Figure 3.7 Portugal Synagogue, 2016. Courtesy of KMKD.

It is during fieldwork that one faces the stark reality of how Turkey deals with its contested heritage. The approach of locals towards both us researchers and towards the buildings proved to be an invaluable source of telling data, as it shows that inhabitants engage with the past and relate it to the present in an effective manner.[39] For example, an abandoned Rum chapel would remain standing, with the *mukhtar* locking its door to prevent vandalism. An Armenian chapel in the neighbouring village, on the other hand, would be razed to the ground and locals may be hostile towards researchers. Indeed, there were some problems accessing Armenian buildings due to the local community's hostility towards outsiders who asked questions on subjects they denied or preferred not to talk about. In another instance, the *mukhtar* of a historic Syriac village (where not a single Syriac was left) was telling a fabricated story of how the Syriacs had voluntarily sold their church to a Muslim citizen, when the reality was that this church was appropriated and unlawfully (but legally) given new ownership after Syriacs were violently driven out of the village. The reasons for this coloured approach to historical buildings are all embedded within the fact that cultural heritage policies and practices are inherently political.

The Rum architectural heritage in cities such as Kayseri, which were strongly affected by the Greece–Turkey Population Exchange of 1923, showed much less damage when compared to cities where the dominant majority of non-Muslims were Armenian. This can be understood as a reflex of wishful reciprocity where the new (exchanged) inhabitants strive to care for the monuments of the earlier community, hoping that their own monuments in their motherland are given the same attention. At the same time, during fieldwork at Rum monuments, locals would come and ask whether we thought these territories would be 'taken back' by Greece. This is probably a reflection of the fact that the descendants of the Rum communities are still alive. It may also mean that these current Muslim inhabitants who descend from families subjected to the population exchange dream of reclaiming their own buildings which remain in Greece.

Figure 3.8 Signage at the church at Ferhatlı, Adana, 2015. Courtesy of KMKD.

Figure 3.9 Signage at the Church of the Holy Trinity, Kayseri, 2015. Courtesy of KMKD.

Treasure-hunting, which I came upon at nearly every site, is not a new phenomenon in abandoned non-Muslim buildings in Anatolia. Since the genocide, rumours that Armenians buried gold under or near their houses resulted in a campaign of ransacking and destruction within these properties.[40] During my fieldwork, I encountered signs placed at a few sites which warned against treasure-hunting, but these appeared to have done little to stop ill-doers (Figures 3.8 and 3.9).

Appropriation of built heritage left behind

The reason behind the acute negligence and state of decay of countless abandoned buildings of non-Muslims in Turkey is also connected to the exceptional measures which the state applied to these buildings after their owners left. A number of laws, decrees and complex bureaucratic tools were legislated in both the Ottoman and Turkish Republican periods, in order to control Armenian movable and immovable properties and remove Armenians from the economy. As in most of Anatolia, 'the physical removal of Armenians to the Syrian deserts proved decisive in separating them from their property, because it was clear that they were not meant to return.'[41] The Liquidation Law of 1915 was mainly aimed at vacant Armenian properties. Properties which could bring rent, such as houses and shops, were to be recorded and liquidated through the Foundations Council. Those which could not bring rent, such as churches, were recorded and liquidated through the State Treasury.[42] Also, according to a decision of the Council of Ministers on 18 March 1925, appropriated schools, places of worship and charities of non-Muslim minorities could all be allocated to local administrations.[43] The lands of Syriacs were seized by Kurdish neighbours or registered as forest lands.[44] The properties left behind by Rums subject to the Greece–Turkey Population Exchange were distributed to those who replaced them, and the surplus was sold. Those that were not sold were registered to the State Treasury.[45]

The predicament concerning what would become of the vacant properties was also solved by reissuing their deeds. In regions where there was a considerable number of abandoned building stock, Muslim citizens pillaged and squatted in these properties. With a decision of the Turkish Civil Code in 1926, those who had been using (i.e., squatting in) such buildings for twenty years were issued deeds of these properties.[46] As many of the rightful owners of the buildings or lands were either dead, in exile or had emigrated, they could not be present to apply for renewal of their deeds. With the issue of fresh deeds to Muslim subjects, the circle of Turkifying properties and possessions of non-Muslim subjects was complete and legalized (Figure 3.10).

However, not all deeds were left to Muslim citizens. For example, after the Armenian monastery complex in Aghtamar Island in Van Lake was abandoned, it was squatted in by an *agha* (local chief) named Agit who then filed for its registration in his name. However, the government rejected his appeal and, instead, registered it to the State Treasury.[47] In recent years, a Muslim journalist whose family came from Van was also put under the spotlight after it was discovered that he had inherited a nineteenth-century church – originally part of the Armenian Varagavank monastery complex –

Figure 3.10 Church from Varagavank monastery complex, Van, 2012. Courtesy of Agos Newspaper.

from his Muslim grandfather.[48] Obviously, this property was one of those that were given/sold to local Muslims after the Armenians were purged. The journalist still owns the church, and no conservation measures have yet been taken to save it, although it remains at great risk of collapse.

It is important to remember that not only houses but also monumental buildings were issued deeds, which made them properties of Muslim villagers or the state. Monasteries, which were built to serve God, were treated as if there was no difference between them and a modest house. These examples provide clear testimony to the state strategies explained in this chapter. As Kurt states, this is a version of violence, where the state has inflicted tyranny by not only removing all physical conditions for a group to survive but also implementing this on a judicial basis through its bureaucratic, ideological instruments.[49]

Conclusion: Emergency as normalcy

The twentieth century witnessed harsh measures dealt towards non-Muslim communities in Turkey, which resulted in a drastic reduction in their population.

The reasons for these measures were economic, sociopolitical and religious. In general, the state sought to build a Muslim bourgeoisie by oppressing the non-Muslims through often legalized yet invariably unjust strategies. Emergency as a state of exception is a useful theoretical framework for understanding what happened to non-Muslim heritage in Turkey, since it justifies exceptional measures as normal occurrences. The Turkish Government defines the state of emergency as a time-limited situation arising from natural disasters, hazardous epidemics or severe economic crises and widespread violent acts targeting fundamental rights and liberties.[50] Given official governmental descriptions of the state of emergency, the situation of non-Muslim built heritage is not classifiable as such, be it via natural disaster, epidemic or any similar crisis. It is not limited to a particular time, as its abandonment, exploitation and decay continues. The state of political flux defined by authorities and state actors hindered any state of normalcy for non-Muslim architectural heritage at risk in Turkey. It caused these buildings to remain in a constant state of ever-amplifying decay – a persistent state of emergency.

However, one curious parallel to the official description does exist: the built heritage in question is in a state of emergency since the rights and liberties of the owners (although never officially equal to the Muslim population) were violated by the state and its subjects. When one looks at how the historic buildings are being treated, a more tangible state of emergency can be traced through the rainwater pouring through a collapsed dome, or a treasure-hunter pit which causes gaping cracks in the load-bearing walls. If this rate of degradation increases, and all buildings are lost, then this state of emergency will probably recede, giving way to a flattened narrative. The multicultural heritage of Anatolia will face a substantial loss if these tensions are not seen as an opportunity for debate and democracy, which can then drive conservation efforts. Threats towards this heritage will cause it to remain a matter of emergency, as long as respectful, non-nationalistic cultural policies are not adopted.

What can be spoken of in this sense is a constant state of crisis and uncertainty, that is, 'emergency', of having to respond to the problem via attitudes that range from neglect to destruction. One manifest constant is that all these approaches are deliberate. These sites of constant emergency thus lose their effect of emergency, normalizing an abnormal situation. Socio-spatial and political trajectories intersect in these buildings and in this sense, emergency is a reflection of a much longer-term spatial production and contestation. Ackerman observes this as 'normalization of emergency conditions – the creation of legal precedents that authorize oppressive measures without any end'.[51] These landscapes thus embody the strange coexistence of a post-conflict situation with a current conflict one. As an example, in early June 2016, the German Parliament recognized the 1915 Armenian Genocide, after which Turkey retaliated by not only recalling their ambassador but also took back archaeological excavation permits of German institutions for that year.[52] Yet, just two weeks later at the Fortieth World Heritage session in Istanbul in June 2016, Turkish and Armenian diplomats presented their cautiously written speeches for Ani, the medieval capital of the Armenian kingdom, to be inscribed as a world heritage site. This shows how non-Muslim heritage in Turkey can be seen as a pawn caught in political movements, heavy-handed ideological frameworks and evolving strategies/agendas of nationalism.

The historic, economic and social results of the nationalization and Turkification process in Turkey included erasing a shocking percentage of the built heritage of non-Muslims as well as the human capital they represented. The architectural heritage studied in this chapter has suffered numerous blows of different nature and force, due to political pressures, social discourses or military interventions. The instances studied in this chapter show that emergency powers are used far from sparingly when it comes to heritage politics concerning non-Muslim built heritage in Turkey. When contextualizing politics of imposed emergency in terms of the architectural heritage, histories of deliberate dispossession and destruction are in striking abundance. As a result, these sites are, in fact, in a state of physical emergency, and at risk of being completely lost due to their materially symbolic, embodied properties. What is lost is not only the rich built heritage – the material proof which carries historical and architectural significance – but also the cultural wealth of Anatolia, with its arts, symbols and traditions.

Notes

1 The protagonists of this chapter are those who have governed the late-Ottoman Empire, and afterwards Turkey, over the last century and a half and four of the

non-Muslim communities that inhabited this geography in much bigger numbers than they now do. These communities are the Rums, Armenians, Syriacs (also called Assyrian or Aramean) and Jews. For the scope of this chapter, only these four groups have been studied, and emphasis has been primarily given to monumental buildings of heritage quality. There exist other non-Muslim minorities in Turkey such as the Georgians, Bulgarians, Yazidis, etc. but they have not been included in this chapter for reasons of brevity and focus. Muslim denominations such as the Alevite and Shiite also have a history of being suppressed by powers of the dominant belief. However, this is not within the scope of this chapter.

2 Banu Pekol, ed., *Kayseri Adana İzmir Elazığ Niğde Bursa: Assessment Reports of Cultural Heritage* (Istanbul: Anadolu Kültür, 2018).

3 Traumascapes, as used in this chapter are 'places across the world marked by traumatic legacies of violence, suffering and loss . . . much more than physical settings of tragedies . . . . Full of visual and sensory triggers'. See Maria Tumarkin, *Traumascapes: The Power and Fate of Places Transformed by Tragedy* (Victoria: Melbourne University Press, 2005), 12. It is interesting to note that Tumarkin's definition mainly focuses on the victims; however, for the case studied in this chapter, the traumascapes affected the perpetrator or later inhabitants, causing them to inflict damage on the buildings.

4 Stuart Hall, 'Whose Heritage? Un-Settling "The Heritage", Re-imagining the Post-Nation', in *The Politics of Heritage, The Legacies of 'Race'*, eds. Jo Littler and Roshi Nainoo (New York: Routledge, 2005), 25.

5 Alois Riegl, 'The Modern Cult of Monuments: Its Character and Its Origins', *Oppositions* 25 (1951): 21–51.

6 V. Gül Cephanecigil, 'Preliminary Remarks on the Late Ottoman Churches in Aintab', *ITU A|Z* 12, no. 2 (July 2015): 131–43.

7 For an in-depth examination of the use of heritage in defining memory, place, identity and cultural expressions, as well as how it can be at the centre of tensions between different identity or power groups, see Laurajane Smith, *Uses of Heritage* (London: Routledge, 2006), chapters 1 and 2. The discussion of how nationalism employs and reconstructs the past in both 'performative' and 'pedagogical' ways is explained by Homi K. Bhabha in *The Location of Culture* (London: Routledge, 2004), 209–19.

8 D. E. Cosgrove, 'Should We Take It All So Seriously?', in *Durability and Change: The Practice, Responsibility and Cost of Sustaining Cultural Heritage*, ed. W. E. Krumvin (London: Wiley and Sons, 1994), 265; S. M. Viñas, *Contemporary Theory of Conservation* (Amsterdam: Elsevier Butterworth Heinemann, 2005), 213.

9 Smith, *Uses of Heritage*, 48.

10 David Lowenthal, *The Past Is a Foreign Country* (Cambridge: Cambridge University Press, 1999) and Rodney Harrison, *Heritage: Critical Approaches* (London: Routledge, 2013) both discuss how the past and its heritage are reproduced in the present.

11 Rodney Harrison, 'Heritage as Social Action', in *Understanding Heritage in Practice,* ed. S. West (Manchester: Manchester University Press, 2010), 245.

12 Carl Schmitt, *Political Theology: Four Chapters on the Concept of Sovereignty* (Chicago: University of Chicago Press, 2005).

13 Giorgio Agamben, *State of Exception* (Chicago: University of Chicago Press, 2005), 9.

14 Michael Hardt and Antonio Negri, *Multitude: War and Democracy in the Age of Empire* (New York: Penguin Press, 2004), 7.

15 Bruce Ackerman, 'The Emergency Constitution', *Yale Law Journal* 113, no. 8 (2004): 1030.

16 Pekol, *Kayseri Adana İzmir Elazığ Niğde Bursa.*

17 In 1906, the non-Muslims living in lands that today belong to Turkey constituted 20 per cent of the total population. By 1927, this number had decreased to 3 per cent. In 2016, the number of non-Muslims came out even fewer: a meagre 0.12 per cent (Toros Alcan, Millet-i Hakime ve Millet-i Sadıka [The Dominant Nation and the Loyal Nation]', in *Yok Hükmünde: Müslüman Olmayan Cemaatlerin Tüzel Kişilik ve Temsil Sorunu* [*Declared Null and Void: Legal Entity and Representation Problem of Non-Muslim Communities*], eds. Rober Koptaş and Bülent Usta (Istanbul: Aras Yayınları, 2016), 24). This drastic reduction is despite Antakya – a city home to a populous non-Muslim community – being incorporated into Turkey in 1939. In order to understand why these numbers plummeted so rapidly, one must look back at how these communities were previously treated in these lands. Although some histories relate to all non-Muslims, this chapter will consider each non-Muslim community separately as some measures were community-specific. These histories are the basis for understanding the state of the built heritage belonging to these centuries-old non-Muslim minorities in modern Turkey.

18 Mutay Öztemiz, *II. Abdulhamit'ten Günümüze Süryaniler* (Istanbul: Ayrıntı Press, 2012), 36; David Gaunt, *Katliamlar, Direniş, Koruyucular: I. Dünya Savaşşı Sırasında Doğu Anadolu'da Müslüman-Hristiyan İlişkileri* (Istanbul: Belge Press, 2007), 257–9.

19 Turkish for granary/storage/barn.

20 Court of Cassation Legal General Assembly 8.5.1974, case no: 1971/2-820, Decision no: 1974/505, *Journal of Court of Cassation Decisions,* August (1975): 16.

21 Samim Akgönül, *Azınlık: Türk Bağlamında Azınlık Kavramına Çapraz Bakışlar* (Istanbul: Bgst Press, 2011), 11. This decision was taken as a response to one of the lawsuits opened by non-Muslim Foundations against the Turkish state concerning the '1936 Declaration'. The state had seized all property these foundations acquired which was not listed in a declaration they had given in 1936. Samim Akgönül, *Türkiye Rumları* (Istanbul: Iletisim, 2016), 318–21.

22 Non-Muslim foundations were finally allowed to acquire new property only with the Fourth EU Harmonization Package announced in January 2003. Gökhan Sarı, *Ermeni Meselesi Işşığında Süryaniler* (Ankara: Barış Platin, 2013), 176.

23 Mehmet Ali Gökaçtı, *Nüfus Mübadelesi* (Istanbul: Iletisim, 2004); Evangelia Balta, *Nüfus Mübadelesi* (Istanbul: Inkılap, 2015); Akgönül, *Türkiye Rumları*; İlay Romain Örs, *İstanbullu Rumlar ve 1964 Sürgünleri* (Istanbul: Iletisim, 2019).

24 Raif Kaplanoğlu, 'Bursa Kiliseleri', *Bursa Araştırmaları Dergisi* 30, no. 8 (2010): 10–25.

25 Yıldız Ötüken, Aynur Durukan, Hakkı Acun and Sacit Pekak, *Türkiye'de Vakıf Abideler ve Eski Eserler IV* (Ankara: Directorate General of Foundations Publications, 1986), 472.

26 Ibid., 709.

27 Hundreds of thousands of Armenians were killed under the reign of Sultan Abdülhamid II (hence the name Hamidian massacres), and tens of thousands converted to Islam while a similar number fled to the Russian Empire. These killings began in urban centres in central and eastern Anatolia but then spread to the west and also to rural districts. Edip Gölbaşı, '1895-96 Katliamları: Doğu Vilayetlerinde Cemaatler Arası Şiddet İklimi ve Ermeni Karşıtlığı', in *1915: Siyaset, Tehcir ve Soykırım*, eds. Oktay Özel and Fikret Adanır (Istanbul: Tarih Vakfı Yurt Yayınları, 2015), 140; Edip Gölbaşı 'The Official Conceptualization of the anti-Armenian Riots of 1895–1897: Bureaucratic Terminology, Official Ottoman Narrative, and Discourses of Revolutionary Provocation', *Études Arméniennes Contemporaines* 10 (2017): 33–63. Later, during WWI, what is now known as the Armenian genocide included both execution and deportation which ended mainly in torture, rape and death for tens of thousands of Ottoman Armenians. Donald Bloxham, *The Great Game of Genocide: Imperialism, Nationalism, and the Destruction of the Ottoman Armenians* (New York: Oxford University Press, 2005).

28 *Takvim-i Vekayi*, No: 2189, 19 May 1331 (1 June 1915): The precise name of the law is Vakt-i Seferde İcraat-ı Hükûmete Karşı Gelenler İçin Cihet-i Askeriyece İttihâz Olunacak Tedâbir Hakkında Muvakkat Kanun [Provisional Law on Steps

to Be Taken Militarily concerning Those Who during Campaigns Oppose the Actions of the Government].

29 Şeyda Güngör Açıkgöz, 'Kayseri ve Çevresindeki 19. Yüzyıl Kiliseleri ve Korunmaları İçin Öneriler' (PhD diss., Istanbul Technical University, Istanbul, 2007), 59–65.

30 Jonathan Varjabedian, 'Efkere: Surp Garabed Monastery', *Efkere*, 3 January, http://efkere.com/places-of-worship/surp-garabed-monastery/.

31 Henry Fanshawe Tozer, *Turkish Armenia* (London: Longmans Green and Co., 1881), 161.

32 Tozer writes of how he heard at night the sound of the semantron, a wooden board, struck with a mallet which summoned the monks to prayers, and how in the early morning he heard chants from the church, especially those of the young boys. Tozer, *Turkish Armenia*, 161–3.

33 Şükrü Ilıcak and Jonathan Varjabedian, *My Dear Son Garabed, I Read Your Letter, I Cried, I Laughed* (Istanbul: History Press, 2018), 5.

34 Raymond Kevorkian, *The Armenian Genocide: A Complete History* (London: I.B. Tauris, 2011), 514.

35 Dickran Kouymjian, 'The Destruction of Armenian Historical Monuments as a Continuation of the Turkish Policy of Genocide', in *A Crime of Silence: The Armenian Genocide*, ed. G. Libaridian (London: Zed Books, 1985), 174–5.

36 Stanford J. Shaw, *The Jews of the Ottoman Empire and the Turkish Republic* (New York: New York University Press, 1991); Ayner Levi, *Türkiye Cumhuriyeti'nde Yahudiler* (İstanbul: İletişim, 2010).

37 Önder Kaya, 'İzmir Sinagogları', *Şalom*, 4 January 2017, http://www.salom.com.tr/arsiv/haber-101636-Izmir_sinagoglari.html.

38 Directorate General of Human Rights and Legal Affairs, *ECRI Report on Turkey* (Strasbourg: Council of Europe, 2011), 32. The Directorate General of Foundations (Vakıflar Genel Müdürlüğü) was founded in 1920 and is a Turkish governmental institution that manages and audits religious foundations dating back to the Ottoman Empire and which still exist today.

39 For an elaborate analysis of the relationship between heritage and affect, see Laurajane Smith, Margaret Wetherell and Gary Campbell, eds, *Emotion, Affective Practices, and the Past in the Present* (London: Routledge, 2018).

40 Uğur Ü. Üngör and Mehmet Polatel, *Confiscation and Destruction: The Young Turk Seizure of Armenian Property* (New York: Continuum, 2011), 71.

41 Ümit Kurt, 'The Plunder of Wealth through Abandoned Properties Laws in the Armenian Genocide', *Genocide Studies International* 10, no. 1 (Spring 2016): 38.

42 Taner Akçam and Ümit Kurt, *Kanunların Ruhu: Emval-i Metruke Kanunlarında Soykırımın İzini Sürmek* (Istanbul: İletişim Press, 2012), 38.

43 *The Ottoman Archives of the Prime Minister's Office: Republic Archives*, 18 March 1925, Decision no: 1039, file no:135-7, 3.29.10.
44 Susanne Güsten, *A Farewell to Tur Abdin* (Istanbul: Istanbul Policy Center, 2016), 18.
45 Nevzat Onaran, *Cumhuriyet'te Ermeni ve Rum Mallarının Türkleştirilmesi: Emval-i Metrukenin Tasfiyesi-I (1914-1919)* (Istanbul: Evrensel Press, 2013), 477.
46 *Turkish Civil Code* (1926), no. 639, http://www.mevzuat.gov.tr/MevzuatMetin/5.3.743.pdf.
47 Onaran, *Cumhuriyet'te Ermeni ve Rum Mallarının Türkleştirilmesi*, 459–61. There is no underlying systematic behind the reappropriation of non-Muslim monuments, as is demonstrated by research into their current ownership in the fieldwork explained in this chapter. Churches/monasteries, etc. have been registered to the ownership of Muslim individuals, the State Treasury, the local Municipality or even the village's legal entity (Pekol, *Kayseri Adana İzmir Elazığ Niğde Bursa*). In some instances where individuals were not granted ownership and the building was registered to the state, there was probably a local dynamic in play.
48 Nesi Altaras, 'Varagavank Manastırı Mehmet Çoban'a Emanet', *Agos*, 22 August 2019, http://www.agos.com.tr/tr/yazi/22814/varagavank-manastiri-mehmet-cobana-emanet.
49 Ümit Kurt, 'Birinci Cihan Harbi Sonrası Ermeni Mallarının İadesi Cebel-i Bereket Örneği', in *Yok Edilen Medeniyet: Geç Osmanlı ve Erken Cumhuriyet Dönemlerinde Gayrimüslim Varlığı*, eds. A. Şekeryan and N. Taşçı (Istanbul: Aras Press, 2017), 203.
50 'Olağanüstü Hal Kanunu', accessed 15 December 2019, https://www.mevzuat.gov.tr/MevzuatMetin/1.5.2935.pdf.
51 Ackerman, 'The Emergency Constitution', 1043.
52 Philip Oltermann and Constanze Letsch, 'Turkey Recalls Ambassador after German MPs' Armenian Genocide Note', *The Guardian*, 2 June 2016, https://www.theguardian.com/world/2016/jun/02/germany-braces-for-turkish-backlash-as-it-votes-to-recognise-armenian-genocide.

4

Emergency as normalcy in mid-2010s Amed/Diyarbakır

Eray Çaylı and Herdem Doğrul

As laid out in detail in the introduction to this edited volume, spatially focused scholarship on normalcy and emergency has decisively problematized the assumption that the relationship between these two phenomena is an antithesis. It has shown that, increasingly throughout modernity, not only have normalcy and emergency been interdependent, but they have also often operated under the guise of one another. Yet, the geographical and historical unevenness characterizing this interdependence, and/or this operation – the uneven ways in which the effects resulting from normalcy and emergency's workings as interdependent forces have been distributed across geography and history – remains underexplored in relevant scholarship, particularly in the case of Turkey. In what follows, we explore this unevenness in a way that dovetails with this book's contextual focus on mid-to-late 2010s Turkey. We discuss the entanglement between normalcy and emergency as it has unfolded in the city of Amed, otherwise known by its official name Diyarbakır. Many Kurds living in the region and elsewhere within Turkey consider Amed as the unofficial capital of northern Kurdistan; simply put, the city is known as the Kurdish capital of Turkey. Demographically, it is the largest predominantly Kurdish-inhabited city in south-eastern Turkey. Our chapter therefore uses the city's Kurdish-language name except when referring to official institutions such as the Diyarbakır Metropolitan Municipality.

The context in which we explore the relationship between normalcy and emergency has two defining features. The first is Turkey-wide; it concerns the intense demolition and construction activity that took place across the country during the mid-to-late 2010s. While this activity gradually increased throughout the late 2000s and early 2010s, it entered a new phase in mid-2012, in the aftermath of which it reached new heights. Mid-2012 was when a piece of legislation known popularly as the Disaster Act was issued, the avowed aim of which is to disaster-proof the country. The second feature that has defined this context is Kurdistan-specific and dates from late 2015. It involves the flare-up of war in northern Kurdistan – in other words, in parts of eastern and south-eastern Turkey. The flare-up of war brought to a halt more than six years of semi-official peace talks which had followed more than two decades of fighting between the Kurdistan Workers' Party (PKK) and Turkey's armed forces. City centres and towns where fighting took place saw immense destruction, including Amed's historic centre Suriçi (literally: within-city-walls). Suriçi is nestled within 5.8-kilometre-long walls whose history stretches back to 3000 BC. Just three months before the start of war, Suriçi's ancient walls and citadel were listed as a UNESCO World Heritage Site, alongside the adjacent Hevsel Gardens that connects the historic district to the Tigris River and an eleventh-century bridge spanning the river. Following the fighting, the central government subjected 80 per cent of Suriçi to urgent expropriation, followed by wholesale demolition and architectural overhaul, including that of its listed buildings. Around the same time, across much of Turkey's Kurdistan (including Amed), democratically elected pro-Kurdish mayors – distinct from the other administrative authority operative at the local level across Turkey, which comprises governors appointed by the Ministry of Interior Affairs – were ousted by the central government, and replaced with so-called 'caretakers' appointed by the cabinet.[1]

Working from these two features that frame the empirical context of our study in order to focus on the extensive demolition and construction activity that has recently taken place in Amed's historic centre Suriçi, we ask the following questions: What sorts of factors lead to the geographically uneven distribution of the entanglement between normalcy and emergency even when the geography in question is within the borders of a single state and thus technically under the same jurisdiction? How might this uneven distribution be understood and challenged through a focus on the built environment? In other words, what is particularly architectural about the uneven distribution of the entanglement between normalcy and emergency, and what are the political possibilities and limitations of understanding it as such? Alongside addressing these questions, we aim to contribute to a set of Turkey-specific discussions on the states of emergency and disaster-preparedness practices the country has witnessed throughout the mid-to-late 2010s, and on the architectural dynamics at work throughout this period. Our main argument is twofold. First, we argue that the entanglement of normalcy and emergency that has recently become salient in Turkey needs to be situated within a history that is much more expansive than just the mid-2010s: namely, this is a history that stretches back to the early twentieth-century dispossession and violence suffered by Turkey's non-Muslim populations. Secondly, we argue that, in the case of Amed, the entanglement between emergency and normalcy is best understood as being grounded in intra-colonial dynamics. However, as we will detail in what follows, in making this argument, our notion of intra-colonialism is not necessarily one that aligns with Foucauldian notions regarding how colonialist methods move from the periphery to the centre or, more broadly, with a Global North and a Global South distinction that imagines each of these geopolitical entities as socially and politically monolithic.

Approaching the entanglement between normalcy and emergency as internal colonization

The way we understand the relationship between normalcy and emergency insofar as it has unfolded within the context of contemporary Turkey is as follows. We not only approach emergency and normalcy as entangled in, rather than antithetical to, one another, but we also understand this entanglement as being distributed unevenly across geography and the bodies inhabiting it. This understanding is relevant to our analysis both contextually and methodologically. The contextual relevance is evident in our empirical focus on Amed: the city that constitutes the sociopolitical and cultural heart of the very region that has been the subject of recurrent episodes of emergency rule. Methodologically, we see this attention as a call to reconsider the framework through which regions such as northern Kurdistan are understood in the scholarship on spatial politics. The uneven disadvantaging of such regions, we suggest, indicates the imperative to consider them through the framework of colonization rather than merely through emergency and normalcy.

In proposing to reformulate in this way the impact of the entanglement between normalcy and emergency on Turkey's Kurdistan, we follow such spatially focused scholars of the region as Joost Jongerden and Zeynep Gambetti. As Jongerden has shown, the idea that Kurdistan has been colonized (both by Turkey and by Western powers) has remained the premise of modern-day pro-Kurdish politics in Turkey since the 1970s, and as such, has featured in much of the relevant scholarship produced in the country since the 1990s, particularly that pioneered by İsmail Beşikçi.[2] Jongerden's work has aimed to nuance this idea by showing that the method of colonization, insofar as it was employed by Turkey's authorities, was intended not only to push out Kurds and Kurdishness but also to settle Turkish-speaking refugees coming in from ex-Ottoman territories.[3] Of particular significance to this method was the '1934 Settlement Act, Law Number 2510'. This piece of legislation was employed for settling Turkish-speaking refugees at various sites of strategic importance, such as within the vicinity of infrastructure and borderlands, as well as for forcibly resettling Kurds (whom the law spoke of as non-Turkish-speaking Turks) in Turkey's western regions.[4] The legislation's assimilationist categorization of Kurds as non-Turkish-speaking Turks and the practice of forced resettlement that it premised upon this category were both legitimized as a civilizing mission that would bring peoples categorized as such up to date with Turks proper.[5] Jongerden has also shown that over time this early Republican policy came to influence much more recent policies, such as the village evacuations that the state carried out in the 1990s as part of their martial strategy against the PKK.[6] Approaching Turkey's Kurdistan and its unofficial capital Amed through the lens of colonization has allowed scholars like Jongerden and Gambetti to analyse counter-policies implemented in the region since the mid-2000s by pro-Kurdish municipalities – policies such as renaming and redesign of urban spaces – as exercises in decolonization.[7] Their many strengths notwithstanding, such analyses of how colonization works and/or is challenged in the region have tended to prioritize large-scale trends whether spatially (the scale of regional geography) or temporally (the long term). As Jongerden and Gambetti themselves acknowledge, this tendency has led to a scholarly neglect of 'the actual production of space':

> an analysis of the relations and practices constituting particular productions of space and the performativity of spatial practices, or how people experience and shape the places they live in, how social relations co-define and institutions occupy geographical location as territory.[8]

In this chapter, we aim to offer an analysis of the latter sort, and do so by approaching the implications that the entanglement between normalcy and emergency has had in Amed through a focus on internal colonization as a method that operates on multiple spatial and temporal scales, including those smaller than the scale of geography and that of long-term processes.

The most frequently cited formulation of colonization as and through methodology is Michel Foucault's, developed through his discussion of the relations between colony and metropole. According to Foucault's well-known formulation, if the world has gradually become a post-colonial one throughout the second half of the twentieth century, this has not meant the complete eradication of colonialism. If anything, this period has seen the methods used in the colony begin to permeate the metropole.[9] Spatially oriented scholars have questioned Foucault's formulation in terms of the sociopolitical flatness deriving from the temporal and spatial hierarchizations that characterize it. Among such scholars, geographer Derek Gregory and anthropologist Ann Stoler have decisively problematized the idea that coloniality and post-coloniality are phenomena which have uniform effects across each of the territories associated with one another, and which are always necessarily separated by the temporal gap that the prefix 'post-' indicates.[10] Meanwhile, the temporalization of the spatial gap separating the colony from the metropole has been problematized for its methodological reproduction of the Orientalist notion that the colony lags behind the metropole in developmental and civilizational terms. As Joe Turner has shown, the reproduction at work here occurs despite the temporal–political inversion of the Orientalist notion, and it does so in two ways. First, the Foucauldian formulation still sees the colony as a pioneering model for methods that are then employed in the metropole. Secondly, it considers colonization as a method which the monolithically imagined geopolitical entity of the Global North implements in the similarly imagined Global South and which only then boomerangs back at the former.[11] We believe that relevant architecture scholarship, which has yet to explore this sort of a problematization of the Foucauldian formulation, could significantly benefit from the non-essentializing approach to the politics of geography and from the non-linear understanding of the political temporality of colonization that characterize Turner's critique.

To indicate potential ways in which architecture scholarship might benefit from such a problematization, it is worth continuing to think with Turner. His alternative to the Foucauldian formulation of the relationship between colony and metropole is to focus on 'how seemingly disparate practices of colonial pacification and social civilisational work come together in novel, yet familiar, ways . . . that not only draw from experiments in . . . counterinsurgency . . . but are also buttressed by older histories of social work's "civilising" mission'.[12] But there is a caveat when focusing on these continuities, one which Turner unpacks through the work of anthropologist Elizabeth Povinelli. Considering contemporary governance practices as colonization requires attention to the 'contingencies, shifting remobilisations and logics' of 'late liberalism' in Povinelli's terms, foremost among which are strategies that promote 'cultural recognition'.[13] These strategies constitute a shift from the manner in which 'liberal states' throughout much of the twentieth century approached the question of race, given that they purport to undo colonialism's racial and gendered hierarchizations. But they still sustain coloniality insofar as their valuation of life and non-life is based upon colonially grounded discourses and practices of developmentalism and civilizationalism, and particularly upon a (racialized and gendered) compartmentalization of subjects into 'developed', 'underdeveloped' and 'undevelopable' constituencies, where the latter constituency is deemed disposable.[14] Turner conceptualizes this compartmentalization as 'internal colonisation': a contemporary mode of governance which 'denies the subjectivity of the internally colonised and draws on [the] orientalist . . . demarcation between the civilised and savage' and which does so at times by purporting to shift away from colonial modes.[15]

We find Turner's conceptualization useful because it helps approach the uneven ways in which emergency is distributed across a given geography and history not through a hierarchization between certain instances of its implementation (i.e., precedents versus antecedents) but, rather, through an emphasis on how they depend on one another to come into existence. Turner's conceptualization, moreover, helps us to understand this interdependence as one premised on the developmentalist and civilizationalist valuation of subjects and the environments they inhabit, which is common to various instances of emergency's implementation and which, as we hope will become evident in what follows, is central to the specific historical and geographical context explored in this chapter. The questions through which we would like to further the sort of enquiry advanced by Turner are the following: What is particularly architectural about the uneven (i.e., intra-colonial) distribution of the entanglement between normalcy and emergency? What are the political possibilities and limitations of understanding it as such?

Violence/peace and construction/destruction in 2010s Suriçi

We would like to begin our empirical analysis of how Diyarbakır's historic centre Suriçi has recently become subject to both near-complete destruction and, subsequently, an architectural overhaul, by recalling the three interrelated forces that shaped the urban environment in Turkey throughout the 2010s: democratization, a so-called 'construction boom' and the purported risk of disaster. In this section we show how these three forces assumed a distinctive significance in the case of Kurdistan, and particularly its sociopolitical and cultural heart – Amed.

Addressing the question of why the destruction of urban areas like Suriçi is so ardently pursued requires attending to the political contexts in which such pursuit takes place. In certain contexts, destruction and overhaul are legitimized on the grounds of poverty. In others, security becomes the pretext. Both these notions have featured prominently in the discourse of urban transformation that has affected Suriçi periodically since 2009. But grasping this discourse fully requires attention to the longer historical context in which it has come to engulf Suriçi. A crucial component of this context comprises the genocides of the early twentieth century. According to the 1914 Ottoman census, Suriçi was home to more than 65,000 Armenians. The town's Armenian population has gradually disappeared in the aftermath of 1915, now numbering at virtually a handful. We wish to reference 1915 and its aftermath here not only as a commemorative gesture, regardless of how important such gestures may be. There is an aspect of this episode that is of a markedly material character and, as such, speaks to our discussion here much more directly than it does as a question of remembrance: the points at which property ownership in Suriçi changed hands profoundly, whether through market dynamics or through direct intervention by governments.

Suriçi's location next to the fertile Hevsel Gardens and at the heart of northern Mesopotamia's trade routes had from the outset rendered it home to the urban gentry, aristocracy and wealthy merchants. This was the case until immediately after the foundation of the republic, which gave rise to modern architecture and town planning. It was then that Amed's urban population began to move outside the walled city, making Suriçi available to new migrants from the countryside and the poor. The resulting demographic transformation unfolded gradually over the following decades – that is, until the military coup of 12 September 1980, and the tragedies that ensued throughout the 1980s and the 1990s. These decades triggered an exponential rise in Suriçi's population, accompanied by a boom in the number of *gecekondu*s built within the walled city.

From this point onwards, Suriçi's story has been one of 'poverty in turn'.[16] That is, families whose material conditions improved moved out of the walled city and the spaces they left behind were taken up by newcomers to Amed from its rural hinterland. In this respect, Suriçi's story is not unique; it has followed a pattern of circulation seen in nearly every one of the world's cities subject to the force of capitalism, coupled with learned assumptions regarding newly built and 'modern' areas of the city being better than existing ones. One of the few factors that might hinder this conventional pattern is the residents' ability to develop relations of production right where they reside. This factor is at work in Suriçi, if only partially. Hevsel Gardens is still an important area for agricultural production, while certain craftspeople, including ironmongers, saddlers, weavers, fishmongers, etc., continue to live and practice their crafts within the walled city. This enables Suriçi to remain vital to the city's livelihood, not only for dwelling purposes but also for those of production. To give one example, more than 300 families who live in Suriçi still make a living by working the land in Hevsel.

Against this background, let us now consider the present historical juncture in the urban transformation of Suriçi. The origins of this juncture stretch back to 2007. On 4 September that year, TOKİ (Housing Development Administration of Turkey) and Diyarbakır Metropolitan Municipality signed a protocol for a project titled 'Urban Renewal of the Band of Protection around Diyarbakır's Historic City Wall'. TOKİ's justification for the project was the elimination of *gecekondu*s surrounding the protection band along the historic walls and thus the implementation of the conservation master plan dating from November 1990 – the city's first-ever conservation master plan that the Diyarbakır Cultural and Natural Heritage Conservation Board had brought into force following Suriçi's designation as Urban Heritage Site in 1988. The emphasis at work here on preservation, conservation and the elimination of buildings deemed unworthy of architectural quality echoes just the sort of developmentalist and civilizationalist valuation of people and the environments they inhabit, outlined in the previous section of this chapter as a prominent intra-colonialist method.

The Urban Renewal protocol signed in 2007 identified 452 rights holders. On 31 March 2008, the protocol's purview expanded, leading to the 'Diyarbakır Alipaşa and Lalebey Neighbourhoods Urban Renewal (Transformation of *Gecekondu*s) Project'. The new protocol of the same name was undersigned by the Governor of Diyarbakır, the president of TOKİ, the Mayor of Diyarbakır Metropolitan Municipality and the district municipality Sur. On 14 October 2009, the same dignitaries signed an additional protocol dedicated to securing the 'healthy' implementation of the two projects mentioned earlier. This protocol identified a further 824 rights holders in Alipaşa and Lalebey neighbourhoods in addition to the 452 dating from the 2007 project, thereby commencing the removal of a total of 1276 rights holders from the whole of Suriçi.

According to the 2009 protocol, expropriation and demolition in Suriçi would be carried out by the Metropolitan Municipality, while TOKİ would construct a new housing estate comprising 1272 flats in the neighbourhood of Çölgüzeli situated eleven kilometres northwest of the walled district. Implementation of the protocol, however, was put on hold due to preparations for a new conservation master plan in lieu of the existing one dating from 1990 – preparations which had been taking place since 2008 and which led the existing conservation master plan to be suspended. The new conservation master plan was approved in January 2012, allowing demolition work to begin in Suriçi. But residents, especially those in Alipaşa and Lalebey, turned down TOKİ's offer and resisted evacuation. This brought the project to a halt, followed by the Metropolitan Municipality's decision to withdraw from the protocol altogether on grounds of its failure to observe the interests of Suriçi's residents.

By this point, the process of demolition that referenced the conservation master plan had already been amply criticized by relevant professional organizations, such as the local chapters of the Chamber of Architects and the Chamber of Town Planners. Despite this criticism, the project had managed to launch. The master plan had predicted the removal of 37 per cent of Suriçi's population. The research and assessment process that led to the master plan had identified only 6 per cent of buildings in the district as risky, whether due to their excessive height or to their lack of structural integrity. But the area earmarked for demolition was much larger than just 6 per cent. This discrepancy was among the factors that led the people to object to the master plan, leading to a pause in the demolition work for the time being.

What to make of the convergence of the local authorities and the central government in this project? What brought together these two forces that are otherwise – ideologically and politically – diametrically opposed to one another? It is possible to call this a partnership of objectives. Regardless of how one names these objectives – elimination, rehabilitation, cleansing, conservation, improvement, etc. – they are all the product of an approach to the city that sees it primarily as a financial asset. A most striking way of illustrating this is to recall the parliamentary question that was raised in May 2009 by Selahattin Demirtaş who, in the aftermath of his ascent to leadership of the pro-Kurdish party in 2010, has come to gain much acclaim in left-leaning circles. Demirtaş, then a member of parliament for Diyarbakır and a representative of the pro-Kurdish DTP, asked, 'how much money TOKİ has transferred to the municipality from the direct sale of lands in Suriçi' rather than questioning the many social disadvantages the project was poised to inflict on the district's residents.[17]

As has recently been observed in many of Turkey's major cities – most infamously in the cases of Sulukule and Tarlabaşı in Istanbul – projects claiming to preserve historic urban centres see their impoverished residents as a threat, and hold the latter responsible for any damage such areas have suffered.[18] The urban poor are then criminalized through various means. Once their criminalization reaches an unpoliceable degree, demolition begins. In many cases, demolition takes lengthy periods to complete, and populations continue to live alongside the rubble whether because they object to transformation projects or because they have got nowhere else to go. The physicality of demolition makes it easier for various other urban actors to stigmatize the areas in which these populations live as hotbeds of crime. Characteristic accusations targeting such populations are that their neighbourhoods are home to drug dealers and addicts, unregistered sex workers, burglars, pickpockets and suchlike. The case of Suriçi has not been exempt from this stigmatization. However, its residents have repeatedly said that the district is precisely the opposite of what its stigmatization has portrayed. They have testified to feeling so safe and secure that they have not found it necessary to even shut their doors. To quote from a series of interviews conducted in April 2015 as part of the Zan Institute's research on Suriçi's neighbourhoods that were subjected to 'urban transformation':

> We regret that we left our place. My place was beautiful; I was born and grew up there. I mean, I did not want to leave. Everyone there was an acquaintance, a relative of mine.... When I got sick or something happened to me, they would all come see me. We visited one another. Now even if we die no one will know, no one will open the door. Here, everyone is a stranger. I had railings built around my windows and balcony just to be on the safe side. I am scared because I am alone. There I was not afraid; they were all acquaintances, relatives, and so I was not afraid. All doors were open [68-year-old female domestic worker].[19]

The same report speaks of a precondition that is observed by certain businesses in the walled city and that precludes the employment of Suriçi's residents.

> As a business in Suriçi we are unable to employ people living here. Our contracts include such a clause. If we are not employing them, then who will? This is why they turn to drugs, pickpocketing, burglary, and such activities [31-year-old male and manager of a business].[20]

As the urban transformation project that began in Suriçi came to a halt, in October 2012 the central government used the second clause of the so-called 'Disaster Act' to designate the entire walled city as a risky area.[21] Opposition to this designation failed to develop at the time. One of the most popular explanations for this failure has emphasized the semi-official peace talks between the government and the Kurdish political movement that came to a halt in 2015 as war flared up. The explanation is that the Kurdish political movement did not want to harm this process by objecting to the government's actions in other arenas. But this is far from being a plausible explanation; the date when the designation was declared was a time when the talks had not yet begun in earnest, and the Kurdish political movement was still in a mode of active resistance, including on the streets of Amed and other towns and cities of Kurdistan and in prisons where thousands were on hunger strike. Therefore, to explain the Kurdish political movement's failure to express strong objection to the risky area designation by way of a resignation with which it allegedly received such developments is not only ill informed but also ill-intentioned, as it prioritizes the Kurds in the assigning of blame for tribulations affecting a Kurdish city. In so doing, such an explanation implies that the Kurdish political movement is underdeveloped in its contrarianism, thereby effectively reproducing in the realm of contrarian politics the developmentalism and civilizationalism that characterizes intra-colonialism.

What, then, are some of the plausible explanations for the Kurdish political movement's failure to oppose the government's designation of Suriçi as a risky area? One explanation is by way of the revised conservation master plan that had been approved only months prior to this designation. No matter how much of Suriçi might be designated as a risky area, the master plan ensured – at least, technically – that wholesale demolition and overhaul were impossible. All government institutions were obliged by law to comply with it. Furthermore, Suriçi had already been listed as an Urban Heritage Site in 1988, requiring the preservation of its streetscape. In sum, no one expected the government to demolish an area protected by its own laws, hence the absence of overt mobilization against the risky area declaration. But the government's contravention of its own laws was exactly what took place in 2012, aided in great part by the fact that the Disaster Act left heritage sites designated as risky areas to the mercy of the Ministry of Culture and Tourism. It was technically the Ministry's duty to comply with heritage statuses and conservation master plans but, in many cases including that of Suriçi, they instead authorized the wholesale demolition and reconstruction that the government pursued in designating such areas as risky.

To return to the explanation debunked previously, regarding how the Kurdish political movement allegedly did not want to harm the peace process by objecting to the government's actions in other arenas, there may have been one way in which the wider political atmosphere affected developments in Suriçi. Note that this atmosphere was not one of calm and quiet. Contrary to what many critics of the peace process have assumed, it was an atmosphere characterized by immense tension, as the government continued to pursue a carrot-and-stick approach including the implementation of isolation policies while the Kurdish political movement, in turn, resorted to methods such as hunger strikes. The political atmosphere therefore obliged the Kurdish political movement to focus on the tensions characterizing this atmosphere. If such issues as Suriçi were placed on the back burner, this was not the result of some hidden consensus between the government and the Kurdish political movement. Rather, it was the result of outright and protracted dissensus obliging the Kurdish political movement to dedicate its attention and energy to such phenomena as hunger strikes.

In sum, the demolitions that began in 2012 led to the removal of 735 households (including property owners and tenants) from the neighbourhoods of Cevatpaşa-Fatihpaşa (the subject of the 2007 protocol) and Alipaşa-Lalebey (that of the 2009 one), and their being moved to TOKİ-built flats in Çölgüzeli. Demolitions then came to a halt, and the urban transformation project to which they were attached was suspended. This remained the case until the declarations of autonomy that took place towards the end of 2015 in towns and city centres across Kurdistan, including Suriçi, and the flare-up of war that ensued. Following the People's Assembly's declaration of autonomy in Suriçi on 14 August 2015, the government declared a curfew for 6–7 September, 13–14 September, and 10–13 October. Further curfews were declared for 28–30 November and 2–9 December, and a final one on 11 December. At the time of writing, the curfew effectively remains in place; despite the government's declaring the end of its operations in March 2017, no one has been allowed entry into neighbourhoods subject to the curfew except contractors, construction workers and government officials.

Address-based population data from 2014 states the total number of residents in neighbourhoods where curfews were declared – Cevatpaşa, Fatihpaşa, Dabanoğlu, Hasırlı, Cemal Yılmaz, and Savaş – as being 26,084.[22] From the declaration of the curfews onwards, this population has been displaced in its entirety. Local representatives from the Union of Engineers' and Architects' Chambers conducted a survey in these neighbourhoods at the end of the second curfew, which fell on 13 October. The survey concluded that while 706 businesses and homes had suffered damage, 693 of these were salvageable by way of simple repairs.[23] At this stage, the fighting had not reached the peak that it would a couple of months later, and heavy weaponry had yet to be employed. This remained the case until 2 December. The fresh curfew declared on this date was followed by the state's deployment of heavy weaponry, turning Suriçi into an all-out war theatre. Throughout this episode of war, information about the neighbourhoods under curfew was entirely inaccessible, except through the state news agency and social media posts by various accounts affiliated with the special forces carrying out the operations.[24] From the visuals circulated by these sources, it has been possible to identify heavy damage inflicted on various listed buildings, such as the Kurşunlu and

Hacı Hamit Mosques, Paşa Hammam, Mehmet Uzun House and Armenian Catholic Church. Despite the numerous press statements, objections and court cases launched by local representatives from the Union of Engineers' and Architects' Chambers, the area has remained inaccessible, and damage has continued unabated. The damage compounded towards the end of February 2016, due to the extensive demolition undertaken as part of the military method of entering armour-heavy machinery into neighbourhoods with close-knit networks of houses and especially into the Hasırlı neighbourhood.

The latest curfew and the military operations accompanying it came to an official end in March 2016, when the minister of Interior Affairs released a statement to that effect.[25] Even then, a comprehensive repair campaign would have been able to reverse the 103 days' worth of severe damage that had been inflicted on Suriçi. But immediately after the interior minister's statement, the government authorized the urgent expropriation of 6292 parcels out of Suriçi's total of 7714.[26] The rest of the parcels were not included in this expropriation because they had already been expropriated as part of the previous episodes of urban transformation underway since 2007. The urgent expropriation was premised on the risky area designation issued in 2012. But this itself is in violation of the Expropriation Act and specifically clause no. 27 thereof. To cite from the Chamber of Architects Diyarbakır Chapter's court appeal for the suspension of Suriçi's urgent expropriation, clause no. 27 of Turkey's Expropriation Act reads as follows:

> Clause no. 27 of Act no. 2942 [the Expropriation Act] identifies urgent expropriation as an exceptional measure where the urgency in question requires the presence of three conditions. Two of these concern the implementation of the Duty of National Defence: urgent expropriation may be declared for the purpose of protecting public welfare and public order as required by the need to defend the homeland or by emergencies subject to special statutes. While the third condition does allow the government to determine whether there is a valid case for urgent expropriation or not, it still requires that the validity in question is premised on the prerequisites of protecting public welfare and public order and thus parallels the first two conditions in this regard.[27]

This urgent expropriation has enabled the sort of extensive demolition that accompanied the entry of armour-heavy machinery into close-knit streetscapes, such as those in the Hasırlı neighbourhood, to engulf the rest of Suriçi's neighbourhoods under curfew. Gradually, these six Suriçi neighbourhoods were wiped off the map. To the extent that the local chapter of the Chamber of Architects has been able to observe the developments in Suriçi, demolition has proceeded without proper planning. On paper, demolition and construction activity in Suriçi is overseen by the Ministry of Environment and Urbanization. But, in practice, the only authority in charge of this activity is the Security Directorate of Diyarbakır Province, that is, the police. According to information that the local chapter of the Chamber has gleaned from engineers working at demolition sites in Suriçi, police chiefs instruct operators of equipment and machinery regarding what or how much needs to be demolished, and listed buildings that have not suffered any damage are taken down gratuitously. In December 2016, while demolitions were still underway, the Ministry of Environment and Urbanization authorized a revised conservation master plan for Suriçi, amending the one issued in 2012.[28] Most of the revisions involved were legitimized on grounds of 'security'. The revised plan prescribed the construction of six new police precincts and the widening of streets. To give one example, Yenikapı Street – infamous for being the site of the murder of the human rights lawyer and president of the local Bar Association Tahir Elçi – is now named Yenikapı Avenue, signalling a substantial widening.[29] Closer scrutiny of the revised plan indicates that the widening of streets is primarily intended to help form something of a 'ring road' that connects the newly constructed police precincts. As such, the plan jeopardizes the streetscape that ensured Suriçi's listed status as an Urban Heritage Site. Indeed, fifty-nine listed buildings situated in related areas have already been demolished.[30]

Conclusion

This chapter has suggested that the unevenness of late liberal distribution of the entanglement between normalcy and emergency – insofar as it has taken place in Turkey and particularly its largest predominantly Kurdish-inhabited city Amed – is best understood as an intra-colonial governance method. Following Turner's notion of internal colonization, we have argued that this method operates in ways that are temporally and spatially non-linear and that are irreducible to such hierarchizations as colony versus metropole or coloniality versus post-coloniality.

We have demonstrated our argument through the historical arc of dispossession that our analysis of Suriçi, Amed's historic centre, has traced.

The purportedly exceptional circumstances at work in the deportation and dispossession of the city's non-Muslims in the early twentieth century left behind an urban vacuum in both a spatial and a socioeconomic sense, as it deprived Amed of a central constituent of its commercial importance. The spatial vacuum was then gradually filled by domestic refugees produced by more recent episodes of emergency rule in the region, such as those of the 1980s and 1990s when armed conflict between state forces and the PKK caused mass rural-to-urban displacement due to much of the fighting taking place in the countryside and to the state's implementation of methods such as village evacuations as part of its military enterprise. The socioeconomic vacuum, meanwhile, became the stuff of developmentalist discourses and practices proclaiming to aim to restore Amed to its former glory. One set of such discourses and practices most relevant to architecture concerns heritage and conservation. As buildings left behind by non-Muslim populations were rendered the stuff of a cosmopolitan past worthy of restoration, Amed's historical cosmopolitanism was reduced to a matter of urban and architectural physicality, while the displaced populations that in the late twentieth century had settled in the historic centre were deemed unworthy of preservation. If this resembled similar interventions carried out elsewhere in Turkey in the name of conservation and heritage protection, such as those discussed in Pınar Aykaç's and Mesut Dinler's contributions to this edited volume, in Amed they had a distinguishing character deriving from the state's martial approach to the wider region of which the city is the sociopolitical and cultural heart.[31]

Therefore, if internal colonization helps us capture how colonialist methods move between different regions within the same borders, it also demonstrates how this movement is differentiated in each region it affects. A case in point concerns the Disaster Act. The ways in which it has been implemented in different parts of Turkey may all have been based upon a certain developmentalist mission, but the nuances between each implementation are not irrelevant to how internal colonization works. In much of Turkey, the developmentalism in question has proclaimed a techno-determinist approach to resilience. Undoubtedly, this proclamation could and should be criticized for being a mere façade. But it is noteworthy that where the Disaster Act has been employed in Amed's historic centre Suriçi – the sociopolitical and cultural heart of Turkey's Kurdistan – it has not even felt the obligation to adopt such a façade. The Disaster Act was implemented here under the guise of protecting and enhancing the historic centre's significance as heritage and its potential as a touristic destination. While this implementation involved a developmentalist mission, the fact that it served objectives profoundly different from resilience and thus from how the Disaster Act was implemented elsewhere in Turkey was not even considered worthy of a rhetorical façade.

We would like to conclude by returning to the question we raised earlier in the chapter regarding what might be particularly architectural about internal colonization as such. A focus on architecture helps show how what we have termed internal colonization operates on scales much smaller than that of geography and the long durée of history. It, moreover, shows how methods initially not specifically developed for internally colonized regions might be made to serve the objectives of internal colonization, and to do so by capitalizing on architecture's twofold significance as both sign or symbol and as embodied experience. As notions of developability and those of disposability associated with them have been assigned to certain regions in which the Disaster Act has been implemented, in Amed's historic centre Suriçi the consequences of this assignment have been much more overtly and promptly violent than they have been elsewhere. If intra-colonization (or the uneven geographical distribution of the entanglement between normalcy and emergency) – insofar as it is considered an architectural phenomenon – affects particular sites, this effect does not always necessarily derive from legislative precedence. That Suriçi has been affected by internal colonization does not, in other words, have to mean that this was where the Disaster Act first appeared. This might, rather, be a matter of how methods developed elsewhere are then implemented in such places as Suriçi to capitalize on architecture's twofold significance as both sign and experience to frame the debate around internally colonized sites. The aim in so doing, we believe, is to make the differential treatment of those subjected to internal colonization not only blatantly evident but also insidiously reproducible even by those proclaiming to contest the government's approach to the built environment.

Notes

1 Tuvan Gumrukcu and Ali Kucukgocmen, 'Kurdish Mayors Replaced in Turkey in Crackdown on Criticism of Syria Assault', *Reuters*, 18 October 2019, reuters.com/article/us-syria-security-turkey-kurds/kurdish-mayors-replaced-in-turkey-in-crackdown-on-criticism-of-syria-assault-idUSKBN1WX1GP.

2 Joost Jongerden, *The Settlement Issue in Turkey and the Kurds: An Analysis of Spatial Policies, Modernity and War* (Leiden: Brill, 2007), 54–7. See also İsmail Beşikçi, *Devletlerarası Sömürge Kürdistan* (Istanbul: Alan Yayınları, 1991).
3 Ibid., 129–30.
4 Ibid., 173–217.
5 Ibid., 198.
6 Joost Jongerden, 'Under (Re)Construction: The State, the Production of Identity, and the Countryside in the Kurdistan Region in Turkey', in *After Civil War: Division, Reconstruction, and Reconciliation in Contemporary Europe*, ed. Bill Kissane (Philadelphia: University of Pennsylvania Press, 2014), 166–7.
7 Joost Jongerden, 'Crafting Space, Making People: The Spatial Design of Nation in Modern Turkey', *European Journal of Turkish Studies* 10 (2009): 13–18, journals.openedition.org/ejts/4014; Zeynep Gambetti, 'Decolonizing Diyarbakir: Culture, Identity and the Struggle to Appropriate Urban Space', in *Comparing Cities: The Middle East and South Asia*, eds. Kamran Asdar Ali and Martina Rieker (Karachi: Oxford University Press, 2009), 95–127.
8 Zeynep Gambetti and Joost Jongerden, 'The Spatial (Re)production of the Kurdish Issue: Multiple and Contradicting Trajectories – Introduction', *Journal of Balkan and Near Eastern Studies* 13, no. 4 (2011): 377.
9 Michel Foucault, *Society Must be Defended: Lectures at the Collège de France, 1975-1976* (London: Penguin, 2004). For a scholarly analysis that uses this Foucauldian lens to approach the case of contemporary Turkey, see Deniz Yonucu, 'The Absent Present Law: An Ethnographic Study of Legal Violence in Turkey', *Social & Legal Studies* 27, no. 6 (2018): 716–33.
10 Derek Gregory, *The Colonial Present: Afghanistan, Palestine, Iraq* (Oxford: Blackwell, 2004); Ann Stoler, *Imperial Durabilities in Modern Times* (Durham: Duke University Press, 2016).
11 Joe Turner, 'Internal Colonisation: The Intimate Circulations of Empire, Race and Liberal Government', *European Journal of International Relations* 24, no. 4 (2018): 766.
12 Ibid., 779.
13 Ibid., 772.
14 Elizabeth Povinelli, *Economies of Abandonment* (Durham: Duke University Press, 2011), 22–7. Turner's discussion here of how subjects are compartmentalized on the basis of developability draws heavily on Cynthia Weber, *Queer International Relations: Sovereignty, Sexuality and the Will to Knowledge* (Oxford: Oxford University Press, 2015), 81.
15 Turner, 'Internal Colonisation', 770–2.

16 Melih Pınarcıoğlu and Oğuz Işık, 'Not Only Helpless but also Hopeless: Changing Dynamics of Urban Poverty in Turkey, the Case of Sultanbeyli, Istanbul', *European Planning Studies* 16, no. 10 (2008): 1354.
17 Selahattin Demirtaş, 'Türkiye Büyük Millet Meclisi Başkanlığına', Türkiye Büyük Millet Meclisi, 7 May 2009, https://www2.tbmm.gov.tr/d23/7/7-7880s.pdf.
18 İclal Dinçer, 'The Impact of Neoliberal Policies on Historic Urban Space: Areas of Urban Renewal in Istanbul', *International Planning Studies* 16, no. 1 (2011): 43–60.
19 Serhat Arslan, Derya Aydın, Hakan Sandal and Güllistan Yarkın, *Sur'da Yıkımın İki Yüzü: Kentsel Dönüşüm ve Abluka* (Diyarbakır: Zan Foundation, 2016), 12.
20 Ibid., 16.
21 TMMOB Diyarbakir Provincial Coordination Board, *2015-2016: TMMOB Destroyed Cities Report* (Ankara: Union of Chambers of Turkish Engineers and Architects, 2017), 46.
22 Union of Southeastern Anatolia Region Municipalities (GABB), 'Damage Assessment & Forced Migration Report: Aftermath of the Urban Armed Conflicts in Southeast of Turkey', Hakikat Adalet Hafıza Merkezi, 30 June 2016, hakikatadalethafiza.org/wp-content/uploads/2016/06/2016.06.30_GABB-Report-EN.pdf.
23 TMMOB Diyarbakır İl Koordinasyon Kurulu, 'Yıkılıp Yeniden İnşa Edilen Tarihî Kent Merkezi Üzerine: Diyarbakır Sur Raporu', *Mimarlık* 399 (2018), www.mimarlikdergisi.com/index.cfm?sayfa=mimarlik&DergiSayi=413&RecID=4348.
24 Eray Çaylı, 'Bear Witness: Embedded Coverage of Turkey's Urban Warfare and the Demarcation of Sovereignty against a Dynamic Exterior', *Theory & Event* 19, no. 1 supplement (2016), muse.jhu.edu/article/610225.
25 Abdullah Karakuş, 'Vatandaş kendisini güvende hissedecek', *Milliyet*, 9 March 2016, milliyet.com.tr/siyaset/vatandas-kendisini-guvende-hissedecek-2206442.
26 TMMOB Diyarbakir Provincial Coordination Board, *2015-2016*, 46.
27 Veçdi Erbay, 'Tuma Çelik: 7 Bin Yıl Yaşanılan Suriçi, 2015'te Kesintiye Uğradı', *Gazete Duvar*, 30 July 2019, https://www.gazeteduvar.com.tr/gundem/2019/07/30/tuma-celik-sur-icin-gec-degil.
28 Ahmet Şahin and Ebru Hasar, 'Askıya alma tutanağı: Diyarbakır İli, Sur İlçesi sınırları içerisinde bulunan 187 hektarlık alan, 6306 sayılı Afet Riski Altındaki Alanların Dönüştürülmesi Hakkında Kanun', Türkiye Cumhuriyeti Çevre ve Şehircilik Bakanlığı, 28 December 2016, diyarbakir.csb.gov.tr/askiya-alma-tutanagi-diyarbakir-ili-sur-ilcesi-sinirlari-icerisinde-bulunan-187-hektarlik-alan-630

6-sayili-afet-riski-altindaki-alanlarin-donusturulmesi-hakkinda-kanun-duyuru-178174.

29 For more on Tahir Elçi's assassination, see BIA News Desk, 'Lawyer Tahir Elçi Commemorated on Fourth Anniversary of His Killing', *Bianet*, 28 November 2019, bianet.org/english/human-rights/216427-lawyer-tahir-elci-commemorated-on-fourth-anniversary-of-his-killing.

30 A report prepared by local representatives from the Union of Engineers' and Architects' Chambers has identified a total of seventeen violations of the law that have marked the government's activities in Suriçi. See TMMOB Diyarbakır İl Koordinasyon Kurulu [Diyarbakır Branch of the Chamber of Architects], 'Diyarbakır ili, Sur ilçesi Koruma Amaçlı Uygulama İmar Planı Değişikliği İtiraz Raporu', 10 January 2017, dimod.org.tr/mimarlarodasi/haber_detay.asp?id=314.

31 For an ethnographic account of how a similar entanglement between the various episodes of dispossession discussed in this paragraph has unfolded in the city of Mêrdîn, Amed's southern neighbour, see Zerrin Özlem Biner, *States of Dispossession: Violence and Precarious Coexistence in Southeast Turkey* (Philadelphia: University of Pennsylvania Press, 2020).

5

Forum in relation to the polis

The case of I.39 and Turkey

Emre Özyetiş

Part one: Introduction

In early September 1977, the head of the junta in Argentina, Jorge Rafael Videla, met with the US president Jimmy Carter in the White House.¹ Videla's visit was designed in such a way that it was not overshadowed by the human rights violations back in Argentina, where the number of people who had disappeared had exponentially increased after Videla had been installed as the president, following the coup in 1976.² In a press conference accompanying the junta leader's visit to the United States, Videla said: 'Whoever speaks the truth will not receive retaliation for telling it.'³

On Human Rights Day, 10 December 1977, acquaintances of people who disappeared in Argentina published a two full-page public statement in the newspaper *La Nación,* directed to the junta administration, where they reminded Videla of the statement he had made in the United States. They declared that they were only asking for the truth.⁴ The truth they were asking for was about the whereabouts of their loved ones: whether they were alive or not, and where they were physically confined, at that very moment. However, it is a safe call to suggest that they knew that they were not going to get the truth from Videla. I think that they were probably calling the bluff of Videla and asserting their right to be *parrhesiastes* (those who use their right to free speech). As citizens of a country which Videla tried to portray as democratic, they claimed their right to *parrhesia* freely, a political act Michel Foucault elaborates with a series of studies on the concept of truth, in the last seminar series delivered before his death in 1984.[5]

The idea of Western democracy has taken its inspiration from the Athenian democracy. In the Athenian democracy, telling the truth was a responsibility that involved participating in the game of *parrhesia*: free speech.[6] Foucault's genealogy of the concept of truth starts by looking at what the equal right of speech, the equal participation of all citizens in the exercise of power, and *parrhesia* all meant for the constitution with which Athenian democracy was defined.[7] These three political constituents were the essential elements of the political system that governed the *polis,* which housed the *agora,* where *parrhesia* appeared. While *parrhesia* is roughly translated as 'free speech' within the political context, *parrhesiastes* is defined as someone who does not just say anything they have in their mind. In the Athenian *polis,* the right to free speech had implications of being a duty that would come from below, directed to an interlocutor who was sovereign and had power over the *parrhesiastes. Parrhesia* was such an obligation for the citizen to practice since there were 'moral qualities' that were attributed to the *parrhesiastes.* To participate in the '*parrhesiastic* game', one had to belong to the right social status that would grant them their moral ground to be *parrhesiastes,* such as being male and not a slave. With one being a so-called well-born citizen of Athens, *parrhesia* involved a game between the truth, *logos* and the *genos* (the birth) at first.[8] But given the social status attached to the *parrhesiastes,* the right to speak freely also implied a moral obligation. Rather than a right to an 'ignorant outspokenness', political *parrhesia* entailed speaking of the truth when the *parrhesiastes* knew that they were speaking the truth.[9] In order for the *parrhesiastes* to participate in the '*parrhesiastic* game', directed towards the sovereign, they had to be responsible citizens who were 'courageous' enough to speak the truth, even if that would risk their status and, in the most extreme form, their lives.[10] In other words, in the domain of politics, a *parrhesiastes* was someone who spoke the truth and took the risk in telling a sovereign a truth that could be disturbing. The political *parrhesiastic* game depended on *parrhesiastes* 'to disclose those truths which would ensure the salvation or welfare of the city'.[11] Hence, this added another relationship between *logos* and *nomos* (the law) to the game. It was the ethical duty of every citizen who had the right and the privilege of being part of the *polis* and the *agora.* As *parrhesiastes,* they were supposed to tell the truth to the sovereign and to criticize them, despite the consequences, given they had to convey the truth if they knew it, for the sake of *nomos*.[12]

Signed by more than 200 friends, family members and acquaintances of those who were missing, the confrontational bulletin published in *La Nación* made Madres de Plaza de Mayo go public with their demand to know the whereabouts of the thousands of people who had disappeared under the junta dictatorship in Argentina. The signatories demanded to hear the truth by claiming the physical *agora* of the *polis*, Plaza de Mayo in Buenos Aires, but also via their confrontation with Videla through the discourse he appropriated, they reclaimed the domain of politics and the right to practise *parrhesia*. Maybe it was a bluff as Videla pretended to be a good tyrant who could demonstrate the litmus test for his good ruling abilities. After all, the junta leader was desperate to portray his administration as if it was committed to being a part of the democratic Western world, in order to continue receiving allocated funds and aid from the US government; for their part, the United States had to pretend as if their foreign policy with Argentina was informed by human rights and not the dirty war politics.[13] Therefore, Videla implied he was capable of playing the *parrhesiastic* game by pretending to offer a *parrhesiastic* contract to those who were not entitled to speak before, and by promising they would not be punished when they speak freely. Whether this was the case or not, the junta eventually lost its capacity to rule over the political domain where *parrhesiastes* were able to emerge. With the military dictatorship losing power and Argentina returning to democracy in 1983, the information concerning around 10,000 documented disappeared people became accessible to the public, and courts began ordering exhumations to be conducted.[14] Depending on how one decided to intervene in the field of truth (graves and cemeteries were among those fields in the case of the 1980s Argentina), it was demonstrated that the truth could still be obscured when improperly handled. Either due to a lack of expertise or because of the complicity of the experts in the crime that was also being unearthed, the truth of this period was still in danger as reported by the Equipo Argentino de Antropología Forense (EAAF, Argentine Forensic Anthropology Team).[15] EAAF was formed in response to this problem as the National Commission on the Disappearance of Persons, which was established after the junta was replaced with the civilian government of newly elected President Raúl Alfonsín, and Madres de Plaza de Mayo reached out to an international team of experts to stop this from happening.[16]

Referred to as the 'the world's first professional war crimes exhumation group', a young team of scientists specialized in archaeology, physical and social anthropology, computer sciences and law (as well as various volunteers) were trained by a group of experts from the American Association for the Advancement of Science.[17] These forensic experts were also the ones who were investigating the exhumed skeletons found in São Paolo in Brazil in 1985. They were there to answer whether the exposed skeleton belonged to Josef Mengele, a physician who was complicit in the Holocaust and crimes the Nazi regime were held responsible for, but who had evaded arrest, unlike Adolf Eichmann who had been taken to court after being captured in Argentina in 1960.[18] Thomas Keenan and Eyal Weizman indicate that this was the moment in the late twentieth century when a forensic discourse within war crimes research emerged.[19] The 'Mengele Investigation', as they claim, 'opened up what can now be seen as a third narrative in war crime investigations – not that of the document or the witness but rather the birth of a forensic approach to understanding war crimes and crimes against humanity'.[20] The thread they trace from the Eichmann Trial to the Mengele Investigation introduces a shift from the witness to forensic aesthetics, which replaces the testimony of the survivor with the testimony of the skull. In the case of the Eichmann Trial, the witness or the survivor's testimony did not require words either: Keenan and Weizman refer to Felman and Dori Laub's book *Testimony* (1992) to point out that 'it was often in silence, distortion, confusion, or outright error that trauma – and hence the catastrophic character of certain events – was inscribed'.[21] In the case of the Mengele Investigation, the testimony of the material, a skull that is remaining from someone who is not alive anymore, is heard with the help of the forensic expert. And this testimony is not a simple utterance of words either. *Mengele's Skull* (2012) is a study of the shift in the way truth is uttered. In the case of the Mengele Investigation, this shift becomes visible in the use of superimposed video images of the skull and video images of Mengele developed by Richard Heimer, a forensic expert in the team of the Mengele Investigation, and through which the experts say what they believe to be the truth.

This method was not just providing the means to test and position what could be declared as truth on a scale of probability similar to what the empirical sciences demanded from the scientist by the methods they appropriated.[22] It also demanded from the scientists and experts a new language with its form and aesthetics enabling the truth to be uttered and heard by the public. The images developed by Heimer 'produced the potential for conviction'.[23] By the 1980s, scientists who had already spoken on behalf of things in criminal courts began to 'appear in human rights cases as expert witnesses'.[24] Referring to this moment as the advent of forensic aesthetics, Keenan and Weizman postulate that the task of scientists and experts involved in the process is no longer only to convince themselves 'but also government lawyers and criminal investigators, as well as . . . the general public'.[25] Hence, to demonstrate the atrocities to be registered as what they are, '[p]ublic opinion itself' was added to the scientific method of forensics as 'another decision-making calculus'.[26] Forensic aesthetics involved the 'arduous labour of truth construction, one employing a spectrum of technologies that the forum provides, and all sorts of scientific, rhetorical, theatrical, and visual mechanisms'.[27]

Their publication *Mengele's Skull* demonstrates the shift from 'the living to the dead, from the witness to the bones or the missing person, from memory and trauma to a forensic aesthetics'.[28] I tend to think of what Keenan and Weizman point out to be a moment of crisis, one that changes the rules of the field on which we as researchers and experts struggle to respond. But what appears as forensic aesthetics amid this crisis, and which the scientist and the expert have become dependent on, is haunting forensic anthropology teams around the globe. It also affects the global human rights discourse in political theory and social sciences as it ends up becoming confined within the domain of philanthropy and NGOs. Experts and scientists, who happen to be academics, plus researchers from a variety of disciplines (including architecture and design) all propose to intervene into the field as the political domain is found in a moment of crisis, if not emergency. This crisis is not a result of a disaster or war but is related to truth and the way one can speak.

For Foucault, the domain in which *parrhesia* could be performed was political. It required a *polis* and an *agora* in which one could claim one's right to free speech and participate in the *parrhesiastic* game, whereas experts are situated in the *forum*, as Keenan and Weizman remind us. Forensics is '[d]erived from the Latin *forensis*, the word's root refers to the "forum," and thus to the practice and skill of making an argument before a professional, political, or legal gathering'.[29] As they continue elaborating on this *forum*, they further demonstrate that it not only requires an *arena* but 'protocols of appearance and evaluation', as well as experts.[30] The EAAF was one of the early examples of this process, which coincided with the Mengele Investigation in São Paolo. They gained sufficient expertise in exhumation in order to identify the bodies of those who had disappeared, as well as developing forensic anthropology investigation methods, both of which aimed at presenting the truth most accurately to those who seek it. As the post-junta government allowed the team to participate in the *parrhesiastic* game, the experts and activists were able to identify people who had disappeared through their methods, and then give them a proper burial afterwards, giving their families and friends the opportunity to mourn for their lost ones. The truth, which was obscured from them before, was able to be revealed thanks to the methods EAAF mastered and utilized. Meanwhile, EAAF became involved in other atrocities that involved human rights violations around the globe, and so they also established forensic anthropology teams in Chile, Guatemala and Peru. Those teams and international bodies such as the UN War Crimes Tribunal became equally invested in the material documentation and demonstration of the massive atrocities, leading to various forums being founded that addressed human rights violations in the late twentieth century.[31]

The study of forensics and its relation to the material and cultural shift within techno-scientific epistemology, coupled with its claim to scientific knowledge (as an empirical and laboratory science), is far beyond the scope of this piece. However, I am perplexed as to the implied direct relationship between the claim to truth and forensic evidence inherently found in the role experts seek to have within human rights discourse. This relationship is too hastily drawn once scientists and experts are ascribed to be *parrhesiastes*. Political *parrhesia* has its roots in Quintillion's description of what was not 'simulated or artfully designed', with the zero-degree of rhetorical figures in rhetoric for the Greeks.[32] On the other hand, as Keenan and Weizman demonstrate, to be able to engage in a conversation in the *forum*, the expert needs to be capable of knowing and following the protocols even if their presence would alter and change those sets of rules eventually. One can assume that occupying a place in the *forum* and speaking from/in the *forum* does not rule out the expert's participation in the *polis* as *parrhesiastes*. Moreover, a *forum* can only be assumed to exist, at least spatially, within an already existing *polis*. Therefore, one can suggest that *forum* and *polis*, the expert and the *parrhesiastes*, could overlap. But the question for me is whether an expert who holds a claim to scientific truth can be considered as a *parrhesiastes*. Can an expert who needs to invent a whole set of protocols and performances within their practice be considered as practising their obligatory right to speak the truth? When the scientist conveys what their experiments postulate, but who is also challenged to convince the general public that their finding is commensurate with scientific truth, how far is this from mastering a persuasive use of language? And can we talk about experts and scientists as *parrhesiastes* once their duty – to tell the truth – does not come from below, and, instead, their place within the human rights discourse is justified by an epistemologically higher ground that claims to be scientific?

In 2002, the EAAF produced a documentary about their practice. Titled 'Following Antigone: Forensic Anthropology and Human Rights Investigations', the documentary demonstrated their capabilities, and stood as a promise to the public, governmental and international bodies that they were set to exist in the forums that were being opened up around the world.[33] With this documentary, the group shared how their practice was directed to an audience – one which they listed as 'courts, judges, human rights lawyers and activists, associations of families of the victims, and students' – in order to provide information about 'how forensic sciences can further human rights investigations'.[34] The EAAF can be thought of as unearthing the truth when they properly bury the remains which were left to disappear. This rough description can imply a straightforward analogy with Antigone, the protagonist in the play by Sophocles (497–405 BC). In the following pages, I will not discuss the content of the documentary, but, instead, I will consider its title and what it implies for spatio-critical research in a field that is undergoing a crisis that amplifies the one in Sophocles' *Antigone,* keeping in mind the questions I posed earlier.

Part two

Sophocles' *Theban Plays* are 'Oedipus the Tyrant', 'Oedipus at Colonus' and 'Antigone'. 'Antigone' is chronologically the last episode of the three, where the tragic destiny of the Labdacus lineage in the city of Thebes comes to an end. Although these three plays do not necessarily present a storyline that allows for them to be presented as a trilogy, they do draw for us a picture of the context in which the tragedy unfolds. In the first episode of the three plays, we know that an oracle had foretold Oedipus' destiny to his parents before Oedipus' birth, and to Laius, the king, and Jocasta, the queen.[35] Laius and Jocasta's insistence on refusing to see the truth that was shown to them by the god of Delphi, Apollo, indicates the first sign of crisis in the domain of *aletheia*, the revealing of truth. Despite being told that Laius was meant to be a childless king for Thebes (the *polis*) to foster, Jocasta and Laius ignore the word of the gods.

After Jocasta gives birth to Oedipus, they seed the curse that would run through their bloodline as they try to bend the prophecy by exposing the child. As the story unfolds itself in 'Oedipus the Tyrant', the prophecy becomes fulfilled when Oedipus becomes determined to put an end to the plague that hits the *polis*: Thebes. Apollo attempts to reveal that the cause of the plague was Laius' murder by Oedipus and his marriage to his own mother.[36] Apollo's human-double, the oracle Teiresias, as well as Creon, who visit the temple are sent to Oedipus to tell him of this cause. However, throughout the play, what keeps the tragedy unfolding is how Oedipus fails to comprehend what is being said about who defiled the land. Despite the mortals' ignorance and efforts to un-hear it, the gods reveal the truth at the end of the play. And this points to the second sign of the crisis *aletheia* is facing: truth becomes possible to be comprehended only after the oracles' words had to be proven by the testimony of the messengers and servants who had seen Oedipus killing King Laius. For the truth to be heard, it needs to be mediated by the mortals.

The tragedy of Antigone opens up with Antigone's sister, Ismene, speaking to Antigone about Creon's decree that their brother Polyneices' corpse is to be unearthed and left as food for animals.[37] We learn that Eteocles and Polyneices, the two brothers of Ismene and Antigone who did not leave Thebes with their father Oedipus and stayed behind to fight over Thebes, are dead. As Oedipus' curse at the end of the 'Oedipus at Colonus' promised, the two brothers killed each other while Eteocles was fighting alongside their uncle Creon, with Polyneices against them.[38] Therefore, Eteocles is granted the right to have an official ceremony, and Polyneices' corpse is banned from being buried and mourned over. The play is the unfolding of the tragedy that follows Antigone defying the law of Creon and eventually committing suicide before Creon lifts his decree for Antigone – who also happens to be Creon's sister Jocasta's child, and his son Haemon's betrothed – to be left to die in a cave.

For many, Antigone signifies a moment of rupture, almost a revolutionary gesture, in contrast to a heroic figure whose kinship and family bonds triumph over a powerful and ruthless tyranny.[39] However, the more it is reflected on, the more it becomes clear that Antigone's devotion to family and blood kinship is not the motivation behind her defiance of Creon. Being the protagonist of Sophocles' last *Theban* play, Antigone, and her rebellion against Creon infused with Greek mythology, opens up a whole range of ways to read her as a political figure.[40] Antigone's revolt against Creon and confrontation with the king problematize the entire notion of justice and its roots. In a sense, the question is about *parrhesia* but not in terms of speaking freely. It is more of an act where doing what is right at a moment when there is no truth to be disclosed or no *polis* or *agora* present to engage in a *parhessiastic* game. The way Antigone acts is similar to what Foucault describes as Socratic *parrhesia* that allows *bios* (life) to enter a relationship with *logos*.[41] This is a *parrhesiastic* discourse that discloses the truth of someone's life: 'how this relation to truth is ontologically and ethically manifest in [her] own life'.[42] Historically, Sophocles' *Antigone* is found at the crossroads of interrogation about the Athenian democracy, as Foucault refers to this moment in history.[43] This is when the Greeks engage in 'a *problematization* of some hitherto unproblematic relations between freedom, power, democracy, education, and truth in Athens at the end of the fifth century'.[44] Foucault does not mention Antigone in his study on the shift of the place of truth's disclosure from Delphi to Athens, and, instead, looks at Euripides' (484–407 BC) tragedies, where Foucault says that the word *parrhesia* appeared for the first time in Greek literature.[45] But EAAF's documentary titled 'Following Antigone' makes me wonder, and causes me to look again at Antigone's revolutionary act through a lens that inscribes the urge to speak freely neither on *genos* nor on *nomos*. Instead, it is her *bios* – the way the truth is ontologically and ethically manifested in her rebellious act. If one follows Antigone, I would argue that would entail leaving the domain of politics willingly or never claiming it unless one dedicates oneself to that domain's annihilation for good, which Antigone's so-called foil Creon thinks to be self-destructive.[46] This would require a more detailed account of what Foucault studies as Socratic *parrhesia* and not a return to political *parrhesia*.

What makes Antigone's defiance more than a question of devotion to family ruling over tyranny is the way Antigone threads her destiny. Antigone does not defy Creon's law only once but does it multiple times on various levels.[47] Antigone not only buries Polyneices but also makes a grave for him and mourns over it. What is more, Antigone makes sure that the defiance is heard and known by others, including Creon.[48] When confronted, without showing any attempt to engage in what Foucault would refer to as a '*parrhasiastic* contract' to guarantee lesser wrath on behalf of the sovereign, Antigone resists and almost insults Creon.[49] Whenever her actions are questioned, or whenever she is reminded of their consequences, Antigone shuts down the conversation and leaves the other party to their doomed end.[50] Without promising or expecting a better way of doing things, Antigone commits herself to what she presents as her destiny, even though she had the chance to observe how her father Oedipus was 'once shunned and abominated by all, god and man alike, for his atrocious crimes of incest and patricide is, in the end, embraced, protected, and honoured by the Athenians and awarded by the gods themselves with everlasting well-being'.[51] Hence, by defying the law of Creon, she unfolds and owns her own destiny. She is in a position to be able to accept her own death. She is able to look at her own death in a manner which is not strategically played out and designed or imposed upon her by the gods, but owned and claimed only by her actions, guided by insurgency rather than the wrath which is incurred in her rebelling against Creon.

If anyone, it is Haemon who gets as close to being someone who performs political *parrhessia*, given his social status and his engagement with his father to remind him of the *nomos* by saying what he believes to be true despite his father's wrath.[52] With her act, Antigone is not a political *parrhesiastes*, although this is not because she does not qualify to be one. For one thing, throughout the play, it is indicated more than once that she transgresses the social role that was ascribed to her as a woman.[53] What is more, her social status as both King Creon's niece and future daughter-in-law would grant her the right to engage in a *parrhesiastic* contract, but she does not seek one. Antigone can confront the sovereign by appropriating the *nomos* and the practices, performances and protocols attached to it. However, this is not a strategic move on Antigone's behalf. Throughout the play, as she imposes herself on a political domain it becomes visible to other figures, such as those who have the right to speak freely but have not spoken up, to speak up against Creon.[54] And when that domain is opened up – when the oracles confront Creon, and when Creon reassesses his decree and decisions, not after Ismene and Haemon speak up to him, but after the oracle Teiresias 'teaches' him the truth – it is already too late.[55] Antigone takes her own life before Creon releases her and allows Polyneices to have a grave. Seeing that Antigone is dead, Haemon kills himself in a rage against his father. Eurydice bleeds herself to death after hearing the news of her son Haemon's suicide.

I believe that what EAAF refers to when they suggest following Antigone is not her death, but the courage to tell the truth. However, I believe Antigone's life and death together implicate an act of courage to manifest the truth, not as an ethical obligation, but as a consequence of her care for self, and therefore, for others. This kind of manifestation of truth is different from the courage to tell the truth as Foucault's account of *parrhesia* suggests.

Part three

After the military coup in 1980, Turkey was ruled by martial law between 1980 and 1983. This is a situation which later became embedded in the constitution of Turkey, effective since 1982.[56] The state of emergency which legally replaced the existing implications of martial law began on 1 March 1984, as Partiya Karkerên Kurdistan (PKK, Kurdistan Workers' Party) commenced its military campaign against the Turkish government.[57] Until November 2002, 'the legal norm' that existed in the rest of the country did not apply to the politicized Kurdish areas. Instead, further implementations of the state of emergency were made, such as village guard systems and the Law on The Combat Against Terrorism.[58]

In early October 1984, following the first major attacks by PKK in Şemdinli and Eruh, Kenan Evren, the head of the military junta that seized power in 1980, went on an 'Eastern tour' that mostly covered the cities where most of the politicized Kurdish population were found.[59] During this visit, Evren gave an interview to the press, published on 7 October 1984.[60] Unlike his Argentine counterpart Videla, who relinquished power in 1981, Evren did not offer a *parrhesiastic* game or contract. Instead, Evren established what the truth was. As the headline of the newspaper that reported his interview described: 'Evren revealed the truth that the public should know.'[61] With the truth revealed, it was declared that the nation had two troubles, one of them being 'the secessionist (separatist) leftist terrorists' – by which Evren was mostly referring to PKK insurgency – and the other being 'the Islamist political movement' that was gaining momentum after the coup.[62] The first trouble Evren postulated was symptomatic of the crackdown on opposition groups in the country, whereupon thousands went missing, with many being declared 'lost under custody'.⁶³ On 27 May 1995, after Hasan Ocak's tortured and murdered body was found in a common grave, a group of peaceful protesters started their sit-ins in Istanbul's Galatasaray Square, and continued them every Saturday, demanding to know the whereabouts of the other disappeared people. Referred to as Cumartesi Anneleri/İnsanları (Saturday Mothers/People), similar to Madres de Playa del Mayo, the group became a symbol of the atrocities the Turkish state had committed since the 1980s.⁶⁴ After the Turkish state's measures against the group's protest turned violent on 13 March 1999, Cumartesi Anneleri/İnsanları had to withdraw their protest from the public square.

Recep T. Erdoğan, a former affiliate of the Islamist political movement which Evren declared as the second trouble in the same interview, rose to power with his party Adalet ve Kalkınma Partisi (AKP, Justice and Development Party) after capturing the largest share of the votes in the November 2002 elections in Turkey. AKP launched a reform process to meet the European Union's Copenhagen criteria, one which indicated signs of a *parrhesiastic* game in which the possibility of a non-violent resolution to the war between PKK and the Turkish State was also hinted at. During this period, in 2009, Cumartesi Anneleri/İnsanları resumed their protest. This was the same year when the trial of a gendarmerie officer, retired colonel Cemal Temizöz, also started, and which implied a possibility of pursuing accountability for state-perpetrated killings and disappearances in Turkey.⁶⁵

However, another round of armed conflict surged in 2015. Erdoğan's rule was electorally threatened after the election held on 7 June 2015, when AKP lost the majority in the parliament for the first time since 2002. After a series of events which distorted the public confidence in the peace talks between the state and PKK, in July 2015 the Turkish government began ordering curfews in the urban areas where the politicized Kurdish base is found, such as Sur, Nusaybin, Cizre and İdil, wherein the number of residents totalled hundreds of thousands.⁶⁶ While the setting for the armed conflict had been predominantly the rural context, between 2015 and 2017, the violence intensified in city centres and the urban context found in the eastern and south-eastern regions of Turkey. During and after this period of urban warfare, the Turkish government appropriated substantial physical interventions to the built environment as military tactics.⁶⁷ The violence was broadcasted via visual, print and social media with images in such a way that it became a spectacle.[68] The conflict and the destruction provided powerful and violent imagery to be disseminated through visual media. Between 2015 and 2017, it was common to come across social media accounts of Turkish Security Forces members who claimed to be on the battlefield, and who posted brutal and degrading images from the operations they had conducted. However, as a consequence of open-ended and all-day extended curfews, physical access to the destroyed neighbourhoods was restricted to the public. What is more, the state of emergency laws had once again begun to be enacted throughout Turkey after a failed coup attempt in July 2016, allowing courts and local authorities to hinder the circulation of information (if not impinged on by proponent actors in the conflict). After the Turkish government declared that security operations were completed, all that was left in the conflict areas was the excavation of millions of cubic metres of rubble and construction sites ready for new buildings. In other words, while the political domain of the *polis* disappeared during the coup in 1980, this time not only the political domain but also the spatial and temporal domains of the *polis* were destroyed as manifested in the aftermath of the security operations.

Part four

On 28 November 2015, the Diyarbakir Bar president and Kurdish human rights lawyer Tahir Elçi delivered his last public statement. Elçi had posted a photograph of the damaged pillars of the Şêx Mutahar Mosque's minaret, one of Diyarbakir's symbols, with a caption reading 'assassination of legs of "four-legged minaret"' on his Twitter account three days before the public statement. Elçi was drawing the public's attention to the damage inflicted on this cultural heritage site, one that was under protection according to the Conservation Plan in Sur District of Diyarbakır. Sur was one of the refuges for those who were forced to leave their villages as a result of the Law on The Combat Against Terrorism during the 1990s, and it was now part of the Diyarbakır Fortress and Hevsel Gardens Cultural Landscape protection and management plan, which UNESCO had included in the World Heritage list in 2015. The damage was caused by the armed conflict between PKK and the Turkish Security Forces after the re-escalated violence in the city centre.

Seconds after the public statement was delivered, an armed confrontation between two PKK militants and the police took place on the adjacent Gazi Avenue. Shooting two police officers dead near the entrance of the street by the minaret, the militants entered the street and escaped the crime scene as they ran past. Another round of gunfire took place between the militants and the police who were following the press statement delivered by Tahir Elçi as the militants fled through the street. Elçi subsequently died after receiving a bullet in the back of the neck. Despite the presence of both the press and the security forces recording the public statement, there was apparently no footage that showed who was responsible for the killing of Elçi. As a result of the state officials' inattentiveness towards investigating the death of Elçi, Diyarbakir Bar Association shared the evidence they had with Forensic Architecture (FA) of Goldsmiths, University of London, in order for their specialized research team to carry out a forensic investigation of the incident.

FA's 'The Killing of Tahir Elçi' report is the collective's first encounter with the Turkish legal system. Their investigation, listed as I.39 in their online database, is a demonstration of what Weizman refers to as reversing the 'forensic gaze' and investigating 'the same state agencies . . . that usually monopolize it'.[69] Regardless, it is also worth noting that in their project, FA avoids any use of language that would cast doubt on their impartiality, and define their role in the investigation, as requested by Diyarbakır Bar Association: namely, to 'unpick the chaotic moments leading up to Elçi's death'.[70] Backed up by four different videos, including sound footage, sound spectrographic analysis and witness accounts from the official investigation, FA models the crime scene using a computer-aided model.[71] With this model, a series of simulations and analyses are undertaken in order to examine who was responsible for the fatal shooting of Elçi. FA's findings were shared with the public prosecutors in a 29-page report, submitted along with the 26'17"-long video that accompanied the report on 13 December 2018, and on 2 February 2019, in a session with the public given in both Turkish and English. In the story which FA published via *Opendemocracy* as well as in the video, FA presents the case by providing the context for it, explaining the evidence they have, how they acquired it, how they handled, processed and analysed it, and what findings they came up with after their analysis. The public was informed about the report in Turkey mostly through online news outlets, which were not controlled by the state, where they streamed the video FA produced.

The narrator in the video speaks over moving images that consist of archival video footage of the press conference, interviews and news, as well as raw footage taken from the shooting scene. These are often incorporated with CAD models and animations accompanied by a timeline used to demonstrate the accuracy and analysis FA made concerning the footage from the crime scene. Right before the models and analysis derived from the model as well as simulations are presented, for a brief period of 5 seconds, we see FA in action. The video is not only a representation of the field and analysis that lead to material evidence. It also provides a representation of the laboratory itself where the field is brought into where FA's methods are developed and used in Goldsmiths, University of London.

The video is edited accordingly so that the models FA produced to simulate the event can be matched within the spatio-temporal context the raw footage already possesses. The intertwined use of models and the raw footage is the source of the material evidence FA draws upon in order to conclude that police officers – 'C', 'D' and 'A' – were potential suspects. In December 2018, the Diyarbakır Bar Association submitted the report to the public prosecutor before sharing it with the public. In February 2019, the Bar shared the report with the public as the public prosecutor's office ignored the calls to launch a new inquiry in light of the findings from the report I.39.

Last part

As mentioned in Part Two, Haemon is the one character who attempts to exercise political *parrhesia* to convince Creon to change his mind and dismiss his decrees. While doing so, Haemon is speaking on behalf of Antigone, whom he refers to as 'a child'.[72] Haemon also reminds Creon that even though he is the king, Haemon and Creon are equals, and in fact, it is Creon that Haemon cares about, rather than Antigone.[73] What is more, Haemon also speaks on behalf of the citizens and suggests that Creon should change his mind because Antigone is innocent, according to the public.[74] Haemon has the courage to tell the truth. But Creon does not seek *parrhesiastes*.[75] Even at the very beginning of the tragedy, Creon's lack of interest in political *parrhesia* is apparent when he dismisses granting a *parrhesiastic* contract to the messenger who first brought Creon the news about his orders being defied.[76] In fact, it is Haemon's attempt to help Creon participate in the *parrhesiastic* game by telling the truth, that makes things irreversibly tragic. After rejecting hearing what Haemon offers to say, Creon orders Antigone to be deserted in a cave.[77] While Haemon attempts to initiate a political *parrhesiastic* game, this is not enough to confront Creon and stop the events that are coming. Antigone's actions, on the other hand, demonstrate what Foucault refers to as 'the courage to manifest the truth about oneself, to show oneself as one is, in the face of all opposition'.[78] Antigone annihilates not only herself but also the political domain, which made others speak, the oracle to intervene, and Creon to lose his hübris. In this sense, she is someone who precedes the political *parrhesia* by opening up space for *parrhesiastes* to engage in the *parrhesiastic* game, which she would annihilate at the end. To me, Antigone appears to demonstrate the Socratic *parrhesia* in Foucault's account.

Forensic Architecture was established in 2010 as a 'research agency' consisting of multidisciplinary researchers and professionals. It is a pioneering research collective whose work has been influencing architectural design and research methods. Since their establishment, the collective has received extensive public attention within art and architectural circles. The collective's major task can be summarized as a desire 'to take over the means of evidence production' by inverting the 'forensic gaze' in order to monitor and challenge the sovereign in the violence they often assume they are entitled to commit.[79] FA has a prominent presence in art and design exhibitions in various galleries and biennales around the world. But with the task they claim, they also require a legal framework that can allow FA to demonstrate their skills and provide expertise services to intergovernmental organizations, various prosecutors and governmental bodies as well as international and local NGOs.[80]

The other but equally crucial task for Forensic Architecture is salvaging the word *forensics*, with Weizman drawing our attention to the word *forum*, from which the etymological root *forensis* is derived. According to Weizman, modernization of forensics 'as a term and practice . . . followed a trajectory of linguistic telescoping'.[81] The forum, which was entangled with the multitude of domains, was reduced exclusively into courts of law. Hence, the word 'forensic' lost the 'public, political element'.[82] To bring criticality back to the *forum*, FA offers the 'forensic turn – the emergent cultural and juridical sensibility of the probative value of physical evidence'[83] with the advent of 'forensic aesthetics' appearing as an opportunity. Forensic aesthetics refers to the mode when things start to appear in the forum by the use of 'different techniques and technologies of demonstration, rhetoric, and performance – gestures, narrative and dramatization, image enhancement and projection'.[84]

In *Forensic Architecture* (2017), Weizman refers to FA's collaboration with the Bureau of Investigative Journalism (BIJ) to analyse patterns of drone strikes by the CIA in the Federally Administered Tribal Areas in Pakistan. Their survey of the archives of BIJ that consisted of 'news reports, witness testimonies, and field research on drone strikes between 2004 and 2014', constituted the backbone of their investigation I.7. FA developed architectural models to 'enhance the testimonies of people who experienced drone strikes' whether they were still in the region or had managed to escape the area in their subsequent investigations I.8, I.9, I.10, which were commissioned by the UN Special Rapporteur on Counter-Terrorism and Human Rights.[85] It is interesting to note that Weizman considers that FA's practice and methods could develop such models to facilitate a medium, one which allows survivors to 'speak out'. In this medium, with their testimonies, they are introduced into the *parrhesiastic* game in its most extreme form, when 'telling the truth takes place in the "game" of life or death'.[86] I believe this is a crucial aspect of claiming the ground for counter-forensics to perform what Weizman refers to as the 'forensic operation' in the field.[87] Unless those who perform counter-forensics can occupy the same terrain as the one who can grant *parrhesiastic* contract to others, or invite them to engage in the game of speaking the truth, FA cannot have an encounter with the sovereign as an equal. I.8, I.9 and I.10 were investigations requested by the UN, so those who undertake the forensic operation were invited to the assembly where they sought to demonstrate the truth, whereupon they were granted the right to design the *forum* in which they could enjoy inviting others into the *parrhesiastic* game. But instead of bringing the politics back to the *polis*, the *forum* seems to be the only site where the *parrhesiastic* game is played out, and this is a play for an audience who is already willing to watch the performance. Forensic operators end up enabling a *forum* at the cost of the rest of the *polis* where people should be speaking the truth freely. We might ask: Can this be similar to the voice material which is given by the expert at the cost of muting the witnesses who have been crying out to be heard while they are alive?

After the report FA published on the killing of Tahir Elçi had been shared with the public, Diyarbakır Prosecutor's office requested a new Forensic

Investigation report from Adli Tıp Kurumu (ATK: the Turkish Institution of Forensics) on 18 March 2019.[88] On 6 July 2019, ATK returned their report without making any changes to their initial one.[89]

I.39 has been part of the exhibition 'Under the Radar' in the Swiss Architecture Museum, Basel. Here the curators present a variety of work that demonstrates 'that architecture is not limited to the construction of houses, but also includes spatial analysis of the territory in which architecture emerges'.[90]

Tahir Elçi's assassination marked the escalation of clashes that resulted in mass deaths after Turkish Security Forces laid siege to various city centres. In the case of Cizre, at least sixty people who were stuck in basements between 23 January 2016 and 8 February 2016 were killed.[91]

On 23 September 2019, Tahir Elçi's family requested the prosecutor's office to open an investigation into the ATK team that was responsible for investigating the killing of Tahir Elçi. They referred to a member of the ATK team in Diyarbakır who had submitted a complaint. In a testimony that was filed on 3 August 2016, the person who made the complaint was reporting that the misconduct occurred during the official investigation, and which resulted in evidence going missing from the report which ATK prepared for the public prosecutor's office.[92]

On the 700th sit-in of the Saturday Mothers, the Turkish Authorities banned the group's gathering, and arrested and detained protesters, including Emine Ocak, the 82-year-old mother of Hasan Ocak. Tahir Elçi was their lawyer before his assassination.

Notes

1 Report from US Embassy to Secretary of State Vance entitled 'Videla's Visit: Videla's Position on the Eve of His U.S. Visit', *ADP*, 2 September 1977.
2 M. Cohen Salama, *Tumbas anónimas: Informe sobre la identificación de restos de víctimas de la represión illegal* (Buenos Aires: Catálogos Editora, 1992), 23.
3 'Solo pedimos la verdad', *La Nación*, 10 December 1977.
4 Ibid.
5 Foucault died from complications related to AIDS on 25 June 1984. Seminars around the concept of parrhesia were Foucault's last public lectures at the Collège de France in 1983 and 1984 before his death. These lectures are compiled and published under the titles *The Government of Self and Others I: Lectures at*

the *Collège de France 1982-1983*, ed. Frédéric Gros, trans. Graham Burchell (Basingstoke: Palgrave Macmillan, 2010) and *The Courage of the Truth (The Government of Self and Others II): Lectures at the Collège de France 1983-1984*, ed. Frédéric Gros, trans. Graham Burchell (Basingstoke: Palgrave Macmillan, 2011). In between those two seminars, Foucault delivered six lectures at the University of Berkeley which are compiled in *Fearless Speech*, ed. Joseph Pearson (Los Angeles: Semiotext(e), 2001).

6 Lionel Pearson, 'Party Politics and Free Speech in Democratic Athens', *Greece & Rome* 7, no. 19 (1937): 41.
7 Foucault, *Fearless Speech*, 22.
8 Ibid., 102.
9 Ibid., 73.
10 Ibid., 15.
11 Ibid., 102.
12 Ibid., 16.
13 W. Michael Schmidli, 'Institutionalizing Human Rights in U.S. Foreign Policy: U.S.-Argentine Relations, 1976-1980', *Diplomatic History* 35, no. 2 (2011): 353.
14 Argentine Forensic Anthropology Team, 'The Argentine Experience', accessed 11 December 2019, https://www.eaaf.org/.
15 Mercedes Doretti and Jennifer Burell, 'Forensic Anthropology in Peace Support Operations', in *International and Comparative Criminal Law Series, Volume 28*, ed. Roberta Arnold (Brill: Nijhoff, 2008), 181.
16 Argentine Forensic Anthropology Team, 'The Argentine Experience'.
17 Thomas Keenan and Eyal Weizman, *Mengele's Skull: The Advent of a Forensic Aesthetics* (Berlin: Sternberg Press, 2012), 56.
18 Ibid.
19 Ibid., 58–61.
20 Ibid., 13.
21 Ibid., 12.
22 Ibid , 36.
23 Ibid.
24 Ibid., 13. The work of Thomas Dwight in the late nineteenth century is seminal in the development of forensic anthropology. One of Dwight's students, George Dorsey, became the first expert witness in a homicide case in 1897, while working at the Field Columbian Museum in Chicago as a Curator. Megan B. Brickley and Roxana Ferllini, *Forensic Anthropology: Case Studies from Europe* (Springfield: Charles C Thomas, 2007), 5.
25 Ibid., 27–8.

26 Ibid.
27 Ibid., 67.
28 Ibid., 70.
29 Ibid., 28.
30 Ibid., 29.
31 See Laura Kurgan, 'Residues: ICTY Courtroom No.1 and the Architecture of Justice', in *Alphabet City 7: Social Insecurity*, eds. Cornelius Heesters and Len Guether (Toronto: House of Anansi, 2001), 112–29; Susan Schuppli, 'Entering Evidence: Cross-examining the Court Records of the ICTY', in *Forensis: The Architecture of Public Truth*, ed. Forensic Architecture (Berlin: Sternberg Press, 2014), 279–316.
32 Ibid., 21.
33 Argentine Forensic Anthropology Team, 'Following Antigone: Forensic Anthropology and Human Rights Investigations', filmed 2002, https://video.alexanderstreet.com/watch/following-antigone-forensic-anthropology-and-human-rights-investigations.
34 Ibid.
35 Sophocles, *The Theban Plays: Oedipus the Tyrant, Oedipus at Colonus, Antigone*, trans. Peter J. Ahrensdorf and Thomas L. Pangle (Ithaca: Cornell University Press, 2014), 711–14, 1171–6.
36 Ibid., 787–93.
37 Ibid., 21–39.
38 Ibid., 1354–96.
39 Ibid., 142.
40 Judith Butler, *Antigone's Claim: Kinship between Life and Death* (New York: Columbia University Press, 2000); Tina Chanter, *Whose Antigone?: The Tragic Marginalization of Slavery* (Albany: State University of New York Press, 2011); Tina Chanter and Sean D. Kirkland, eds, *The Returns of Antigone: Interdisciplinary Essays* (Albany: State University of New York Press, 2014).
41 Foucault, *The Courage of the Truth*, 102.
42 Ibid.
43 Ibid., 73.
44 Ibid.
45 Ibid., 37.
46 Sophocles, *The Theban Plays*, 149.
47 Chanter, *Whose Antigone?*, 9–10.
48 Sophocles, *The Theban Plays*, 86–7, 509.
49 Ibid., 497–507.

50 Ibid., 83, 543–9.
51 Ibid., 65.
52 Ibid., 636–8.
53 Ibid., 60–72, 484–6.
54 Ibid., 536–7, 711–23.
55 Ibid., 991.
56 Bezci Egemen and Güven Gürkan Öztan, 'Anatomy of the Turkish Emergency State: A Continuous Reflection of Turkish Raison d'état between 1980 and 2002', *Middle East Critique* 25, no. 2 (2016): 164.
57 Ibid., 164–7.
58 Ibid., 173.
59 Ibid., 172.
60 'Türkiye'nin Başında İki Bela Var', *Milliyet*, 7 October 1984.
61 Ibid.
62 Bezci and Öztan, 'Anatomy of the Turkish Emergency State', 172.
63 İHD, 'Kayıpları Unutmadık', 2003, accessed 11 December 2019, http://www.ihd.org.tr/wp-content/uploads/2007/11/kayiplari_unutmadik.pdf.
64 The group was awarded the International Hrant Dink Award in 2013 and referred to as showing, 'an unprecedented resistance so that others won't have to suffer similar pain. . . . [T]hey became and still continue to be defenders of truth.'
65 Human Rights Watch, 'Time for Justice: Ending Impunity for Killing and Disappearances in 1990s Turkey', 3 September 2012, https://www.hrw.org/report/2012/09/03/time-justice/ending-impunity-killings-and-disappearances-1990s-turkey.
66 Between June and November 2015, Turkey survived a number of terrorist attacks as the Turkish state declared war against PKK. This was after two police officers were killed in Ceylanpınar on 22 July 2015. HPG (a fraction of PKK) first claimed responsibility but then PKK denied responsibility on 6 August 2015. An investigation of the incident by the parliament was refused after AKP and MHP voted against the proposition. On 24 August 2019, the former prime minister Ahmet Davutoğlu referred to this period and started a debate on 'Turkey's bloodiest summer'. 'Ex-PM Davutoglu Ignites Debate on Turkey's Bloodiest Summer in 2015', *Yerepouni Daily News*, 26 August 2019; 'Parliamentary Inquiry for Investigation of "Ceylanpınar"', *bianet*, 6 March 2018.
67 Güneydoğu Anadolu Bölgesi Belediyeler Birliği [South-east Anatolia Union of Municipalities], 'Nusaybin Sokağa Çıkma ve Sonrası Durum ile İlgili Bilgilendirme Notu [Southeastern Anatolia Region Union of Municipalities, Information Note on Nusaybin Curfew and After]', 2016, accessed 11 December

2019, http://hakikatadalethafiza.org/kaynak/nusaybin-sokaga-cikma-yasagi-ve-sonrasi-durum-ile-ilgili-bilgilendirme-notu; International Crisis Group, 'Türkiye'deki PKK Çatışmasını Yönetmek: Nusaybin Örneği' [Governing PKK Conflict in Turkey: The Case of Nusaybin], 2017, accessed 11 December 2019, https://d2071andvip0wj.cloudfront.net/243-managing-turkeys-pkk-conflict-turkish.pdf.

68 Mehveş Evin, 'Terörle Böyle mi Mücadele Edilecek?', *Diken*, 4 April 2016, http://www.diken.com.tr/terorle-boyle-mi-mucadele-edilecek/.
69 Ibid., 64.
70 Forensic Architecture, 'CGI Crime Scene Reconstruction Opens New Leads in Kurdish Activist Killing', *Opendemocracy*, 8 February 2019, https://www.opendemocracy.net/en/cgi-crime-scene-reconstruction-opens-new-leads-in-tahir-elci-killing/.
71 Forensic Architecture, 'Report: Investigation of the Audio-visual Material Included in the Case File of the Killing of Tahir Elçi on 28 November 2015', 13 December 2018, https://content.forensic-architecture.org/wp-content/uploads/2019/03/FA-TE-Report_12_English_public.pdf.
72 *Antigone*, 693–4.
73 Sophocles, *The Theban Plays*, 634–741.
74 Ibid., 733–5.
75 Ibid., 726–7.
76 Ibid., 316.
77 Ibid., 773–80.
78 Foucault, *The Courage of the Truth*, 339.
79 Eyal Weizman, *Forensic Architecture: Violence at the Threshold of Detectability* (New York: Zone Books, 2017), 64.
80 Ibid.
81 Ibid., 65.
82 Ibid.
83 Ibid., 84.
84 Ibid., 96.
85 Ibid., 36.
86 Ibid.
87 Ibid., 95.
88 Tahir Elçi Vakfı, 'Savcılık Adli Tıp'tan yeni rapor istedi', published 3 April 2019, http://www.tahirelcivakfi.org/savcilik-adli-tip-tan-yeni-rapor-istedi/.
89 'Adli Tıp Kurumu, Tahir Elçi Dosyasını Geri Gönderdi', *T24*, 6 July 2019, https://t24.com.tr/haber/adli-tip-kurumu-tahir-elci-dosyasini-geri-gonderdi,829411.

90 Forensic Architecture, 'Under the Radar', accessed 11 December 2019, https://forensic-architecture.org/programme/exhibitions/under-the-radar.
91 TIHV, 'Cizre Field Report, 31 March 2016', accessed 11 December 2019, http://en.tihv.org.tr/wp-content/uploads/2017/10/Cizre-Field-Report.pdf.
92 Tahir Elçi Vakfı, 'Vakfımızdan Suç Duyurusu', published 23 September 2019, http://www.tahirelcivakfi.org/vakfimizdan-suc-duyurusu/.

6

Between the guests and the hosts
Spaces of illegalized migration in Turkey

Merve Bedir

the foreigner is first of all foreign to the legal language in which the duty of hospitality is formulated, the right to asylum, its limits, norms, policing, etc. He has to ask for hospitality in a language which, by definition is not his own, the one imposed on him by the master of the house, the host, the king, the lord, the authorities, the nation, the State, the father, ... This personage imposes on him translation into their own language, and that's the first act of violence.[1]

Turkey's constantly changing national politics and legal context have treated migrants differently according to their identity and class, as well as the international political context in place during their period of arrival. While political and legal actors have referred to migrants as 'guests', some have been granted citizenship, others have been relocated to 'developed' countries, and still others have remained in transition/unregistered, indefinitely. The Turkish branch of the United Nations High Commissioner for Refugees (UNHCR) was founded in 1960 to liaise with the Turkish State on matters of refuge,[2] and to organize the registration, interview and relocation processes of the migrants who seek asylum.[3] The first regulation concerning foreigners and international protection was introduced in 1994.[4] However, since then, several circulars – policies with limited impact on a particular period or case – have temporarily suspended or altered this regulation and its implementation, within the limitations of the circulars. One consequence of 11 September 2001 has been the implementation of increasingly stringent international policies of asylum, which has resulted in periods of stay for migrants in Turkey gradually increasing from three months to six years.[5] The first law on migration and asylum in the history of Turkey, 'Law Nr. 6458; Law on Foreigners and International Protection',[6] which was fully accredited within the European Union framework, has recognized those notions of asylum and refuge, although it exempted the migrants arriving from non-European countries.

In this chapter, first and foremost, I approach 'emergency' in relation to migration as a matter of law. Dwelling on freedom of movement as a universal human right, I use the term 'illegalized migration' to highlight that the illegality of some migrants and migration is a product of the laws of the nation state, rather than an intrinsic feature of migrants.[7] Furthermore, I propose that the idea of migration as emergency is rooted in the very existence of the modern nation state, enabling the nation state to extend its sovereignty beyond and outside the domain of universal human rights, and therefore to define certain migrants as illegal. The absence and/or inadequacy of the established legal frameworks that deal with migration and citizenship in Turkey – and the arbitrary implementation of existing legal frameworks and tools – continuously leave certain migrants outside the law, which leads to a state of absolute uncertainty for them. The exemption of the non-European migrants from Turkey's law on foreigners and international protection also emphasizes emergency being an embedded assumption within the state's philosophy of defining citizenship. Lastly, emergency is embedded in Turkey's principle of presenting itself as a country of transition, but not relocation, because it does not take the responsibility of accepting migrants as asylum seekers and giving them refuge (especially up until the migration from Syria). These inherent assumptions on migration as emergency in the legal context have led to the possibility of a continuous illegalizing of migration, and a continuous uncertainty for migrants about their future. Going back to the idea of freedom of movement as a universal human right, this chapter also aims to show how the constituents (migrants and citizens) deal with this emergency and uncertainty. This occurs by putting the universal rights of the migrant to the fore, and by focusing on the migrant as a social and political subject, wherein the representation of the migrant is acknowledged as being that of the citizen – not only from a position of responsibility but also from within the other existing but less-used legal frameworks in Turkey.

Secondly, I approach the idea of migration as emergency for the modern nation state, not only as a matter of defining legality/illegality but also as a matter of what constitutes citizenship. Mechanisms of the nation state are established based on the idea of building (good) citizenship through language, education, culture and so on. Even if this ideology is becoming more and more decayed today, the good citizen is still the basis of the nation state's construct and the migrant, by his or her very nature, is an emergency for this construct. This construct positions the migrant not only as an emergency for the state but also for the good citizen. In this respect, I utilize the notion of 'hospitality' to present the several dimensions of the emergency, and the resulting uncertainty for the migrant: not only from a legal perspective, which concerns the sovereign, but also from a sociopolitical and cultural perspective, which concerns other migrants and citizens. I adopt the discourse of hospitality to explain the political, social and cultural insinuations of the notions of guest and host, in relation to illegalized migration. I aim to present the spaces of hospitality, and how emergency and uncertainty become mediums of hostility towards the migrant, as well as how these notions are appropriated by various constituents in order to interchange the roles of hospitality and recreate the potentials of living together.

The arguments presented in this chapter are based on different cases from 'Vocabulary of Hospitality', my ongoing project that aims to look at the infrastructures and landscapes of illegalized migration. The chapter focuses on Gaziantep, a city in south-eastern Turkey where migrants from Syria constitute 20 per cent of the population.[8] The first case presented concerns the national border and migration towards the city, the second is about a camp for migrants from Syria and the third deals with a kitchen set up by women from Syria and Turkey, all of which refer to, and are localized within, Gaziantep. My main discursive references are Carl Schmitt[9] on the notion of emergency, Immanuel Kant[10] and Jacques Derrida[11] on the notion of hospitality, and Bülent Diken and Carsten Bagge Laustsen[12] on the notion of camps. My ultimate aim in this project is to emphasize the political agency of solidarity, including how the roles of host and guest can interchange, and how the potentials of uncertainty can be employed by the constituents to defeat the uncertainty created by the nation state, moving towards the idea of living together.

On emergency and hospitality

According to Schmitt,[13] the basic principle of politics is the distinction between 'us' and 'them', and the spatial order of the world is conceptualized based on the division of 'us/inside' and 'them/outside'. Considered in the context of migration, the notions of 'host' and 'guest', 'citizen' and 'migrant', 'state' and 'asylum seeker' replace how Schmitt defines 'us' and 'them'. Schmitt continues to explain that a state of emergency – which in our case is the act of migration and the arrival of migrants at the border of the nation state – is declared by the sovereign power, in this case 'us', (i.e., the nation state), and applies to the outsider, in this case 'them' (i.e., the guest/migrant/foreigner at the nation state's border). By declaring a state of emergency, the sovereign (host) suspends the law, creating an ambiguous, uncertain territory, and a condition of lawlessness towards the guest.

In the context of migration, it is important to elaborate further Schmitt's theory on emergency and uncertainty by linking it with the notion of hospitality. As Kant explains in *Perpetual Peace*,[14] the right of hospitality is a matter of nation state and philanthropy; by asking the guest (migrant) their name, they are enjoined to both the state and to the law, which guarantees their identity and provides them the rights to reside. They go 'inside' the law, to be legally responsible persons, and hence are still subject to the law (laws of hospitality). However, they remain 'outside' the law (as is clearly seen in the case of Turkey) because they remain in temporary protection, exempt from the rights to work, from social security and from citizenship. Kant continues to explain that universal hospitality is a matter of human rights, that is, the right of the guest to mobility and shelter, without asking who they are, or without a requirement of philanthropy (the law of hospitality). As Diken and Laustsen also explain, the nation state keeps the migrant 'inside' by making them subject to itself, but also keeps them 'outside' by keeping them as guests, and not letting them participate in the law.[15]

Here it is also important to realize that the guest introduces a different world to the host's space of sovereignty, which is defined by both the nation state and the citizen. The guest represents alternative values, cultural practices and behaviours that might or might not suit that of the hosts, which makes the guest into an enemy. The guest is positioned on the 'outside' – not only in legal terms but also culturally. The host (domestic, homely, local or national) and the guest (newcomer, stranger, occupier) contradict each other, and this is where the laws of hospitality, which Kant describes as philanthropy, come to the fore. The nation state is built on the idea of the 'good citizen', whereupon all its mechanisms are devised for this purpose, via legal structures, education, work and leisure, and by organizing culture and daily life. The guests have to learn the values, customs and languages, etc. in order to live together with the good citizens, but they still may or may not become a citizen (legally) or a good citizen (socially and culturally). This means that a newly arriving migrant (guest) is already an emergency for the modern nation state, because the migrant is unexpected and does not fit the nation state's established understanding of the good citizen. This means universal hospitality (the law of hospitality) is impossible, since giving the migrant the right to reside without philanthropy is impossible for the nation state. The 'inside' and 'outside' entangle both on legal basis and culturally.

The way in which Derrida discusses the notions of 'host' and 'guest' helps us to further dissect Kant's laws of hospitality in relation to illegalized migration, that is, the relationships between the host (the law maker, the sovereign, the nation state) and different guests (categories of migrants) across the spaces of the nation state border, the camp and the city.[16] The word 'guest' comes from the same linguistic origin as the words 'host', 'ghost', 'hostile', 'hostage', 'hospitium', 'hospitality', and also describes the social and cultural relationships among the different constituents of the nation state, hosts and guests (citizens and migrants). The meaning of guest goes back to the root word *hostis* in Latin, meaning guest, stranger and foreigner. The meaning of foreigner also includes that of enemy. The meaning of guest incorporates host or stranger, with an implication of hospitability and cure. The third meaning, hostage, reverses the hostility of the first, as the aggressiveness is defined in terms of the receiver, the victim. The host sometimes becomes the hostage.

Finally, it is necessary to explain what the camp stands for spatially.[17] The camp is where the sovereign creates bare life in order to defend the security, health and well-being of people – treating its inhabitants as potential enemies and outsiders for sustaining its sovereignty. The walls of the camp symbolize sovereignty, while the transgression of the walls represents the shape of the exception. In the camp, exception is the rule (the law), and the camp is the principle of organization.[18] People are excluded from the right to representation, and each person is reduced to the form of bare life. They are assumed to not perform politically, participate in decision-making, and are therefore held as hostages of the sovereign. This chapter considers only the camps built to control migration, where the camp constitutes a grey zone of uncertainty where the migrant (guest) inhabits a threshold. This occurs due to the migrant's inside/outside position in relation to the hosts (the state and the citizen), such as whether the migrant is a true subject of the state or of human rights, or if the migrant is an enemy who threatens the host with their exploitation of healthcare, education and other public resources.

The nation state's border is where people are identified as hosts (citizens) or guests (migrants), and it is the nation state's borders that are reproduced as the borders of camps, neighbourhoods and cities, in order to further define, expand or limit the laws of hospitality. The camp is the space of management and confinement, where the migrant is hostage, shares guest-hood, or becomes a ghost, while the city and/or the neighbourhood is where the migrant can possibly become a host. My research was dedicated to revealing the inherent hostility in the laws of hospitality of the nation states and international legal frameworks, as well as building the law of hospitality (universal/unconditional hospitality) and creating the space for an interchanging role of hosts and guests. Thus, the chapter presents and discusses these relationships and their spaces based on cases in Gaziantep, Turkey.

The border: Hospitality and the nation state

A national newspaper's 28 August 2014 issue mentioned the removal of 85 Arabic nameplates in Gaziantep, and the police manager's explanation by saying: 'Our investigation showed that many of these shops run by Syrians had Arabic nameplates on their windows. This makes the appearance of an Arabic city. We had warned them initially to translate those into Turkish, so it shows that it is a Turkish city. After this warning, if the nameplates were still untouched, we removed them.'[19]

Turkey's establishment as a modern nation state was strongly bonded to the definition of modern Turkish citizenship, and those who did not fit within this definition based on ethnicity, religion and other reasons were often ignored, left unseen, undocumented, or else made invisible throughout its history. From this perspective, the arrival of any migrant who did not fit the definition of citizenship was already considered an emergency for the nation state. The Islamic Revolution in Iran, the fall of the Soviet Union, the wars in Afghanistan and the former Yugoslavia, coupled with civilian conflicts in the African continent and the Balkan region all triggered major migration trends towards Turkey. In each case, Turkey granted citizenship to certain migrants, while the UNHCR registered the majority of the others for relocation. This meant that certain people were legally entitled to host-hood, while others became permanent guests.

The 1994 regulation adopted a transitory approach, where migrants settled temporarily in one of the thirty-six (later, up to sixty-two) different 'satellite cities' in Turkey, and on the basis of registration and periodical reporting at the police department and the UNHCR.[20] This settlement scheme continued until they were either repatriated or sent to a third country by UNHCR with obtained refugee status. This policy then led many migrants, who were referred to as 'urban refugees,' to live in cities with temporary residence. The implementation of satellite cities in Turkey is a precise manifestation of an understanding that the migrant is a guest and continuously temporary within the satellite city. The first law on migration, asylum and citizenship in the history of Turkey, 'Law Nr. 6458; Law on Foreigners and International Protection' was prepared within the European Union accreditation process and implemented in April 2014.[21] The law defined more than ten categories[22] with respect to categorizing and processing different migrants, based on their country of origin, motivation to migrate, status of transition, expectation of relocation and so on. One category in particular defines 'immediate temporary protection to be provided to foreigners in cases of large influx into Turkey, and in those where they cannot return to their country', and has been applied to the migrants from Syria. In addition, migrants under temporary protection do not have any prospect of refugee status, permanent residence, work permit or citizenship, nor do they know how long their temporary protection will last, as this is determined by the state.

Since the beginning of the Syrian War in 2011, Turkey has become the largest host country in the world, with 3,644,342 people registered under temporary protection, the majority of whom reside in major cities and towns, and close to the border with Syria.[23] Gaziantep is one of these border cities, where both camps and urban environments provide temporary protection.

Migrants from Syria constitute 22 per cent of the city's population (437,844), and only 3 per cent of this figure is located inside the camps.[24] Most of the migrants from Syria in Gaziantep have come from Aleppo, which Gaziantep was actually a part of during the Ottoman Empire.[25] The German–Ottoman railway from Berlin to Baghdad was still under construction in the period leading up to the First World War. After the war, the railroad was dismantled, and the approximate line of the national border followed the railroad footprint, separating extended families, relatives and friends who were originally from the Vilayet of Aleppo into the respective cities and nationalities of Turkey and

Figure 6.1 Berlin–Baghdad Railway, c. 1850.

Syria. As the recent civil war continued in Syria, Gaziantep was therefore the first destination for migrants from Aleppo, precisely because of the hundreds of years of relationship between the two cities. The Syrian migrants were seen to be moving closer to their friends and families in Turkey, but this time legally becoming their guests under temporary protection orders.[26]

In 2016, after signing the EU–Turkey Action Plan on migration[27] covering issues of the return of irregular migrants from Europe to Turkey and the resettlement of migrants from Syria, Turkey started implementing a new set of policies, including providing citizenship to eligible migrants from Syria, as well as implementing a mobility restriction regime, limiting their movement only to the cities they were registered in.[28] This has meant that the migrants cannot leave the cities they are registered in without taking permission from the State Department of Migration. This context attests to the guest-hood of migrants under temporary protection, effectively taking them hostage, whereupon the borders of a city spatially reproduce the borders of the nation state. Between the national and international law, and the agreements between the EU and Turkey, universal hospitality is suspended in practice; migrants are given the right to hospitality, but only under the rules of hospitality governed by a nation state, which in turn illegalizes universal hospitality (i.e., illegalizing migration) (Figure 6.1).

The camp

Until the start of the war in Syria in 2011, building camps in order to host migrants had not been a policy of the Turkish state, except in a few previous cases: for example, the two or three camps in Turkey managed by the UNHCR, and another few camps built on the Iraqi side of Turkey's border managed by the state during the First Gulf War to stop potential Kurdish migrants from entering Turkey.[29] Since April 2011, following the declaration of an open-door policy for migrants from Syria, Turkey started building camps in the border cities (twenty-six camps in total), as well as reception and detention centres (currently two and thirty-seven centres, respectively).[30] Nine of these centres were built under the agreement with the European Union within the Migrant Relocation and Resettlement Scheme.[31]

The border camps have been planned, constructed and managed by the State Agency for Disaster Management of Turkey (AFAD) based in Ankara, and have been named as 'hospitality centres'. AFAD's head office in Ankara included an architecture and management team, while the 'migrants' governor'[32] resided in Gaziantep and the local management teams were appointed to the cities with camps.[33] These camps were designed as either tents for bigger numbers of people or as containers for a family in each. The tent camps were organized around large tents on streets with common toilets and showers, as well as around other common spaces for healthcare, education, retail (mainly supermarket), prayer, infrastructure and so on. On the other hand, within the container camps each unit was designed to have its own bathroom, while the other common spaces were organized the same as in the tent camps (Figures 6.2 and 6.3).

Figure 6.2 Nusaybin Tent City, June 2013. Capacity: 2,000 tents and 6,000 people.

The gate of the hospitality centre represents two things. First, it appears as a threshold, separating and connecting the inside and the outside, wherein the threshold transcends the separation between the inner and the outer.[34] Secondly, it appears as a facade, whereupon the host introduces itself to the constituent. Nizip Hospitality Centre's gate has a Turkish flag on the left corner followed by the text 'Nizip Container City, Hospitality Centre', written only in Turkish in a large font. The border of the camp literally copies the national border of the state. Moreover, this facade shows the state's limits of hospitality, that is, the identity that the guest has to acknowledge is a Turkish identity, while the location itself does not aim to be identified as a 'camp' for 'migrants'. However, the hospitality centre has the classic layout of a camp.[35] It is a space encircled by layers of fences and overlooked by watchtowers, while within it rows of tents or containers are laid out in such a way as to enhance visibility and monitor behaviour, ensuring there are no curves or blind spots (Figure 6.4).

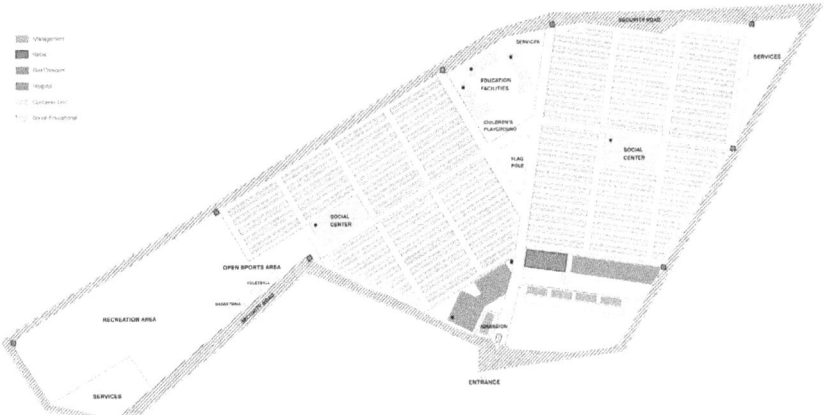

Figure 6.3 Harran Container City, January 2013. Capacity: 2,000 container units and 13,540 people.

Figure 6.4 Nizip Hospitality Centre ID Card.

The identification of the migrants is done by using ID cards (in Turkish) which include a photograph and other information (such as name, surname, ID and tent/container number, father's and mother's names, date and place of birth and gender). One could think that the only thing that differentiates this ID from the ordinary Turkish citizen ID is that it includes a tent/container number, but the back side of the card states that the ID card is valid only within the camp territory. The migrant is therefore enforced to inhabit a territory designated for them, but within that territory they are registered and identified in the same way that the citizens of Turkey are. The migrant's ID card represents both guest-hood and camp as an extra-territory of uncertainty, while also representing the guest's (migrant's) position as being both inside and outside relative to the hosts (the state and the society). The threshold condition – the entanglement of the inside and outside within the idea of the camp – can also be observed with regard to the labour condition and characteristics in the hospitality centre. The hospitality centre administration is located inside the centre, while the managers and workers go to their houses outside, only to sleep. They must speak at least two languages in order to communicate with the migrants. The migrants are allowed to leave the centre daily: they leave early in the morning and come back at 10.00 pm at the latest. Many migrants work informally (undocumented, and without social security) in the workshops and fields in the settlements forty-five minutes away from the camp. This kind of labour and time-space distribution creates the possibility of the administration and migrants making acquaintance with one another.

The camp is considered to be the space for complete isolation of the migrant from public life. In the hospitality centre, however, this point is contested. First, people create space for themselves through small-scale agriculture projects that they undertake behind their tents and in some other parts of the centre. This effort is supported by the trees planted by the management within the centre. Secondly, people change the outside areas of their containers or tents, creating shaded space to sit outside and hang out, or make space for simple agriculture upon the facades of containers. Finally, the hospitality centre has spaces for open-air functions and common areas, including a school, a children's playground area, a sports area, a health care centre, a multipurpose centre (with a computer room, sewing room, laundry room and other functions), plus a mosque/masjid and a market. Some of these are dignified spaces with adequate tools and proper equipment. Nevertheless, the centre lacks space – the space for privacy of people, and also the space to encounter, gather and socialize. All spaces in the centre have a defined function and are to be used only for that. The other activities happen because the hospitality centre's management allows them to happen. The hospitality centre has no space for participation or representation but does allow the possibility of social relations to take place (Figure 6.5).

In the hospitality centre, the design of individual containers, tents and outside spaces resembles a city, with proper infrastructure and detailing (such as a finished floor complete with cladding and drainage, waste collection, lamp posts, solar panels for hot water in common kitchens and toilets, children's play areas, sports facilities and so on). Container and tent units have satellite dishes to receive news from the outside, which means there are TVs and/or radios in the units. However, the spatial differentiation shows that the urban qualities of the centre are contested with the mentality of a camp: not only in terms of the outside borders with watchtowers, but also within the camp borders (i.e., turning different functions into zones, and separating between them the women's and men's areas by using fences – sometimes with barbed wire on top – and CCTV cameras watching the different zones). The tents and containers are fixed to the ground, so they cannot be moved around. Nothing in the centre is abandoned or disposed of in any way, except the migrants themselves (Figure 6.6).

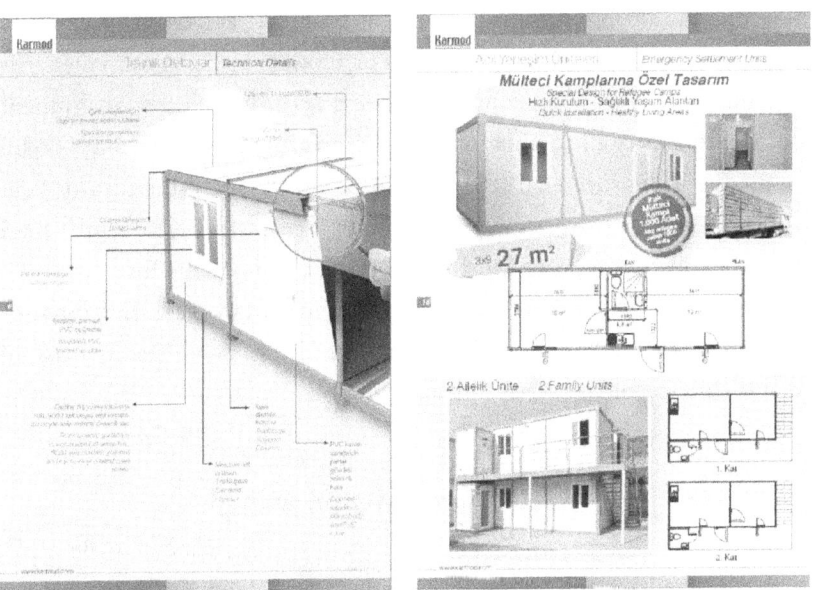

Figure 6.5 Drawings of a container unit, 2013. Karmod technical catalogue.

Figure 6.6 Photo of Nizip Hospitality Centre from the nearby hill.

Nizip Hospitality Centre sits among hills, a few on one side, while one of the major rivers of Anatolia runs along the other side. A road slopes down between two hills, giving a vista to the centre from above. The location of the centre is far from the city, and easily accessible from the main highway between Gaziantep and Aleppo. That being said, the hills add to the experience of being monitored/watched from above, especially when viewed from the hospitality centre itself. The selection of this location supports the idea of remoteness, exclusion and 'outside-ness' of the migrants (guests), as the centre is experienced as 'an island on its own'.[36] However, in being connected to the city with state-provided buses, and by being close to the international highway, the hospitality centre remains 'inside.' On the one hand, migrants can travel to the city, while on the other hand, new migrants can be both brought to the camp and deported from it. The four basic characteristics of camp life consist of living on undocumented work or allowances, being prevented from obtaining decent working conditions, living according to the government's choice of residency and maintaining minimum geographical mobility.[37] While the power of the sovereign (the host) is beyond the law, the idea of being inside and outside permeates every aspect of the guest's life, for a time frame that is unknown to anyone but the sovereign. For migrants from Syria, this time frame now spans almost a decade. The guest remains at this threshold of inclusion and exclusion, even if they start to lead an almost 'normal' life inhabiting the container, the camp and the city.

The Kitchen and 'cityzenship'

In Turkey, the laws of hospitality have established an ambivalent context for migrants, but alongside this, a variety of relationships have developed among different migrants (guests) and citizens (hosts). Sometimes they are enemies of each other, while at other times they mobilize against the host (sovereign power), based on shared feelings and issues among the citizens and migrants, such as working conditions, children's education, public health, racism, segregation and violence against women. In Gaziantep, where the population from Syria reaches a fifth of its entirety, it is an everyday experience to see cars on the street from Aleppo and Syrian migrants hanging out at the historical castle, coupled with new labour investment by Syrians in the city and/or students from Syria graduating from universities.[38]

As migration from Syria towards Gaziantep has increased, the number of researchers, teachers, social organizations, charity organizations, NGOs, international aid organizations, financial, management and monitoring organizations have also increased. Their goals have been humanitarian and not political. However, this position of humanitarianism is also paradoxical, because while the humanitarian attitude takes the side of the migrant and supports them, the basis of action is still founded upon guest-hood and the limits of hospitality which the state defines.[39] Considering that the war within (and migration from) Syria is ongoing since 2011, more and more individuals and organizations are dedicating humanitarian support for migrants, and so the migrant becomes a near-permanent interest for the humanitarian organizations. Thus the paradox of guest-hood is sustained in Gaziantep, whereupon the sovereign power and humanitarian organizations start to complement each other in continuing the temporary protection of the migrant. From this, the question of dealing with emergency and uncertainty consolidates around creating the space of hospitium, or universal hospitality, by putting the rights of the guest to the fore and by focusing on the migrant/guest as a social and political subject, whereupon the representation of the migrant is acknowledged as that of the host.

At the end of 2014, a solidarity kitchen was initiated by a transnational women's group in Gaziantep, of which I was also a part. This kitchen is located in the Bey neighbourhood. It is located down a side street that leads to Atatürk Boulevard, within the ground floor of a heritage building owned and used by the Kırkayak Cultural Centre, a registered NGO in the city. 'The Kitchen' was created as an epilogue to two years of activities by women that made use of different spaces in the city. These activities included self-defence workshops, performative group therapy sessions and meetings with different Turkish and Syrian NGOs about what can be done to create better conditions for living together in the city. The women who set up the kitchen come from different backgrounds in Gaziantep and Aleppo, and they either know each other from Aleppo or they are the users of the Cultural Centre, but all have participated in different previous activities. The first gathering towards The Kitchen was made via the initiative of a small group of women, which enabled all those who were interested in coming together for a conversation, although the idea was not necessarily to set up as a kitchen. This particular idea and others emerged and evolved over time. The number of people joining the conversations gradually reduced, but the core group remained at around eight to ten people, going up to sixteen to twenty at times. Germany's opening of its doors in 2015 caused some of the members to leave, but The Kitchen continued its activities and grew back to its former size soon after. Later activities included cooking, walking in the city, expeditions to other sites and organizations, conversations on culture and cultural production, language, daily life, women's issues, migrants' issues and so on.

One of the main directions of conversation in The Kitchen was the historical connection between Gaziantep and Aleppo. The fact that Gaziantep was once part of Aleppo, and the realization that this cancels out what is commonly thought today – namely, that the people from Gaziantep are the hosts to those from Aleppo – brought the conversation towards the idea of what we named 'cityzenship' (*hemşehri* in Turkish and Arabic), thus defining the socio-spatial condition of being from the same city. Cityzenship is also a concept acknowledged by Turkey's 'Law Nr. 5393; Municipality Law', which maintains that people living in the same city are bonded with the concept of belonging to the same city, meaning they therefore have the right to participate in the decision-making mechanisms in/regarding the city.[40] However, this law, and the particular aspect of the law on local representation, has often been overlooked and neglected. The social and legal dimensions of cityzenship made it one of the main discourses that The Kitchen communicated later on, emphasizing how the Municipality Law brings forward an understanding of universal hospitality, living together in the same city and the representation of cityzens. The Kitchen took the notion of cityzenship as a basis and reflected on a contract of hospitality as a physical space, not as a question of nationality (original belonging) but as a question of collective belonging to the city, with The Kitchen assuring those who gathered the right to remain and participate in decision-making. This approach was about sharing the common struggles

Between the Guests and the Hosts

of being a woman in the city, as well as leaving out categorization related to migration by acknowledging collective belonging, and the continuously interchanging roles of hospitality.

The physical kitchen as a space was created by renovating an existing room on the ground floor of Kırkayak Cultural Centre. The space opens directly onto the street and has its own entrance, making it accessible both before and after the opening hours of the cultural centre. The outside door is not locked, making it possible for people to come in, cook, produce, organize activities or rest during different times of the day. The space is composed of two rooms: a smaller back room that stores food and equipment, and a front room that has a free space in the middle and auxiliary enclaves embedded in the walls. The front room is square in plan, with a free flow space in the middle, making

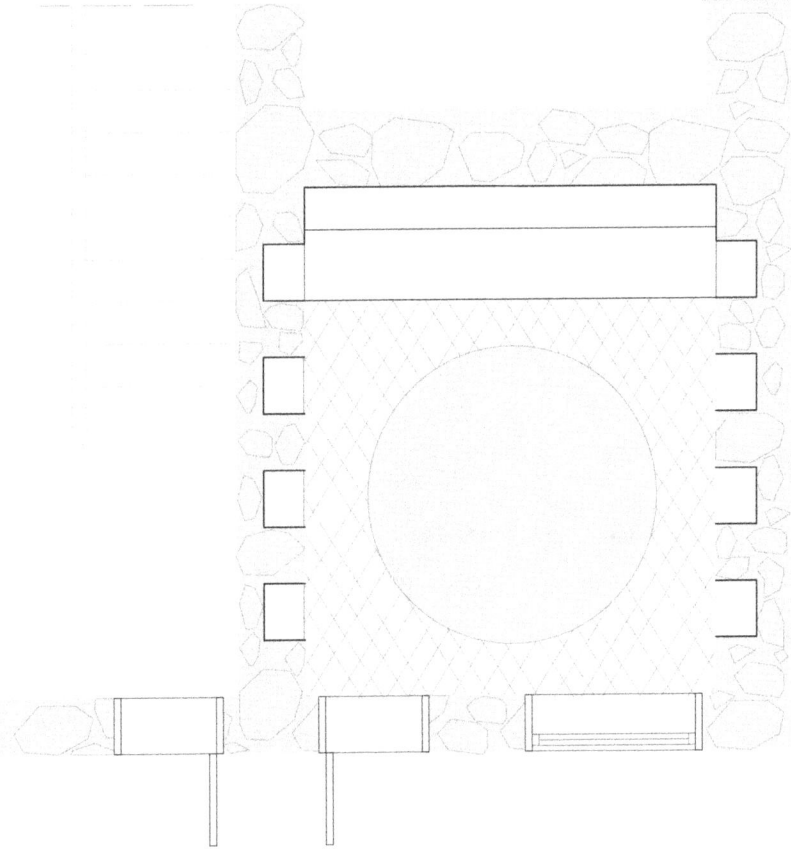

Figure 6.7 Plan of The Kitchen, 2014.

the space suitable for changing activities. The use and design of the spaces are decided collectively, experienced through self-observing the use of space during common activities. The load-bearing walls constructed with stone were in part cladded with wood. This was locally sourced, using a local processing technique to create auxiliary enclaves in the wall. These enclaves are used as temporary storage for stools, floor-tables, jars, books etc. The wooden cladding is easy to clean, and together with the original stone walls creates an intimate interior. The floor cover is not only decided based upon the functions and activities of/for women but also to suit the cultural conditions – such as eating on the floor or gathering around a circular floor-table. It was also decided to set up a niche by the window place overlooking the street, and to use this space as the display facade, presenting to the outside various temporary displays of banners and posters (Figures 6.7 and 6.8).

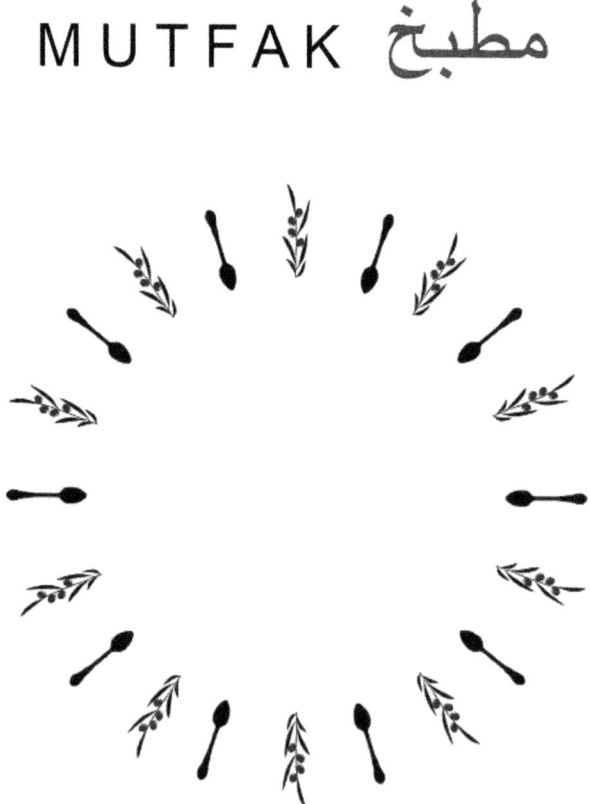

Figure 6.8 Logo of The Kitchen, 2014.

The Kitchen functions as a space of sharing and sustaining the struggle for host-hood, for women from different backgrounds, both from Gaziantep and from Aleppo, based on their common issues. Working as a network, women mobilize and organize workshops, as well as undertaking continuous cooking activities. Food is not perceived as a cultural commodity, but appears as a metaphor for production, constituting a space in itself for cooking up and preparing ideas of living together in the city. The Kitchen in this instance also performs as a space of hospitium, or universal hospitality, putting the rights of the guest to the fore. Furthermore, it also focuses on the migrant/guest as a social and political subject, where the representation of the migrant is acknowledged as that of the host – not only from a position of responsibility, but also from within the existing legal frameworks (Municipality Law).

Epilogue

This chapter has sought to examine the infrastructure and landscapes of illegalized migration, legal structures and their lack within the context of emergency, and the resulting uncertainty this generates for the migrant. Related to this concern, this chapter has also provided an exploration of the potential of uncertainty, that is, the potential of living together within the context of uncertainty and the agency of solidarity. 'Law Nr. 6458; Law on Foreigners and International Protection' in Turkey categorizes migrants and defines a strong hierarchy of who deserves to be considered legal, and how far they deserve to be protected depending on this legal hierarchy.[41] When migrants are of concern, the hierarchy which is underlined by the Turkish national law is reinforced by an extant hierarchy within the international protection system that privileges those who qualify for official refugee status over those who do not. The ongoing 'migration crisis' in Turkey and along the borders of Europe needs to be confronted through the perspective of the heightened borders created by these highly hierarchical national and international definitions and laws of hospitality, and the inherent hostility embedded within them.

The international migration politics which followed 11 September 2001, coupled with the European Migrant Relocation and Resettlement Scheme,[42] mean that 'Fortress Europe' might no longer be the walls between Greece-

Bulgaria and Turkey, but that Turkey itself might become the border wall of Europe. The question of guest or foreigner concerns the issue of national borders, territory and sovereignty, all of which define the rules of hospitality. The sense of protecting one's home can often go as far as xenophobia. Anyone who becomes a threat to sovereignty at home can be seen as an enemy. Those guests who are stuck at the border without being acknowledged by respective nation states or by the European Union become ghosts. This can make them hostile, and the host can run the risk of becoming a hostage too. For the guest, sovereignty of the state is not only about suspension and exclusion. The guest is excluded from the law but remains subject to it, that is, they are included by being regulated and ordered.

Borders perpetuate themselves as hospitality centres, reception centres and detention centres (i.e., specialized structures serving as camps), as well as via other urban spaces of representation, such as upon the nameplates or public space screens written in Arabic. This extends the legal territory of uncertainty, wherein people are excluded from the assumed space of the citizen – one who is also assumed to be an extension of the nation state. The camp becomes evidence of the violence embedded in the pride of hospitality, and where the migrant is rejected from host-hood. The migrant is the subject of mobility and displacement locally and globally, and life in the camp points to exclusion and immobility. The camp is a near-permanent transitory space because of the migrant's inside/outside position in relation to the sovereign, in such a way that the camp is frozen into a state of temporariness, transformed by the guest within, but only lasting for as long as the host wills. On the other hand, The Kitchen is where the right to being host is performed by migrants, where women can gather (whether migrant or citizen) in a registered building, such as a cultural centre in an urban context. Their right to being host is facilitated by the cultural centre's hospitium (universal hospitality), and developing resilience is explored within the kitchen as a space, and within an understanding of cityzenship, transcending the limits of legal space.

When uncertainty is inherent in the legal structure, its limits extend to all parts of life, whereupon uncertainty is reserved not just for migrants but for all those that are in solidarity, and those engaged in the field. In April 2015, research on migration was declared illegal in Turkey, unless an official permission was obtained from the Ministry of Interior; however, the details of this process were never made clear. In December 2015, the ban was lifted, but none of the institutions in Turkey were informed of this decision. For this reason, continuing the work in the hospitality centre in Gaziantep wasn't possible, although this research had initially aimed to look at daily life in the camp. As a last note, the question of ethics regarding research and fieldwork on migration is itself underlined with conditions of uncertainty, that is, how the researcher positions themselves in relation to fieldwork, especially if they come from the same background as the host (the citizen). Considered as a researcher with the same background as that of the host, as the author I position myself as one who is able to reveal the infrastructures of illegalized migration, meaning the perpetuated borders that separate people, whether they are physical or invisible. Secondly, by taking part in the women's collective and helping to set up The Kitchen, I also position myself in solidarity with the migrants in regard to the representation of themselves, sharing the common struggles of being a woman in the city yet avoiding the categorization related to migration by acknowledging the collective character of belonging to a city.

Notes

1 Jacques Derrida, *Of Hospitality* (Stanford: Stanford University Press, 2000).
2 In this text, 'refugee' is used in the meaning stated by UNHCR 1951 Refugee Convention: Someone who, 'owing to a well-founded fear of being persecuted for reasons of race, religion, nationality, membership of a particular social group or political opinion,' is outside the country of his nationality, and is unable to, or owing to such fear, is unwilling to avail himself of the protection of that country.
3 UNHCR, 'Syria Regional Refugee Response: Turkey, Operational Portal Refugee Response', June 2019, accessed 9 April 2020, https://data2.unhcr.org/en/situations/syria/location/113.
4 Official Newspaper, nr. 22127, 30 November 1994. 'Türkiye'ye İltica Eden veya Başka Bir Ülkeye İltica Etmek Üzere Türkiyeden İkamet İzni Talep Eden Münferit Yabancılarile Topluca Sığınma Amacıyla Sınırlarımıza Gelen Yabancılara ve Olabilecek Nüfus Hareketlerine Uygulanacak Usul ve Esaslar Hakkında Yönetmelik', accessed 9 April 2020, http://www.multeci.org.tr/wp-content/uploads/2016/12/1994-Yonetmeligi.pdf.
5 Richard Ek, 'Giorgio Agamben and the Spatialities of the Camp: An Introduction', *Geografiska Annaler Series B: Human Geography* 88, no. 4 (2006): 363–86.

6 Official Newspaper, nr. 28615. 11 April 2013. 'Law Nr. 6458: Law on Foreigners and International Protection', accessed 9 April 2020, https://www.resmigazete.gov.tr/eskiler/2013/04/20130411-2.htm.
7 Harald Bauder, 'Why We Should Use the Term "Illegalized Immigrant"', *RCIS Research Brief* 1 (2013): 1–7.
8 Mülteciler (Refugees), 'Türkiyedeki Suriyeli Sayısı', 2019, accessed 9 April 2020, https://multeciler.org.tr/turkiyedeki-suriyeli-sayisi/.
9 Carl Schmitt, *Political Theology: Four Chapters on the Concept of Sovereignty* (Cambridge, MA: MIT Press, 1985).
10 Immanuel Kant, *Perpetual Peace: A Philosophic Essay*, trans. M. C. Smith (New York: Macmillan, 2001 [1795]).
11 Derrida, *Of Hospitality*.
12 Bülent Diken and Carsten Bagge Laustsen, *The Culture of Exception: Sociology Facing the Camp* (London: Routledge, 2005).
13 Schmitt, *Political Theology*, 55.
14 Kant, *Perpetual Peace*, 137–8.
15 Diken and Laustsen, *The Culture of Exception*, 80.
16 Derrida, *Of Hospitality*, 37, 43–5, 55, 107.
17 Diken and Laustsen, *The Culture of Exception*, 5–7.
18 Ibid., 65.
19 Metehan Özcan, Abd Nova, Basem Nabhan and Auguy Lufuluabo, *Vocabulary of Hospitality Exhibition Catalogue* (Istanbul: Studio X Publications, 2014). Take Place is a collective artwork by Metehan Özcan, Abd Nova, Basem Nabhan and Auguy Lufuluabo, commissioned for the first exhibition of Vocabulary of Hospitality in Istanbul, in 2014. The work is about the names given to the streets and squares of the city by the migrants living in the city.
20 Official Newspaper, no. 22127, 30 November 1994.
21 Official Newspaper, no. 28615, 11 April 2013.
22 These categories include *applicant* (asylum seeker), a person who has made an international protection claim and a final decision regarding whose application is pending; *conditional refugee*, a person allowed to reside in Turkey temporarily until they are resettled in a third country; *subsidiary refugee*, a person who has international protection but is neither a refugee nor a conditional refugee; *temporary protection*, immediate temporary protection to be provided to foreigners in cases of large influx into Turkey, and in those where they cannot return to their country; *humanitarian resident*, a one-year residence permit to cover extraordinary circumstances; *victim of human trafficking resident*, a thirty-day residence permit that covers the period of most vulnerability of an

immigrant being smuggled. In addition, there are the categories of *stateless person*, who does not have any citizenship; *refugee-like-person*, who carries the characteristics of a refugee but is still not eligible to apply for asylum; and *irregular migrant* and *undocumented migrant* refer to the unregistered migrant, who has an irregular pattern of migration.

23 UNHCR, 'Syria Regional Refugee Response'.
24 Ibid.
25 Nevra Akdemir, 'Üç Büyük Göç Dalgası ve Gaziantep'in Mekânsal Sürekli Yeniden İnşası' [Three Main Migration Waves and Gaziantep's Continuous Spatial Reproduction], in *The Migration Conference 2017: Programme and Abstracts Book*, eds. Fethiye Tilbe, Elif Iskender and Ibrahim Sirkeci (London: Transnational Press, 2017), 209–10.
26 Ömer Faruk Kavuncu, *Suriyelilerin Sosyal Uyumunda Sivil Toplumun Rolü* (Gaziantep: BEKAM, 2018), 42.
27 European Parliament, 'EU-Turkey Statement', 2016, accessed 9 April 2020, https://ec.europa.eu/home-affairs/sites/homeaffairs/files/what-we-do/policies/european-agenda-migration/proposal-implementation-package/docs/20160420/report_implementation_eu-turkey_agreement_nr_01_en.pdf.
28 UNHCR, 'Türkiye'deki Suriyeli Mülteciler için Sıkça Sorulan Sorular, İkamet ve Hareketlilik Bölümü', 2017, accessed 9 April 2020, https://data2.unhcr.org/en/documents/download/59167; 'Suriyelilerin İstanbul'a kaydı durduruldu', Deutsche Welle, 6 February 2018, https://www.dw.com/tr/suriyelilerin-istanbula-kayd%C4%B1-durduruldu/a-42465450.
29 Celia Mannaert, 'New Issues in Refugee Research, Irregular Migration and Asylum in Turkey', Working Paper No. 89 for Evaluation and Policy Analysis Unit, United Nations High Commissioner for Refugees. 2013, accessed 9 April 2020, https://www.unhcr.org/3ebf5c054.pdf.
30 'We will Continue Our "open door" policy for Syrians', *Anadolu Agency*, 3 April 2013, https://www.aa.com.tr/en/turkey/we-will-continue-our-open-door-policy-for-syrians/258882
31 Ahmet Senar, 'Geri Kabul Anlaşması', *AB ve Turkiye*, 2014.
32 'Migrants' governorate' was a bureaucratic position that existed in 2014 but was cancelled later on. Similarly, AFAD, while it is still responsible for the management of the camps, is not responsible for the administration of migrants from Syria. This duty is transferred to the State Migration Department.
33 Ahmet İçduygu, 'Syrian Refugees in Turkey: The Long Road Ahead', *Transatlantic Council on Migration: Migration Policy Institute*, 2015, accessed 9 April 2020, www.migrationpolicy.org/transatlantic.

34 Georg Simmel, 'The Bridge and the Door', in *Rethinking Architecture: A Reader in Cultural Theory*, ed. N. Leac (London: Routledge, 1997), 64–68.
35 Wolfgang Sofsky, *The Order of Terror: The Concentration Camp* (Princeton: Princeton University Press, 1997), 52.
36 Richard Sennett, *The Fall of Public Man* (London: Faber and Faber, 1986), 170.
37 Diken and Laustsen, *The Culture of Exception*, 88.
38 'Suriyeliler Halep Özlemini Antep Kalesi'yle Gideriyor', *Hürriyet*, 16 March 2017, https://www.hurriyet.com.tr/suriyeliler-halep-ozlemini-antep-kalesiyle-gi-4 0396639; 'Suriyeli Ambalaj Firmasından Gaziantep'e Yatırım', *Anadolu Agency*, 17 November 2018, https://www.aa.com.tr/tr/ekonomi/suriyeli-ambalaj-firmasindan-gaziantepe-yatirim/1314006.
39 Diken and Laustsen, *The Culture of Exception*, 54.
40 Official Newspaper, no. 25874, 3 May 2005, 'Law Nr. 5393; Municipality Law', accessed 9 April 2020, http://www.resmigazete.gov.tr/eskiler/2005/07/20050713-6.htm.
41 Official Newspaper nr. 28615, 11 April 2013.
42 European Migrant Relocation and Resettlement Scheme, 2016.

7

The politics of normalcy

Examining the festival on the island of Imbros/ Gökçeada

Sevcan Ercan

Introduction

This chapter uses the concept of normalcy as a lens through which to examine a prominent ethno-religious festival on the island of Imbros/Gökçeada. The festival in question consists of a set of events associated with the Assumption Day on 15 August, and which is celebrated by the displaced Rum[1] community of the island. In recent years, this festival has re-emerged as a site of importance for the island community as a whole, including the Rum diaspora. However, it has also become subject to a set of emergency controls imposed by the Turkish state – a situation which has increased in severity since the failed coup attempt in 2016. Taken together, the process of revitalization and the state of emergency have had the effect of altering the traditional and historical make-up of the festival. This leads to the question: What does a 'normal state' of this festival look like? In order to address this query, I examine the festival within the scope of two different temporal frames. The first constitutes the period of the last decade (2010 to the present), during which the festival has been governed by exceptional emergency measures. The second frame involves looking at the festival from a wider historical angle, one that discusses the internal dynamics of the festival as an *exceptional* religious and social gathering.

Imbros, an island within the Aegean Archipelago, is currently inhabited by a minority Rum community, living alongside a Turkish majority. The Rum community used to constitute the sole community living on the island, but due to the anti-minority policies of the Republic of Turkey they were systematically displaced, especially between 1963 and 1980. Since the late 1990s, however, several Rum rituals have been revitalized on the island by the Rum diaspora, which has had many effects – the most central of which is initiating a return of the Rum community. Drawing on my research on Imbros and its diasporic locales conducted between 2016 and 2018, this chapter assesses the festival as the most important of the revitalized rituals, given that it has been key to the Rums' return to the island.[2]

Considering the concept of normalcy in relation to the festival functions as a way of problematizing what is normal – or what a normal version of this festival looks like – discussed in the context of the everyday. As the chapter will discuss, there are a number of ways to reflect on the topic of normalcy within the framework of the everyday, one of which is provided by Lefebvre's critique. Furthermore, in examining this topic across two periods of time, this discussion addresses two further issues. The first issue concerns how today's revitalized festival can be situated in relation to a longer-term history, one which includes a broader understanding of both the state of normalcy and the everyday. Following from this, I reflect upon how the politics of normalcy at play in the production and perception of this historically charged public event (the festival) has changed.

Normalcy and the island of Imbros

As a way of responding to the theme 'architectures of emergency', this chapter approaches the concept of emergency by reflecting upon what constitutes the state of normalcy. This is primarily because addressing the state of emergency involves reflecting on a set of (supposed) dichotomies, such as the relations between normalcy and emergency, normal and abnormal, normality and exceptionality, natural (as normal) and unnatural and so on – a situation which appears to be intrinsic to any discussion seeking to problematize the idea of emergency.

Correspondingly, the relationship between emergency and normalcy has been widely debated and theorized, especially during the last two decades. As one of the central debates, the theory of exceptionalism in relation to the concept of emergency suggests an understanding of emergency as the exception and suspension of the rules and norms. One of the main advocators of this view, Giorgio Agamben, clarifies that the state of exception, of which the current rise of emergency regimes is considered a product, has become 'a paradigm of government'.[3] In other words, as Agamben argues, 'the voluntary creation of a permanent state of exception (though perhaps not declared in the technical sense) has become one of the essential practices of contemporary states, including so-called democratic ones'.[4] Similarly, others also consider the concept of emergency with reference to the dichotomy between norms (as the normal state of things) and exceptions (as the state of emergency), arguing that emergency and normalcy are entwined in today's politics either by the constant use of the language of war in daily life, or through the practice of any kind of emergency rhetoric.[5]

However, the emphasis on the concept of normalcy in this chapter is not only due to this particular interrelation between normalcy and emergency – one which is realized and debated by the aforementioned researchers – but is first and foremost due to the ambiguity of the idea of normal which can be identified within the social and spatial context of the island of Imbros. The reason for this ambiguity is twofold. The first reason is linked with Imbros' natural condition of being an island. Studying small islands in the context of history and heritage studies, Gillian Carr and Keir Reeves state that 'small islands', the category to which Imbros belongs, are often not considered as nations in their own right but, rather, as small outposts of other kingdoms, countries and nations, and thus have often been relegated either as interesting case studies or unimportant curiosities.[6] This overlooking or fetishizing attitude towards islands, which Carr and Reeves define as 'the mainstream, mainland perception of these "small" places', complicates the understanding of normalcy or the normal state of things associated with an island context.[7] The second reason that can help explain the particular ambiguity in terms of defining the 'normal' within the context of Imbros originates from Imbros' controversial status which emerged at the end of the First World War through the Treaty of Lausanne, signed in 1923.

The 1923 Treaty of Lausanne was the final peace treaty which concluded the First World War. In recognizing the borders of the new Turkish nation state amid the collapse of the Ottoman Empire, this treaty also determined that only two islands from among the hundreds which populated the Aegean would henceforth belong to Turkey.[8] Located near the entrance to the Dardanelles, these two islands – Imbros and Tenedos – became Turkish territory under special conditions. The conditions stipulated by the Lausanne Treaty ensured that the native Rum (Anatolian Greek) communities – the main ethnic groups inhabiting both islands – would henceforth be acknowledged as an ethnic minority of Turkey, duly protected with administrative autonomy.[9] In the meantime, a widespread and compulsory population exchange between Turkey and Greece began.[10] While this exchange caused both the displacement of approximately 1.5 million Rums and the creation of a seismic historical condition – one that continues to reverberate today – it also exempted Imbros, Tenedos and Istanbul. The category of 'exception' has thus become an embedded condition of the island since then, given that until 1963 Imbros' Rums led their life on the island as a minority within the Republic of Turkey, but as the majority on their own island. Considering this situation was unprecedented among the other settlements in Turkey which maintained a Rum population after the 1923 exchange, how the state of normalcy appears on Imbros stands before us as an ambiguous case.

In other words, rethinking the concept of normalcy as it is understood in relation to emergency provides us with a critical lens to look into the specific political, social and spatial aspects of the festival which have been influenced and shaped by the politics of normalcy implemented on the island. However, when used as a term, 'normalcy' maintains such a loose grip over its various meanings that it would remain unproductively broad unless one explicitly focuses on a certain context and a specific set of mechanisms through which to understand it. With this in mind, this chapter presents a multilayered exploration of 'normal' which is framed by a critique of Imbros' everyday, while the exploration of normal is conducted through an analysis of a local ethno-religious festival on Imbros.

Rethinking normalcy in relation to the everyday

In the task of rethinking the concept of normalcy, perhaps the most imperative proposition appears to be that normalcy is contingent on the variations in the norms that render a condition as acceptable or desirable – in other words, as 'normal'. Hence, what is considered normal (including its suggested opposite) is often not absolute but, rather, ever-changing. In line with this statement, studies addressing the issues of body politics, including race, gender and disability, may often provide a more illustrative criticism of normalcy, showing not only that the norms are prone to change but also that the very idea of the normal is shaped by particular features of society, rather than existing as a condition of human nature.[11]

On that note, Lennard J. Davis's *Enforcing Normalcy* provides one of the key studies shaping the theoretical underpinnings of my approach towards the concept of normalcy. Davis describes normalcy as a concept which is tied inexorably to 'the assumptions we make about art, language, literature and culture', suggesting that the notion of normalcy generates the idea of disability, as well as the ideas of race, class and gender.[12] For Davis, in order to understand the disabled body, 'one must return to the concept of the norm, the normal body'.[13] This is because 'the "problem" is not the person with disabilities; the problem is the way that normalcy is constructed to create the "problem" of the disabled person'.[14] Asserting that normalcy is a social construct, Davis explains that normalcy as we know it is constructed through the emergence of the idea of *norm* – a concept within which deviations are wished to be minimized while the average appears to become a kind of ideal.[15]

As a result, as Davis explains, the development of normal, including the very structure on which the norms rest, tends to be normative, causing the normalcy to be constantly enforced in public venues.[16] In Davis's argument, the public venues under discussion are the novels (books) where instances of normalcy are regularly checked, and where normalcy becomes part of 'the notion of progress, of industrialisation, and of ideological consolidation of the power of the bourgeois'.[17] While Davis's argument on the issues surrounding normalcy concerns the politics regarding the body and its representation, his discourse is also applicable to other areas. In fact, his analysis of normalcy shows that the critique of the assumptions about what constitutes the norm is a way of understanding how normalcy is constructed at a given time in a given setting. For instance, the discourse of normalcy within the context of the everyday evidently promotes the application of normative measures under the guise of security or emergency. Consequently, a form of hegemony of normalcy constantly suppresses any deviance from the various conceptions of the sovereign powers regarding the everyday.

In order to realize such normative practices generated by the discourse of normal in the context of Imbros, one can simply observe the main gatherings of Imbros' Rum community on the island. As one of the most prominent communal gatherings, the festival under discussion has had to undergo several changes due to the hegemonic practices of normalcy exercised by the sovereign powers on the island. These are currently mobilized through the local authorities, both by the process of providing permissions for public events and by the ways in which these permission-givers participate in these events. Nevertheless, the discourse of normalcy in relation to the festival is not only complicated by this relatively recent involvement of the local authorities as the regulator of public events, but it is also challenged by the very nature of these rural festivals. In fact, the festivals on Imbros had already been considered as *exceptional* social and religious events, having functioned as a break to the 'normalcy' of the everyday. Addressing the differences between the festival and everyday life, Henri Lefebvre describes such celebratory events as follows:

> Peasant celebrations tightened social links and at the same time gave rein to all the desires which had been pent up by collective discipline and the necessities of everyday work. In celebrating, each member of the community went beyond himself, so to speak, and in one fell swoop drew all that was energetic, pleasurable and possible from nature, food, social life and his own body and mind.[18]

In continuing his analysis of the festivals, Lefebvre notes that 'the festivals contrasted violently with everyday life, *but they were not separate from it*'.[19] He articulates this by saying: 'The regular place given in the country calendar to festivals and specific tasks represented the regularity of human actions – their punctual accomplishment – and appeared to guarantee and assure the regularity of the seasons'.[20] Lefebvre's remarks on the differences of festive days from other days in rural communities (particularly those of Greece and Southern Italy) are comparable with the Rums' descriptions of their experience of the past festivals. But what is more important than this is the ability of festivals to contrast with the uniformity of everyday life while remaining an integral part of it. Thus, for Imbros, this characteristic of the local festivals has enabled these celebrations to gain prominent roles after the displacement of the local Rum community from the island.

In short, between the 1970s and 1990s, the festivals on Imbros had largely ceased to be celebrated by the Rum community, up until the revitalization of some during the late 1990s. By the 2000s, the festival in question had already become a kind of state of exception. This was due to the creation of a perception of this festival as a deviation from the normalcy of everyday life, despite its long history on the island, while at the same time it was also enabling a partial return of the Rums to the island. The significance of normalcy in relation to the festival is therefore twofold. On the one hand, the discourse of normalcy, which excludes the festival from the everyday on Imbros, is materialized as a set of normative security measures regulating the public events associated with the festival. The normalizing and abnormalizing power of these measures acts as the main mechanism under which the hegemony of normalcy operates, whereas the discourse of normalcy is fully deployed in the control of the public space by the Turkish authorities. On the other hand, since the festivals are considered to be exceptional yet integral to the everyday life on Imbros throughout history, this particular festival has provided the now-diasporic Rum community of Imbros with a series of possibilities. This means that the festival is not only revitalized as a special ethno-religious celebration happening during a specific period of the year but also indicates that the manner in which festivals as such are celebrated can alter the normalcy of the everyday.

In the following sections, the festival is examined by looking into the politics of normalcy at play during the organization and celebration of both its present and past iterations. By doing so, a spatial ethnography of the festival is created, and then examined through the lens of normalcy, the politics of which appears to shape the festival's social and spatial features.

The revitalization of the festival

Between 1963 and 1965, as part of the last wave of anti-minority policies (often referred to as the 1964 Exiles), the Turkish state approved the deportation of 12,000 Turkish citizens who belonged to the Rum population of Turkey.[21] Together with the Greek citizens who were living in Turkey with a permanent residence permit at this time, the number of people who faced deportation in this period was about 30,000.[22] This number, however, does not include those family members who were forced to leave the country with their loved ones. The 1964 Exiles of the Rum populations of Turkey were the last of the truly explicit episodes of the anti-minority policies enacted by the Turkish state.

In 1965, despite these deportations having begun in 1963, there were still more than 5,000 Rums living on Imbros.[23] Yet, this number had dropped to

300 by the early 1990s.²⁴ This displacement of the Rums of Imbros occurred simultaneously with (and due to) the Turkish state's emplacement of non-Rum communities on the island, itself a process which was realized with increasing intensity during the period that elapsed between 1963 and 2000. The majority of the Rum community were displaced from the island between 1963 and 1980,²⁵ and are therefore considered to be a part of (and subsequent to) the 1964 Exiles. As stated earlier, after the displacement of the Rums during this period, the festivals on Imbros stopped being celebrated to any great extent. In the meantime, the displaced Imbrians²⁶ started to emigrate to other countries, where they established associations and societies in order to rebuild Imbrian communities in these new localities. With the help of these associations, a developed collective sense of the Imbrian diaspora was subsequently created. The Imbrian diaspora adopted narratives which continued patriotic feelings, and cultivated a sense of being indigenous islanders, while many embarked on legal struggles to regain not only their material losses on the island but also their Turkish citizenship.²⁷ Indeed, as a result of the Imbrian associations' continuing demands for an immediate and effective recognition of their inheritance rights regardless of nationality, including reclaiming their Turkish citizenship and their expropriated properties, several people have regained their citizenship and the ownership of their former houses.

By the 1990s, the hostile policies targeting Imbrians had begun to ease, and the weight of the pressure on Imbrian existence on Imbros started to diminish. As a result, possibilities arose to visit the island and to support the few Imbrian elders who are still living there. By the end of the 1990s, the Imbrian diaspora had started to gradually revive the old rituals and traditions.²⁸ This was evidently a very ambitious decision, and thus required constant effort to combine secular and profane elements in order to attract different generations of Imbrians to the island while avoiding generating new conflicts with the Turkish authorities. In order to revitalize the festival, the diaspora organized trips to the island during the month of August. This move was also evocative of the past traditions of island life, during which August had been an exceptionally eventful and lively time. Each year, more and more people joined these trips, and, at some point, the Imbros Associations began to arrange bus services to the island – these collected Imbrians from Athens and Thessaloniki and brought them across during the first week of August and then returned them by the end of August. The August events consist of a series of liturgies and social gatherings, at the centre of which is the festival of the Panagia (meaning the Virgin Mary). As one member of the Imbrian community noted, the decision by the diaspora to attend this festival collectively represents a critical decision in changing the power dynamics on the island.[29]

Changing the everyday through emplacement

On 6 September 2014, *T24* published an article about a classified 1964 National Security Council (in Turkish *Milli Güvenlik Kurulu*, and hereafter NSC) report which revealed the NSC policies that aimed to change the demographics of Imbros.[30] The report had been found in the archives by Erhan Pekçe, a lawyer working on the protection of minority rights in Turkey. It mentions a series of measures and projects that were adopted, or planned to be adopted, to 'Turkify the island [Imbros]' and provide the (Turkish) immigrants with the necessary economic, social and moral support for their settlement on the island in 1964.[31]

In fact, between 1963 and 2000, Turkey had embarked on a series of emplacement practices on the island, aiming to both directly and indirectly manipulate the island's demographic structure. The spatiality of these emplacement practices included the establishment of public institutions (one of which was a highly controversial open prison), the emergence of new settlements, such as state-built villages, and other major infrastructural projects, such as the reservoir and the airport. In addition to the communities and individuals who were directly brought to the island through these projects, the island also attracted immigrant populations during the construction of the public institutions and infrastructure projects. These immigrant groups, coming largely from the rural areas of south-eastern Anatolia, began to occupy some of the Rum villages during the 1970s.

The dispossession of the Rums from their agricultural lands by the mechanisms of expropriation was that which enabled the emplacement practices mentioned previously to be implemented on Imbros. Public institutions – such as the state farm, the open prison and the army base – all appeared on the island less than a decade after the expropriations first started in 1963. Over half of the cultivable land, plus a significant percentage of the total island, was expropriated for these public institutions by the end of the 1970s. As the most critical institution in the displacements of the Imbros

Rums, the open prison with a farm was established on the agricultural lands of Schoinoudi/Dereköy in 1965.[32] In addition to the prison farm, a state farm was also founded in April 1966. This combined emplacement of both prison farm and state farm seized the economic activities of the Rums to a great extent.

Furthermore, a total of five villages embody emplacement practices in the form of new settlements on Imbros. The state-built town of Gökçeada could perhaps also be considered as an additional example, given that it includes most of the public buildings and the lodgings of public employees appointed to the island, plus the summerhouse districts for tourists. In her article on the concept of emplacement and exiles, Liisa Malkki suggests that the system of territorial nation states invents its own national order of things, and it is this which shapes the processes and practices of emplacement.[33] As a product of the national order of things considered in the context of the Turkish nation state and the regulations of the 1934 Settlement Law, the concept of *İskan Köyleri* [State-Built Villages] has become a common spatial form since the very beginning of the Republic. One of the controversies about the 1934 Settlement Law, which is still a main part of the settlement legislation of Turkey, was its stated purpose of dissipating and supporting Turkish culture throughout the whole territory of Turkey.[34] Similarly, the law indicates that any immigrants who do not have a sense of belonging to Turkish culture, or who are 'either an anarchist, spy, or nomadic gypsy', or whose citizenship was revoked in the past, would not be allowed to settle in Turkey.[35]

In short, through its intention to populate the Turkish territory with people having a close affinity to 'Turkishness', the law in Turkey has been able to regulate the transnational and intrastate mass movements of people according to the clear and unambiguous purpose laid out in the 1934 Settlement Law. Judicially, the subjects of emplacement practices taking place on Imbros are people whose resettlement processes the Turkish state officially helped and determined. As such, there were two main types of state-brought groups. The first group were people whom Turkey evacuated from their villages on the mainland due to local floods, earthquakes or infrastructural projects. Given that their migration to the island took place under imperative conditions, these state-brought residents of Imbros were neither from a privileged background nor had a stable income at the time of their resettlement. The other group consists of muhajirs/muhajir – the term used for people who had immigrated from the Balkan regions, mostly from Bulgaria and Macedonia, to Turkey.[36] The resettlement process of the muhajir Bulgarians on Imbros was completed in 2000 as part of the last mass migratory movement from Bulgaria to Turkey between 1989 and 1992, forming a smaller part of Imbros' population.[37]

To conclude, between 1963 and 1980, the public, social and economic life on the island changed dramatically, due to both the top-down emplacement practices and the self-emplacement of the immigrant/occupier groups. The modern state of Turkey showed its hand swiftly by using its institutions and its technological power through its public institutions and public employees. The state has employed an increasing number of public employees brought from the Turkish mainland on the island since 1963. The constant theme of these public projects has been to modernize and enhance mechanisms of local production on the island, alongside developing infrastructure projects and facilitating the arrival of new occupants. Life on Imbros had been considered an idiosyncratic form of rural living which was duly identified as outdated and inefficient by the state, with the decision taken as a way to legitimize the new policies disposing of this rural life. Although most of the projects, except for the prison, were perhaps seemingly innocuous institutions, the ways in which the Turkish state deployed these projects effectively controlled and restricted the Rums' lives on the island, disposing of their old ways of living.

However, the open prison was closed in 1992 when the island's military status was abolished, while the state farm was already inactive by 2000. In the meantime, the rushed, top-down construction process of the state-built villages generated a settlement model in which projects reduced the spaces of human condition to a shelter (a typical house) and a mosque. The residents of these villages felt estranged due to several reasons, varying from the ill-chosen locations of their villages through to the poor architectural and infrastructural features of their village houses. Indeed, the new villages did not supply decent cultural, social and living spaces for their residents. As a result, although the emplacements have caused the displacement of the Rums and thus the disruption of the everyday life created by the Rum community, they failed to establish a functioning everyday life for the new residents of the island in the long run.

Constructing normalcy with the Revitalized Festival

Today, the general structure of the Rum Orthodox Christian year is partially subrogated by the diasporic cycle on Imbros. This situation causes one specific summer festival to gain a prominent role above others, and which goes beyond the major feasts of Christmas and Easter. This contemporary festival – the festival of the Panagia (also known as the festival/feast day of the Assumption of the Virgin Mary throughout the Christian world) – takes place on 15 August in Agridia. Located on a higher hill than the other four villages on the island, Agridia, along with Agioi Theodoroi, constitutes the two key villages of Imbros that maintain an active Imbrian community, culture and a ritual tradition. Since the onset of the 2000s, the festival of the Panagia has continued to expand its significance, both for the Imbrian diaspora and its overall impact on the island.

Since its initial revitalization in the late 1990s, the festival has been in a constant state of flux due to the differences between the aspirations of the Imbrian diaspora and the objectives of the Turkish authorities/other parties related to Imbros. Despite their changing circumstances, however, the Imbrian diasporas have maintained several important features of their festival tradition. For example, they continue to incorporate different spaces and places on the island during the festivities, such as churches, cemeteries, squares and chapels, through a series of rituals taking place consecutively or (as in 2018) simultaneously during August each year. That being said, one difference which does stand out is that, after the revitalization, these festival spaces along with the rituals are intertwined with diasporic symbolism. By the early 2000s, the festival of the Panagia (also named as the Panigyri of the Panagia) was already a gathering of more than 2,000 Imbrians on Imbros. As one of the first researchers who studied the displacement of the Rum community of Imbros, Giorgos Tsimouris defines this festival as a pilgrimage for Imbrians, emphasizing its organized manner but also its emotional and religious significations.[38] Another researcher, Elif Babül, describes the festival as playing 'a central role in the Rums' return to the island'.[39] Similarly, Ozan Say, in his 2013 study on the rituals of Imbros, focuses on the programme of the festival as 'a new phenomenon' for Imbrians that connects members of the community.[40]

In the research conducted during the late 1990s and the early 2000s, the festival is described as 'a highly charged political arena'[41] or 'an open contestation'.[42] Tsimouris, for example, states that the festival is 'where the returnees assert their long-term attachment to the island in an attempt to undermine the tourist misrepresentations disseminated by the local authorities and tourist guides'.[43] Deploying the pilgrimage metaphor, Tsimouris interprets the duality of the existing situation in Imbros as 'tourism versus pilgrimage', describing the attempts of Imbros' local government as an act of folklorizing the return of the Greeks, and as a counter-movement to Imbrians' collective pilgrimage.[44] For Babül on the other hand, the embedded contestation of the festival is created by the local Turkish authorities who are claiming to show an act of tolerance by allowing the existence of the festival, and thus of other cultures.[45] Babül also interprets the festival as 'a way of claiming belonging to and on Imbros' for the diasporic Imbrian community.[46]

The festival is gradually being extended by the diaspora in order to increase their visibility, a process which includes the Turkish authorities – such as the mayor of the island and the district governor – being strategically invited to these extended events.[47] In the meantime, stories of the multicultural character of the island are freely and abundantly deployed in Turkish politics, yet without acknowledging past Imbrian displacement. Accordingly, reports such as the one on 'preserving the bicultural character of the two Turkish islands as a model for co-operation between Turkey and Greece in the interest of the people concerned'[48] or projects like the movement of Cittaslow[49] picture the island as the ultimate tourist destination for those looking for authenticity and natural beauty.[50] The particular state of normalcy that is constructed and maintained within the contemporary festival first unveils itself through the policies of the Turkish state. More specifically, the local authorities demand a series of security measures, imposing formal permissions (given by themselves) on the use of the public space for communal gatherings, especially of the Imbrians.

One of the many spatial implications of this situation is the existence of the constabulary checkpoints temporarily built a few kilometres before the entrances of the villages where the festivities take place. As part of this, during the evening of 15 August, Agridia, which is located on top of a hill, is closed to any traffic, and the participants of the festival are required to walk a few kilometres up to the village in order to attend the festival. Moreover, the idea of permission itself comes with the possibility of situations where the permission is not given. For instance, during the 2016 festival season, the already existing tension between the local authorities and Imbrian associations coincided with the general turmoil in the political arena of Turkey due to the coup attempt of 15 July of that same year. The year also marked the twenty-fifth anniversary of Patriarch Bartholomew in the patriarchate, and several celebrations had already been organized in his honour, including a concert, opening ceremonies of newly refurbished buildings and a newly built union building in the village of Schoinoudi, plus several talks and gatherings. In 2016, this concert took place with the absence of 'protocol', meaning the absence of the mayor and the district governor. This situation, together with several local newspaper articles accusing the festivities of the Imbrians of being ill-timed (due to the recentness of the coup attempt), forced the associations to go underground on the next day of the concert.

The other implication of this newly constructed normalcy of the festival is a new emphasis that is put on the sacred spaces involved in the festivities and liturgies. The extended significance of Agridia's Panagia church during the festival can be referable to this sense. Today the Panagia church is considered to be the place where new generations of Imbrians are introduced to their community's history and traditions within an orthodox Christian setting, and in terms of this new function its architecture is inextricably linked with the physical spaces of the island. As such, the well-maintained and lively presence of the church is set against a background that consists largely of dilapidated or ruined and unoccupied buildings, and creates a theatrical atmosphere through which the displacement of Imbrians is enacted. The Panagia rituals also generate a tourist presence in both the church and churchyard by attributing authentic reputations to the Imbrian community's rituals. Aside from triggering some small-scale reactions among Imbrians, the tourist presence is often tolerated as long as it does not hamper the rituals.

Searching for the historical normal of the festival

Orthodox Christian religion began to be practised on Imbros in the second century.[51] Although the history of the Church of Imbros until the eleventh century is based on scant and incomplete evidence, it is widely believed that there has been a continuous Orthodox Christian presence on Imbros from the second century onwards, and which has endured the rule of different empires.[52] Likewise, since 1923 when the Republic of Turkey was established, and when

Imbros became a part of it, the Imbros church has maintained its status as a metropolitan church.[53] The metropolitan church of Imbros and Tenedos, which operates under the Ecumenical Patriarchate of Constantinople, is located in the county centre of the island. In terms of the calendar of the Christian religion, the particular event which constitutes the main event of the festival under discussion is the annual celebration of the Assumption of the Virgin Mary (the Assumption Day) – the dogma of Mary's bodily assumption into heaven is observed throughout various Christian countries worldwide. The liturgies related to the Assumption Day take place in churches and chapels which are dedicated to the Panagia. The principal church of Agridia village (named as Tepeköy by the Turkish authorities) is one of these Panagia churches, and the main venue of ceremonies and liturgies in contemporary Imbros.

In her study of social experience and religion in rural Greece, Laurie Kain Hart mentions two principles of religious activity and thought in Orthodox Christian religion.[54] The first is 'the calendrical cycle of festivals in celebration of the birth, life, death, and resurrection of Christ and the birth, life and dormition of the Panagia (the Virgin Mary)'.[55] For Hart, the Church inherited this calendrical cycle – an organic framework linked with natural and economic cycles – from the pagan cults, and this syncretism had a crucial impact on the Christian theology of the time.[56] The second major scheme of religious activity and thought, as summarized by Hart, involves the reverence of saints in particular localities such as churches and monasteries.[57] In Imbros this was further deployed in the little chapels, called monasteries by the Rum community, scattered all over the island. Each had been dedicated to either local or universal saints. Imbrians were visiting these monasteries for different purposes throughout the year.

Hence, the ritual year of the Orthodox Christian religion is produced by a conjunction of a non-Christian ritual history (belonging to the particular locality), a popular social and economic calendar and a Christian teaching.[58] Thus, when considered as an amalgamation of these secular and religious, local and universal phenomena, a local ritual calendar is, to some extent, idiosyncratic in terms of the hierarchy of importance of the liturgical events. In Imbros' Orthodox Christian calendar, summer was associated with festivals, which are called *panigyri* [πανηγύρι] (translated into Turkish as *panayır*) of the Panagia and saints, during which feasting occurred in abundance.[59] Each village on Imbros had its annual festival on a different day in summer according to the holy figure or saint to which its principal church is dedicated. This festival season also coincided with the period in which Imbrians resided in the *damia* districts – a district of summer houses (*dami*) of the island surrounded by fields, meadows and orchards and used mainly for animal husbandry but also for agricultural activities. *Dami* is both an architectural form and a particular kind of spatiality with which Imbrians created a rural life, spreading across the island through a network of settlements (villages and *damia* districts) and individual buildings (chapels, monasteries, individual *damis*). Thus, the festivals were occurring in the period when the community was at its most mobile.

Drawing on other studies of the *panigyri*, it can be said that the necessities of the agrarian cycle shaped the annual cycle of the rituals into a final form, where the summers on the island gained a particular social and religious significance.[60] Hart defines a similar situation in Richia (a rural settlement in Greece) as one where 'patterns of abundance and scarcity define the year'.[61] However, this calendar had been interrupted by the displacement of Imbrians, and, except for a few prominent days such as the festival of the Panagia, many festivals have since disappeared. Yet the prominent festival season continues to be the summer festival period largely due to its historical significance and its convenient timing for those Imbrians who can visit the island only during the summer months. In this context, parts of the religious calendar have been reinvented in circumstances in which liturgical cycles did not neatly correspond with new diasporic ones. Consequently, the hierarchy of liturgies on Imbros differed from other examples in Greece or elsewhere.

Conclusion: The festival as normalcy

As a social and spatial materialization of a state of exception which exists in relation to the everyday, the festival serves as a concrete way to understand the otherwise conceptual framework of normalcy. By looking over the historical and contextual material just outlined, we can clearly see that the festival is subject to constant ongoing change, and yet this does not diminish its status as a regular gathering point for the Imbrian community.

With this in mind, the festival provides us with a way to perceive how normalcy is a construct. First, normalcy of the everyday involves the notion of exception – this can clearly be seen in the form of the festival as it has existed in its various manifestations. The politics of normalcy which controls the everyday relies upon an awareness of an exceptional element, that is, normalcy does not make any sense without an understanding of the opposite contained within itself (abnormal, exceptional, emergency etc.). The festival is by definition a site/state of exception. That is its 'normal' condition. Thinking in these terms, we realize that the current state of emergency in Turkey merely changes the terms under which the festival on Imbros is deemed to be exceptional, but not the fact that it is exceptional – for it has always been this.

Secondly, what we also observe from this chapter is that the festival's reassuring regularity as a planned site of exception reveals how the politics of normalcy operates as a set of mechanisms, governing both what counts as normal and what counts as exceptional. We can see that this applies to the individual Imbrian, his/her community and the apparatus of the Turkish state. While the exterior framework under which the festival operates as a site of exception can and does change over time, what does not alter is that the festival effectively thrives under it – it requires such conditions in order to be what it is, that is, a festival of importance for the Imbrian diaspora. Finally, in setting up a contrast with everyday life on the island, the festival acts as a site in which normalcy can be reconstructed. This offers us a way to understand Lefebvre's earlier point, whereupon 'the festivals contrasted violently with everyday life, *but they were not separate from it*'.[62]

Notes

1   There are different nomenclatures associated with this community. Vassilis Colonas uses the term 'the Greek-speaking, Orthodox [Christian] communities of Asia Minor' to refer to a larger group that also includes those people of Imbros; Alexis Alexandris identifies them as 'a Greek Imbriot community'; and Baskin Oran prefers to use the term Rums, which, according to Oran, 'denotes almost-exclusively Orthodox [Christian] population of Byzantine descent of the Ottoman Empire and Turkey', for referring to these islanders and several other communities. Vassilis Colonas, 'Housing and the Architectural Expression of Asia Minor Greeks Before and After 1923', in *Crossing the Aegean*, ed. Renee Hirschon (New York and Oxford: Berghahn Books, 2008), 164; Alexis

Alexandris, 'Imbros and Tenedos: A Study of Turkish Attitudes Toward Two Ethnic Greek Island Communities Since 1923', *Journal of Hellenic Diaspora* 7, no. 1 (1980): 5–31; Baskın Oran, 'The Story of Those Who Stayed', in *Crossing the Aegean*, ed. Renee Hirschon (New York and Oxford: Berghahn Books, 2008), 98.

2   Sevcan Ercan, 'Finding the Island of Imbros: A Spatial History of Displacement and Emplacement' (PhD diss., University College London, 2020).

3   Giorgio Agamben, *State of Exception* (Chicago: Chicago University Press, 2005), 1–31.

4   Ibid., 2.

5   John Freejohn and Pasquale Pasquino, 'The Law of Exception: A Typology of Emergency Powers', *International Journal of Constitutional Law* 2, no. 2 (2004): 210–39; Philip Heyman, *Terrorism, Freedom, and Security: Winning without War* (Cambridge, MA, and London: The MIT Press, 2003), Kindle.

6   Gillian Carr and Keir Reeves, eds, *Heritage and Memory of War: Responses from Small Islands* (Routledge: New York, 2015), introduction, Kindle.

7   Ibid.

8   'Treaty Series No. 16: Treaty of peace with Turkey, and other instruments signed at Lausanne on July 24, 1923, together with agreements between Greece and Turkey signed in January 30, 1923, and subsidiary documents forming part of the Turkish peace settlement', Parliament Papers, accessed 21 June 2016, http://parlipapers.chadwyck.co.uk/fullrec/fullrec.do?id=1923-026125&DurUrl=Yes.

9   Article 14 of the Treaty of Lausanne. 'Treaty Series No. 16'.

10 'Convention Concerning the Exchange of Greek and Turkish Populations', *The American Journal of International Law* 18, no. 2 (April 1924): 84–90, http://www.jstor.org/stable/2212847.

11 There are numerous examples for this kind of approach found in studies of gender, race and class. For example, in the edited volume *The Intersections of Whiteness* the contributors interrogate how 'the normalcy of whiteness' is constructed and maintained in different contexts. Evangelia Kindingen and Mark Schmitt, eds, *The Intersections of Whiteness* (Oxon and New York: Routledge, 2019).

12 Lennard J. Davis, *Enforcing Normalcy: Disability, Deafness, and the Body* (London and New York: Verso, 1995), 158.

13 Ibid., 23.

14 Ibid., 24.

15 Ibid., 23–32.

16 Ibid., 42–4.

17 Ibid., 49.

18 Henri Lefebvre, *The Critique of Everyday Life* (London and New York: Verso, [1961] 2005), chapter 5, Kindle.
19 Ibid., original italics.
20 Ibid.
21 Rıdvan Akar and Hülya Demir, *İstanbul'un Son Sürgünleri: 1964'te Rumların Sınırdışı Edilmeleri* [*The Last Exiles of Istanbul: The Expatriation of Rums in 1964*] (İstanbul: Doğan Kitap, 2014), 44; Samim Akgönül, *Türkiye Rumları: Ulus-Devlet Çağında Küreselleşme Cağına Bir Azınlığın Yok Oluşu* [*The Greeks of Turkey: The Process of Eliminating a Minority during the Era of Nation-States*] (İstanbul: İletişim Yayınları, 2012), 283.
22 Tahsin Yücel, ed., *Rum Olmak Rum Kalmak* [*Being Rum Remaining Rum*] (İstanbul: İstos Yayınları, 2016), 9; Akgönül, *Türkiye Rumları*, 284–94.
23 In 1965, the population of Imbros totalled 5,941 people – 3,220 of them were living in Rum villages, and the rest (2,721) were living in the town centre which consisted of two Rum neighbourhoods and a few housing blocks for civil servants working on Imbros. Many people living in the country centre were Rums. 'Çanakkale İmroz İlçelere göre Şehir ve Köy Nüfusları [City and Village Populations of Çanakkale Imbros]', 1965 Genel Nüfus Sayımı Veri Tabanı [Database of 1965 General Census of Population], Türkiye İstatistik Kurumu [Turkish Statistical Institute], accessed 21 March 2019, http://rapory.tuik.gov.tr/21-03-2019-17:25:44-11512968171252922092697253647.html?.
24 Giorgos Tsimouris, 'Pilgrimages to Gökçeada (Imvros), a Greco-Turkish Contested Place: Religious Tourism or a Way to Reclaim the Homeland', in *Pilgrimage, Politics and Place-Making in Eastern Europe: Crossing the Borders*, eds John Eade and Mario Katic (Surrey and Burlington: Ashgate, 2014). Kindle.
25 These dates which were taken from the Imbrian Syllogos' website differ slightly in various sources. 'Σύλλογος Ιμβρίων [The Imbrian Syllogos]', Imvrians on the Net, accessed 20 March 2019, http://www.imvrosisland.org/imvros.php?catid=2.
26 The displaced Rums of Imbros created the Imbrian diaspora within which they use the name Imbrian to refer to the members of their community.
27 'Το Ιμβριακό Ζήτημα Σήμερα', Imvrians on the Net, accessed 20 March 2019, http://www.imvrosisland.org/imvros.php?catid=2; Interviews at the Imbrian Association in Athens, 9–19 May 2016.
28 Interviews with Imbrians during the August festivities, August 2016, August 2017 and August 2018.
29 This person is also a member of the board in the Imbrian Association of Athens who is also involved in the organization of the annual events. Ibid.

30 Melike Çapan, '1964'ün 54. Yılında İmroz'dan Gökçeada'ya; Rum Tanıklar Anlatıyor: Kıbrıs'ta Ne Olsa Ceremesini Gökçeada Çekti', *T24*, 6 September 2014, https://t24.com.tr/haber/1964un-54-yilinda-imrozdan-gokceadaya-rum-taniklar-anlatiyor-kibrista-ne-olsa-ceremesini-gokceada-cekti,604197; MGK Kararı [NSC Decision], no. 35, 27 March 1964, Imbros and Tenedos Studies Association Archives.
31 MGK Kararı [NSC Decision], no. 35, 27 March 1964.
32 The Ministry of Justice decided to establish an open prison on Imbros on 13 August 1965. Then, this was approved by the Cabinet on 25 August 1965. For the archival record of this decision, 30-18-1-2 / 188-51, Archives of the Republic of Turkey [Türkiye Cumhuriyeti Başbakanlık Cumhuriyet Arşivi] (hereafter AR). Other archival records on this prison: 30-18-01-02 / 198-57-4-1, AR; 30-18-01-02 / 198-57-4-2, AR; 30-18-01-02 / 198-57-4-3, AR; 30-18-01-02 / 198-57-4-4. AR.
33 Liisa H. Malkki, 'Refugees and Exile: From "Refugee Studies" to the National Order of Things', *Annual Review of Anthropology*, no. 24 (1995): 495–523, www.annualreviews.org.
34 Official Newspaper, 'The Settlement Law' [İskan Kanunu], law no. 2510, 14 June 1934, *Resmi Gazete*, no. 2733, 21 June 1934, http://www.resmigazete.gov.tr/arsiv/2733.pdf. For the most up-to-date version, see, law no. 5543, 19 September 2006, http://www.mevzuat.gov.tr/MevzuatMetin/1.5.5543.pdf.
35 'The Settlement Law', article 3.
36 Theo Nichols et al., 'Muhacir Bulgarian Workers in Turkey: Their Relation to Management and Fellow Workers in the Formal Employment Sector', *Middle Eastern Studies* 39, no. 2 (2003): 37–54, https://www.jstor.org/stable/4284291.
37 In the settlement law, Muhajir is a category to define people who immigrated to Turkey under special conditions, such as individuals who have Turkish ancestry but are living abroad, or any nomadic or tribal groups who show loyalty to Turkish culture. Muhajir Bulgarians became particularly evident among the Turkish labour force when several thousands of muhajirs migrated to Turkey between 1989 and 1992. Nichols et al., 'Muhacir Bulgarian Workers in Turkey', 37.
38 Tsimouris, 'Pilgrimages'.
39 Elif Babül, 'Belonging to Imbros: Citizenship and Sovereignty in the Turkish Republic' (Masters diss., Boğaziçi University, 2003), 101.
40 Yaşar Ozan Say, 'Celebrating the Saints in Imbros: The Politics of Ritual and Belonging in Turkey' (PhD diss., Indiana University, 2013), 105. The programme that Say mentions is for 9–23 August 2010.
41 Tsimouris, 'Pilgrimages'.
42 Babül, 'Belonging to Imbros', 100.
43 Tsimouris, 'Pilgrimages'.

44 Ibid.
45 Babül, 'Belonging to Imbros', 101–2.
46 Ibid.
47 Ibid., 102.
48 Andreas Gross, 'Gökçeada (Imbros) and Bozcaada (Tenedos): Preserving the Bicultural Character of the Two Turkish islands as a Model for Co-operation between Turkey and Greece in the Interest of the People Concerned', Committee on Legal Affairs and Human Rights, Parliamentary Assembly, 2008, accessed 15 February 2018, http://assembly.coe.int/nw/xml/XRef/Xref-DocDetails-EN.asp?fileid=12011.
49 The island has officially become part of the movement of Cittaslow since 2011, although its process began in 2006. 'Gökçeada', accessed 17 June 2018, http://www.cittaslow.org/network/gokceada.
50 Erol Saygı, *Gökçeada/Imbros/Ίμβρος* (Izmir: Erol Saygı, 2010); Öztürk Bayram, *Gökçeada: Yeşilin ve Mavinin Özgür Dünyası* (Gökçeada: Gökçeada Belediyesi, 2002).
51 Meliton Karas, 'İmroz'da Dini Hayat ve Kiliseler [The Religion and Churches on Imbros]', in *İmroz Rumları: Gökçeada Üzerine [Rums of Imbros]*, ed. Feryal Tansuğ (İstanbul: Heyamola, 2013), 50–1.
52 Ibid., 50–79; Aleksandros Zafiriadis, *Η Ιστορία της Εκκλησίας Ίμβρου* [*The History of the Imbros Church*] (Athens: En Athinais, 1938).
53 The information was provided by the priest of Agioi Theodoroi villages, Asterios Okoumousis. Karas also mentions an Imbros metropolitan bishop who was in charge in 1923. Karas, 'İmroz'da Dini Hayat', 57.
54 Laurie Kain Hart, *Time, Religion, and Social Experience in Rural Greece* (Lanham: Rowman & Littlefield, 1992), 90.
55 Ibid.
56 Ibid., 91.
57 Ibid., 90–1.
58 Ibid., 225.
59 Interviews with Imbrians during the August festivities, August 2016, August 2017 and August 2018. Hart also associates the summer months with festivals. Hart, *Time, Religion, and Social Experience*, 229.
60 Hart, *Time, Religion, and Social Experience*; Say, 'Celebrating the Saints in Imbros'; Giorgos Tsimouris, 'Reconstructing "Home" among the "Enemy": The Greeks of Gökçeada (Imvros) after Lausanne', *Balkanologie: Revue d'études pluridisciplinaires* 5, nos 1–2 (2001): 1–15, http://journals.openedition.org/balkanologie/727.
61 Hart, *Time, Religion, and Social Experience*, 239.
62 Lefebvre, *The Critique of Everyday Life*, original italics.

8

Coda

Establishing authority over historic areas under emergency

Mesut Dinler

Preface

Written in lockdown due to the Covid-19 emergency, this chapter develops a concept of emergency not as a response to extraordinary circumstances but as a tool to concentrate power. Focusing on the historic quarters of Istanbul (mainly on Fener and Balat districts in the historic peninsula), the main aim of the chapter is to discuss how various power structures have increased their authority over historic urban settings in Turkey through the exploitation of the conditions of emergency. Aligned with this conception, the recent COVID-19 experience presents a metaphor for the chapter to contend with, since it shows that the condition of emergency generates the context where extreme and unthinkable actions are not only envisaged but also fully implemented. In a recent article, Yuval Noah Harari responded to Covid-19-related emergency measures by arguing that emergencies 'fast-forward historical processes'.[1] Similarly, many contemporary thinkers have been alarmed by the predominant power structures' tendency to exploit emergency situations in order to bypass legal and *normal* procedures in favour of capitalist markets.[2] Despite the fact that emergencies may turn into situations where power is manifested in its clearest and most violent form, it should also be remembered that emergencies have the potential to trigger forms of resistance that may disturb the status quo. For instance, the criticism against the capitalist abuse of the Covid-19 emergency has already formed solidarity initiatives.[3]

The history of the preservation of Fener and Balat districts recounts a similar historic narrative, where the concept of emergency generates a milieu for power to be practised and solidarity movements to flourish. In the early 2000s, like many other historic areas of Istanbul, these two districts were presented in the mass media as sites under urgent need of intervention due to their so-called deteriorated social and physical condition. The representation of such areas as shabby quarters has come to serve as a strategic pattern in Turkey from the mid-2000s onwards, providing something of an emergency premise that legitimizes the authorities' interventions in urban space. Bartu Candan and Kolluoğlu recognize this pattern as a common feature of 'neoliberal urbanism' which manifests itself through 'the emergence of the so-called "spaces of decay", "distressed areas", and privileged spaces', and which thus depends on social segregation.[4] Such emergencies fabricated the need for urgent interventions that were permitted through the legislative restructuring of the preservation-related regulations. Simultaneously, neighbourhood solidarity initiatives were formed to fight against the rights violations and brutal actions of power holders. In approaching emergency as a tool for concentrating power, this chapter also attends to its potential to trigger activist initiatives that disturb power holders.

Introduction: Defining the urban heritage in Turkey

Since the 2000s, the relationship between cities and the neoliberal economic state structure has been the focus of various academic studies.[5] However, the preservation of the historic cores of cities multiplies the complexity of this relationship because the goal of historic preservation is generally perceived as an obstacle in front of 'rapid' development.[6] In recent years, several European policy documents have highlighted that heritage can function as a tool for 'sustainable development' (through creating 'economic growth and jobs, social cohesion and environmental sustainability').[7] However, in contexts like twenty-first-century Turkey, where much of the economic growth is driven by the construction sector, the lack of preservation-oriented urban policies and practices entails indifference, especially towards non-monumental architectural heritage. Moreover, the expectation of rapid change and development also exceeds the willingness to safeguard urban heritage.[8] As a result, urban heritage sites tend to be viewed as commodities rather than a sustainable resource.[9]

In Turkey, what we have witnessed since the early 2000s is the commodification process of urban heritage under the central and local management scheme of the Justice and Development Party (AKP – *Adalet ve Kalkınma Partisi*). Bora argues that the tremendous interest of AKP in the construction sector is a familiar pattern of right-wing conservative political parties.[10] He traces this interest back to the 1950s Turkish Democrat Party regime, under the governance of which Istanbul's historic character had irreversibly changed. Another similar pattern one can detect in the urban programmes of these two governments is how they utilized emergency conditions for heritage destruction by bypassing legal processes to safeguard heritage when they were at the peak of their power. For instance, in the Democrat Party period, the *Development Law* was promulgated in 1957, and this introduced regulations regarding town planning.[11] This law not only diminished the authority of local authorities, giving more power to the central government for urban planning,[12] but also generated *mail-i inhidam* (possibility of collapse) reports, which permitted the destruction of structures that posed a danger due to their poor structural condition.

In the 1950s, any structure that obstructed a road construction would be given a *mail-i inhidam* report.[13] In 2012, on the other hand, *mail-i inhidam* reports were used as a tool for urban regeneration. Law No. 6306: *The Law on Regeneration of the Areas at Risk of Disaster* (Disaster Law) made it possible to demolish a structure which was identified as a risk under *mail-i inhidam*. One of the most violent examples of the Disaster Law took place in the historic centre of Diyarbakir, a predominantly Kurdish city. One year after the inscription of the city castle and the surrounding landscape in the UNESCO World Heritage List with the label 'The Diyarbakır Fortress and Hevsel Gardens Cultural Landscape', a violent armed conflict ruined the city, and the restructuring of the historic town centre became possible with the Disaster Law.[14] This law paved the path for urban regeneration projects where low-rise apartment buildings started to be demolished and replaced with high-rise residential structures. Thus, urban heritage has become not only the main fuel of the state's financial structure but also a raw material to design and implement urban regeneration projects.

Making of urban authority in a neoliberal state

The passage to a neoliberal state structure has a common historical background in developing countries: quite often, a military coup is orchestrated by the army and supported by the upper class when the strength of the power structures is threatened by social movements. As occurred in Latin America during the 1970s, the 1980 military coup d'état in Turkey generated the circumstances needed for the country's passage to a neoliberal economy, one in which the state guarantees individual entrepreneurial freedoms and skills within an institutional framework of free markets and free trade.[15] As mentioned earlier, cities play a strategic role in the process of neoliberal restructuring because, according to Breener and Theodore, 'cities have become strategically crucial arenas for neoliberal forms of policy experimentation and institutional restructuring'.[16]

As Turkey was transforming itself into a neoliberal state, Istanbul was being promoted as the main city to attract global investments. Coupled with the privatization of public institutions against an economic background of fragile growth, constant inflation and public sector debt, processes of gentrification became the most common experience.[17] Even though the start of neoliberalism in Turkey can be dated back to the 1980 coup d'état, AKP policies and implementations differ from those of the previous periods.[18] According to Karaman, this difference is due to the ability of AKP in merging neoliberalism with political Islam.[19] Kuyucu also affirms that compared to other advanced neoliberal states where 'administrative decentralization' and 'entrepreneurial urban policies' are encouraged, Turkey differs because power has remained centralized in the hands of AKP especially after the 2010 constitutional referendum.[20] This process gained momentum with the Gezi protests, and accelerated during the conflict with the Kurdish movement, coupled with the failed coup attempt and 'the state of emergency' which followed, all of which helped concentrate power in one single centre giving little or no space for local administration.[21] Moreover, the short-lived decentralization process of the early 2000s was a requirement for EU membership, something which was already considered an abandoned goal in the 2010s.[22]

Instrumentalization of urban heritage for a centralized authority

Despite the more-than-a-century-long history of preservation legislation within Turkey,[23] the post-2005 changes have marked a turning point for the practice of urban conservation.[24] This situation has arisen because these changes have enabled large-scale urban interventions in historic areas through the private sector bypassing normal processes defined in the law.[25] In the early 2000s, despite these ill-defined processes there were positive developments in urban conservation. This was the period when the AKP regime had embraced a decentralization process aligned with the EU perspective in urban policy-making. These developments were achieved mainly through legislation changes proposed within the Conservation Law (Law No. 2863, which is the umbrella law for managing cultural heritage in Turkey since 1983). In 2004, Law No. 5226 introduced local conservation offices, along with a financial scheme for conservation projects, and encouraged the communication between central and local authorities as well as NGOs.[26] Although the implementation process for these policies was not clearly defined (especially for participation processes; even though the participatory decision-making was a request of the law in conservation and planning, the tools were not defined[27]), this law could possibly generate a sustainable conservation scheme only if another change in the law which occurred in 2005 did not dominate the urban conservation practice. In 2005, Law No. 5366, infamously known as the Renewal Act, introduced further changes to the Conservation Law.[28] In addition to its lengthy and confusing title, namely 'Preservation by Renovation and Utilization by Revitalization of Deteriorated Immovable Historical and Cultural Properties (*Yıpranan Tarihi ve Kültürel Taşınmaz Varlıkların Yenilenerek Korunması ve Yaşatılarak Kullanılması Hakkında Kanun*)', the law raised concerns because its aim was written as 'renewing the sites within the boundaries of urban conservation sites which have become deteriorated during time'. In fact, even the Istanbul Historic Peninsula Site Management Plan states that:

> Law No. 5366 is criticized for encouraging 'renewal' that are not in line with the concept of 'conservation', for providing room to develop projects in different renewal areas with different characteristics in terms of the size and characteristics of the area that are outside the conservation plan decisions and for lacking the content to reinforce the socioeconomic structure of the region. The same criticisms are present also in the recommendations of the UNESCO World Heritage Committee starting from 2006 on the Historic Areas of Istanbul.[29]

It should be noted that the changes in the historic environments were part of a larger land management programme that included not only the transformation of urban areas but also the creation of an urban sprawl of Istanbul to an extent which threatens the ecological balance of the Marmara region.[30]

Even though the 2005 Municipalities Law[31] had given power to local municipalities, the 2012 Metropolitan Municipalities Law[32] retrieved and passed this power to metropolitan municipalities. As local municipalities lost their already-limited power, a milestone in power dynamics arrived with the Disaster Law (Law No. 6306).[33] This law equipped TOKİ (*Toplu Konut İdaresi*), the Housing Development Administration of Turkey, and the 2012-founded Ministry of Environment and Urbanization, with even more power to declare 'transformation zones' to mitigate mainly the earthquake risk. TOKİ was established in 1984, but until 2002 it had a limited role, mainly providing credits for social housing projects. After 2002, it was reformed under the Prime Ministry with extensive authority in urban planning, housing and urban renewal of historic sites. The Ministry of Culture and Tourism was the main body responsible for decision-making regarding all historic buildings and sites before the Disaster Law; however, this law invested TOKİ and the Ministry of Environment and Urbanization with an absolute authority over 'transformation zones' that were mainly the historic sites under disaster risk.

Thus, TOKİ and the ministry have become equipped with extensive authority in urban and territorial planning and have become dominant actors in the decision-making and implementation processes. These two bodies can designate any zone as an 'area under risk' and can launch the transformation process at any time and in any circumstance.[34] Moreover, they do not have to involve the municipalities in the process unless the municipalities launch the transformation process themselves.[35] As mentioned in the Istanbul Historic Peninsula Management Plan,[36] even though the law states that the opinion of the Ministry of Tourism and Culture should be consulted for the listed buildings and areas, the Disaster Law is designed for the total reconstruction of these sites.

The recent traumatic memories of earthquakes and the poor structural quality of the building stock in Istanbul have become a tool of justification for the immense urban transformation of the city. The discourses of urgency and emergency helped create the framework under which urban interventions could become acceptable at any cost. However, despite the concrete necessity for preparedness for earthquakes, the implementation projects demonstrated a conflicting goal. As will be explained later, displacement of inhabitants in historic areas and replacement of historic residential fabric with shopping malls, offices, car parks etc. was not an act of earthquake preparedness but, rather, an outcome of AKP-era urban policies that merged neoliberalism with political Islam under a centralized power.

Practising power: Renewal of heritage sites

The earlier-mentioned set of legal changes functioned as the main steps of the construction process of a powerful central authority over historic areas. It is noteworthy that the theme of 'risk' is a constant in this process; in the early periods of AKP governance, it was the local authorities who were given power to define what/where risk is, coupled with the tools to change it. Step by step, this power became concentrated in the hands of the central regime (mainly the Ministry of Environment and Urbanization and, as will be discussed further in what follows, the Cabinet). During this power exchange from local to central authority, the implementations following the legal changes not only created an irreversible change in the cityscape, but also included public campaigns, forced displacements, public resistance and frustratingly long court processes.

Following the Renewal Act (Law No. 5366), up until 2018, forty-seven renewal site decisions were published in the Official Gazette (Figure 8.1). As part of the renewal process, the metropolitan municipality (or the district municipality[37]) defines the boundaries, but the main body that approves the boundaries and designates the 'renewal site' is the Cabinet. After the designation is published in the Official Gazette, a renewal project is then prepared (mostly outsourced to a private company), and implemented, by TOKİ, a private company or directly by the municipality.[38]

In these renewal sites, the physical and social character of the area was presented as emergencies that needed to be intervened in immediately. In a way, the macro-scale transformation of Turkey was reproduced on a smaller scale across all urban areas of Istanbul. The impact of this transformation was immersive for each site: for instance, in the İstiklal Street, the main artery of the Beyoğlu district, urban memory has become completely lost through the disappearance of the small-scale businesses that once defined the character of the street.[39] For the Sulukule district, on the other hand, the social and physical impact of the project was much greater. The renewal project for Sulukule, a

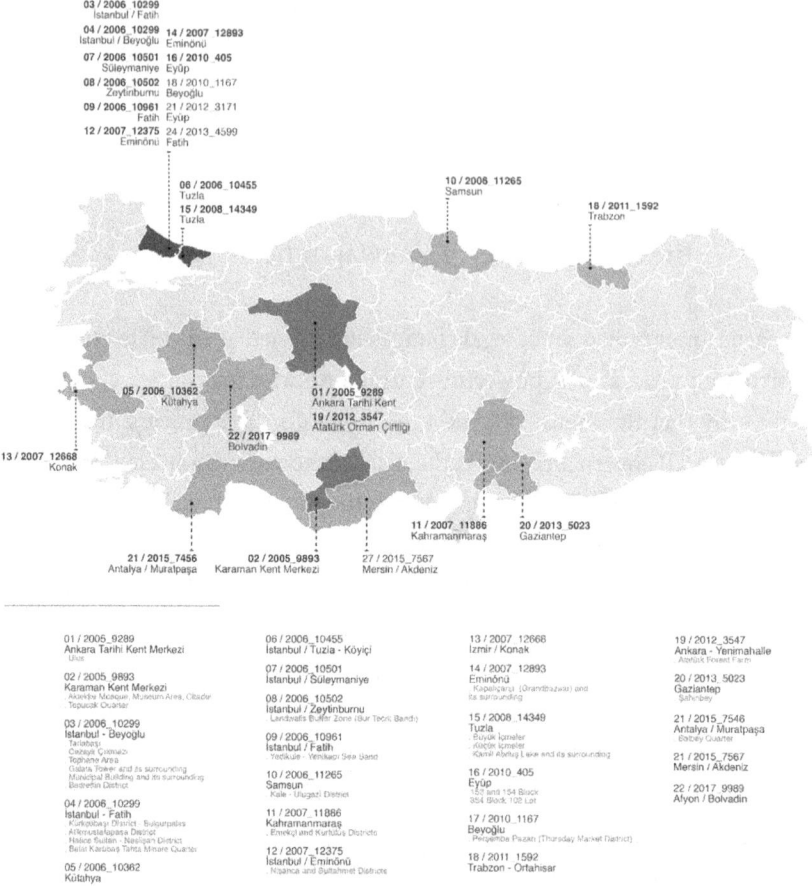

Figure 8.1 Spatial distribution of the renewal sites. Source: Özgün Özçakır, et. al., 'Political': 10. Republished here courtesy of Özgün Özçakır.

Romani neighbourhood on the borders of the historical peninsula adjacent to the Theodosian Walls,[40] was approved by the Istanbul Metropolitan Municipality in December 2016. According to the local municipality (the Fatih Municipality):

> These neighbourhoods have not only been physically ruined but also become homelands for socio-economic problems. [. . .] Sulukule has been occupied by low income and low cultural groups who came as immigrants without having a sense of belonging to the city. There is no trace of a homogeneous culture in the neighbourhood.[41]

Thus, the Sulukule is a distinctive case because the reason for the emergency, as presented by the authorities, is due not only to the physical condition of the site but also to the character of its inhabitants (i.e., the Romanis). To overcome this problem, TOKİ forcibly relocated the Romanis to a new district constructed on the outskirts of Istanbul (app. 40 km away), and completely renewed the site with identical residential projects that were alien to its historic character.[42] The Sulukule Urban Renewal Project, similar to experiences in other renewal sites, was cancelled in 2019 after the construction was fully completed and the Romani community was displaced. The unspoken (but also obvious) goal of the project was the replacement of the inhabitants with a richer class. However, the project did not achieve either 'Preservation by Renovation' or 'Utilization by Revitalization', and it also failed to achieve this hidden goal. The new buildings have, instead, begun to be used by Syrian refugees, after property owners divided each building into as many units as possible in order to rent them to as many people as possible.[43] Similarly, in Tarlabaşı, both within the publications of the municipality and in the mass media channels, the neighbourhood was represented as a site with high crime rates which was a strategy that could eventually present an emergency excuse for urban interventions.[44]

This process also continued in the Fener and Balat districts. These two neighbouring districts are found along the Golden Horn, upon the waterfront of the historic peninsula of Istanbul, and were also designated as renewal sites in 2005 (Figure 8.2). Urban projects in these two districts show how urban heritage

Figure 8.2 Fener and Balat. Source: Google Earth, 2018.

has been conceptualized and managed in Turkey since the 1980s. The experience in Fener and Balat is noteworthy because, unlike other renewal sites, the appeal for the cancellation of the project became accepted by the court.

Fener and Balat: Two historic districts

Fener and Balat districts are bordered by the fifth-century city walls along the Golden Horn. As the currently available archaeological data suggests, the earliest settlement here dates back to the seventh century BCE. Already urbanized in the Byzantine era, these two districts have long suffered from fires and earthquakes (Figures 8.3 and 8.4).[45] In fact, even in the nineteenth century, natural disasters

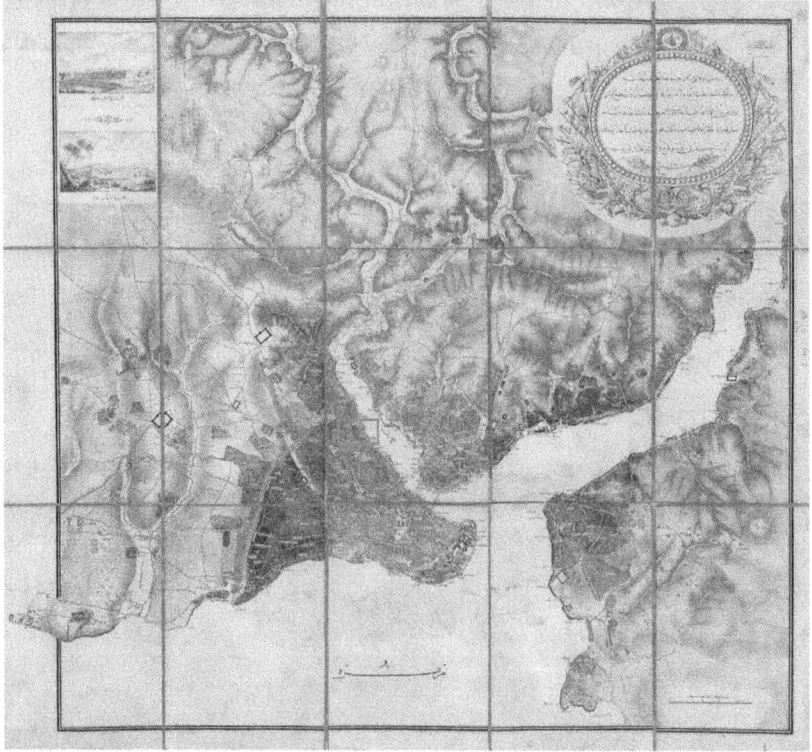

Figure 8.3 Helmuth von Moltke's 1837 Istanbul map. The frame indicates Fener and Balat. Moltke was a German engineer who had been commissioned for the regulation of the urban fabric. He had prepared this map as the first step of his project. Source: Istanbul Metropolitan Municipality, Atatürk Library, *Daru'l-hilafetü'l-aliye ve civarı haritasıdır*, Location No.: 956.101.563 MOL 1268 k.1/, Item No.: Hrt_000041.

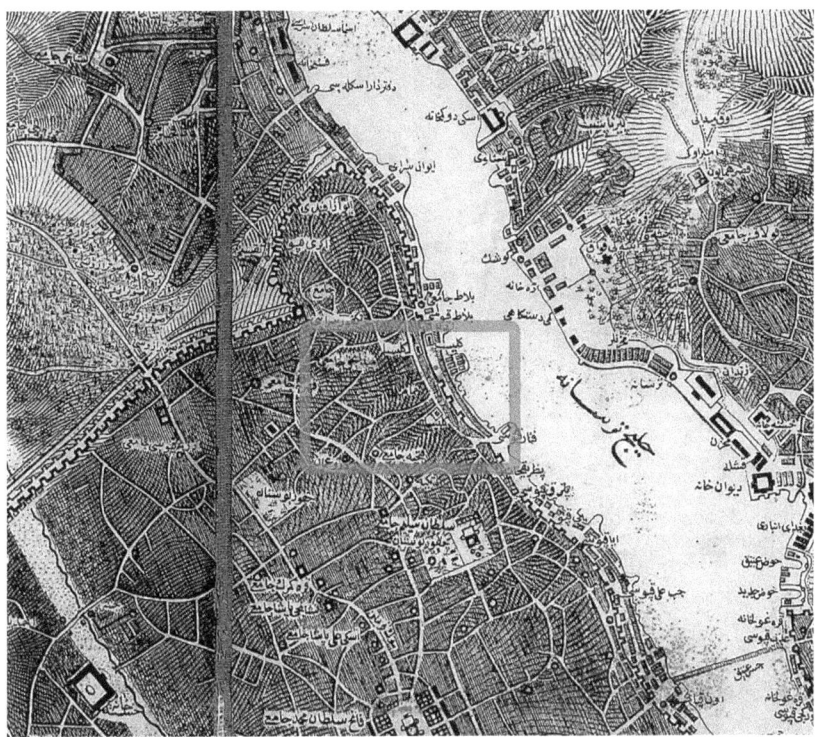

Figure 8.4 Fener and Balat in Helmuth von Moltke's 1837 Istanbul map. Source: Istanbul Metropolitan Municipality, Atatürk Library, *Daru'l-hilafetü'l-aliye ve civarı haritasıdır*, Location No.: 956.101.563 MOL 1268 k.1/, Item No.: Hrt_000041

were treated as emergencies that justified the urban transformation of Istanbul as part of the broader modernization of late-Ottoman society. A common implementation of this urban process was the replacement of the organic street network with the grid pattern which was supposed to provide easier access during emergencies.[46] Both districts had suffered from continuous fires which started and spread easily due to the timber-frame structures found therein, and so, as a precaution against fire, building codes subsequently required masonry construction in place of the burnt-down, timber-framed buildings (Figure 8.5). However, this worsened the impact of earthquakes, especially that of the 1894 earthquake, which is one of the most catastrophic events of the city's history.[47] Even though building codes in construction technique (*Ebniye Nizamnameleri*) were formulated as precautions against emergencies, due to the diversity of disasters, the main outcome was the change of the urban fabric rather than provisions for emergencies.

Figure 8.5 Masonry houses in Balat District. Source: *Archive of University of Bologna.* (Creative Commons) Reached through Europeana.

Fener was populated by Roums (Anatolian Greeks) and Balat by Jews even before the Ottoman conquest of Constantinople in 1453. The turn of the twentieth century witnessed rising nationalism in the second constitutional era of the Ottoman Empire, yet the Roum community continued to live in Fener until the 1940s, whereas the Jewish community in Balat was immediately affected by the nationalist rise. Although both districts were home to a multiethnic and multireligious population, this difference (between Fener and Balat) was due to several reasons.[48] First, the Roum community in Fener held high-ranking bureaucratic positions in the Palace, mainly due to their language skills. Moreover, infrastructure-wise, public services were significantly better compared to Balat even though the two districts are adjacent.[49] However, the main reason for the strong tie between the Roum and the district of Fener is the existence of the Greek Orthodox Patriarchate in Fener.[50] Although the 1923 Lausanne Treaty proposed a population exchange, imposing a compulsory migration of Roums in Turkey to Greece and Turks in Greece to Turkey, Istanbul was exempt from this exchange – thus, the impact on Fener was not strong.[51]

One of the most significant changes in the urban character of both districts came with the French urbanist Henry Prost's 1936–7 Istanbul Master Plan, in which Prost proposed that the shores of the Golden Horn become developed as an industrial zone, mainly due to its marine access and the small-scale industrial sites it had hosted since the late-Ottoman era.[52] However, in terms of displacement of non-Muslim communities, rather than the redevelopment of the Golden Horn as an industrial area, the 1942 Capital Tax (*Varlık Vergisi*) proved much more disastrous. This created regulations for high taxes to be levied on non-Muslim communities and worked to such an extreme extent that most of the non-Muslims had to sell their properties and leave the country.[53] However, the most violent campaign against the minorities was yet to come. On 6 and 7 September 1955, a lynch mob was formed against the Roum community of Istanbul. Minorities' houses, places of worship, shops and even cemeteries were attacked and destroyed within a few hours. This systematic, government-organized, tragic act of violence forced the non-Muslim minorities to leave their homes and immigrate to Europe. Ironically, during the same period, the government had set aside a budget for the repair of the Byzantine monuments, including those that were converted to mosques, for the Tenth International Byzantine Studies Congress that was held in Istanbul from 15 to 21 September 1955.[54] Although international participants to the congress were able to visit these Byzantine structures, the violent effects of the September events probably had a bigger impact on their impression of Istanbul. In Balat on the other hand, the 1948 establishment of Israel in the Middle East caused a demographic change, because a part of the predominantly Jewish community of Balat left Turkey and settled in Israel.

As the inhabitants of both districts gradually left their homes due to the above-mentioned nationalistic events, a new migration wave from rural-to-urban areas started to fill their spaces in the 1950s and 1960s. The main reason for this migration wave was the industrialization in the agricultural sector driven by US aid under the Marshall Plan. Machines replaced manpower, and consequentially this change in the mode of agricultural production reshaped the urban character of the city.[55] The migrants who came to Fener and Balat were mainly from the Black Sea and the Central Anatolia region.[56] As the migrants of the 1950s and 1960s moved into newly developed areas of the city in the following decades, a new community arrived with a new migration wave in the 1990s from the East and South-East Anatolia.[57]

Urban projects in Fener and Balat

In the mid-1980s, Fener and Balat became the subjects of a new episode of planning interventions.[58] The Golden Horn Coastal Rearrangement Project

(GHCRP) was developed in 1984, promising to improve the sanitary condition of the Golden Horn. Due to its marine access and the small-scale industrial sites it had hosted since the late-Ottoman era, the Golden Horn had already been earmarked as part of Prost's 1936–7 Istanbul Master Plan for redevelopment into an industrial zone proper. Along with the industrialization, migration also worsened the poor conditions of the site. Infrastructure was insufficient and technical/sanitary equipment was not satisfying the need of the increasing population. In fact, the bad odour diffusing across the whole city from the Golden Horn's industrial sites was a major urban problem throughout the 1980s.[59]

The cleaning of the Golden Horn was an ambitious project implemented as part of a larger urban programme in Istanbul, one that came in the aftermath of the 1980 coup d'état aligned with the neoliberal turn of Turkey. Due to new economic policies implemented via recommendations of the IMF (International Monetary Fund), Istanbul was now benefiting from central state finance – with the aim of creating a new investment centre for global capital – more than it had ever benefited throughout the entire Republican period.[60] The local elections of 1984 initiated the mayoralty of Bedrettin Dalan, the leading actor in the GHCRP, and under his mayoralty, private investments were encouraged to launch urban projects that were promoted in the newly emerging mass media communication channels. Dalan's projects on Istanbul reflected the dream of transforming Istanbul into a global megacity from a local leading city. A series of urban renewal projects (construction of Tarlabaşı Boulevard, GHCRP, landfills and constructions of coastal roads on the shores of Bosporus) that had been forgotten for over thirty years were brought back on the agenda in order to be implemented: some neighbourhoods dating back to the nineteenth century were demolished, while small ateliers which had been located in the city centre for centuries were removed.[61]

The impact of the GHCRP on Fener and Balat was the expropriation and demolition of various structures along the Golden Horn, including industrial sites, waterfront mansions (*yalı*), small neighbourhoods and the taverns (*meyhane*) for which especially Fener was known. In place of the demolished structures, a long, wide coastal green band was introduced along the shores of the Golden Horn, separated from the neighbourhoods by a parallel road. According to Pinon, the design of the coastal public space was quite problematic: the landscape design was regarded as 'pitiful', and its only benefit to dwellers was that it was 'a wide meadow to look at'.[62] In a report prepared after the Habitat II Conference held in Istanbul in 1996, GHCRP was heavily criticized as follows:

> Opening these parks to public only had given them a meadow to watch. During the organization process of the project, architects did consider neither public needs/social activities nor positive/negative impacts of the project. As a result, many small commercial activities have either reached their minimum or disappeared. In the last years many of the active banks in Balat have been closed. As it may be clearly seen, rearrangement of Golden Horn shores neither rehabilitated these districts nor improved the living standards of the public.[63]

This report not only criticized the GHCRP but also generated a roadmap towards a rehabilitation project for Fener and Balat, with the provision that the project would serve as a model for future implementation in other historic areas.

The need for such a model was one of the outcomes of the Habitat II Conference. As a result of the action call of Habitat II, the issue was raised of selecting a pilot project that would demonstrate that the 'future of the historic districts did not stick between regeneration – that would simply mean demolishing and then reconstructing – and restoration projects on touristic purposes' is not just a dream.[64] Aligned with this strategy, Fener and Balat districts were selected as the sites for the pilot. Following this, the Fatih Municipality launched coordination meetings with experts from the Municipality and UNESCO World Heritage Center Coordination Agency in order to prepare a feasibility study to determine the extent and the methodology of the project. The study lasted a year and was financed by the European Union; it was conducted by the French Institute for Anatolian Studies with the support of Fatih Municipality and UNESCO. Accordingly, an urban implementation strategy was proposed with four main pillars: housing for every individual, liveable human settlements, participatory planning and gender equality.[65] After several interruptions the project was completed in 2008.[66] Despite its efforts to achieve both the individual and the social well-being of the inhabitants, and to improve the socioeconomic conditions together with the physical condition of the site, the project's main output was the restoration works undertaken on a limited number of historic residential structures in Fener and Balat.[67] Even though the project was formulated to function as a model, the designation of the area as a 'renewal site' following the Renewal Act (Law No. 5366) meant that a renewal project was prepared even before the completion of the rehabilitation project.[68]

Renewing Fener and Balat

Similar to what happened in the 1980s, the Fener and Balat districts would represent only a very small section of the change in 2000s Istanbul. Moreover, the neighbourhood initiative was successful in stopping the implementation of the renewal project through a legal process. The project reveals the political underpinnings of cultural heritage, and helps to manifest the relationship between cultural heritage and power dynamics in the context of neoliberalism.[69] As the rehabilitation programme helped these sites to become popular attraction centres, their fame attracted a capitalist interest that could now freely operate in the historic environments. As the central authority manufactured the necessary framework of urban 'renewal', the actors that operated this framework were those who could establish close relationships with the same central authority. In other words, once central power is established, the closer one gets to the centre the easier it is for one to win a contract for an urban renewal project. For instance, following the designation of Fener, Balat and Ayvansaray districts as 'urban renewal areas' in 2006, the district municipality (the Fatih Municipality) prepared a tender and the contract was won by GAP İnşaat – the same company which won the contract for the renewal of Tarlabaşı. GAP İnşaat was a subgroup of Çalık Holding, the then-CEO of which was the current Minister of Economy and the son-in-law of the current Turkish president and the head of AKP. A visual mapping project of the *Networks of Dispossession* initiative shows the network of projects for which Çalık Holding won the contract (Figure 8.6).

After the site was designated as a renewal site, GAP İnşaat handpicked the most famous architectural firms of the country and commissioned each to design a number of building blocks. This was the same project management pattern used in Tarlabaşı. The municipality did not share these projects with the inhabitants and only after a lawsuit could the local residents learn what was proposed for Fener and Balat.

Figure 8.6 The visual mapping of 'the firm behind plans to demolish historic Tarlabaşı and Fener-Balat neighbourhoods', created by *Networks of Dispossession* initiative. Available online: http://mulksuzlestirme.org/index.en/

It should be noted that despite the earlier European Union grant to improve social conditions together with the physical conditions, the lack of support from the Fatih Municipality prevented it from achieving this goal.[70] In fact, even the dozens of houses that were renovated with the grant were proposed to be demolished in the renewal projects. Despite the fact that the inhabitants of Fener and Balat lacked experience in organizing and illustrating urban protest movements (similar to inhabitants in other historic areas of Istanbul),[71] the previous forced displacement in the above-mentioned heritage sites guided them. As a result, the renewal project triggered a public movement to stop the project. On 4 August 2009, the FeBayDer Association (Fener-Balat-Ayvansaray Property Owners and Tenants Association for Rights Protection and Social Assistance [*Fener-Balat-Ayvansaray Mülk Sahiplerinin Ve Kiracıların Haklarını Koruma Ve Sosyal Yardımlaşma Derneği*]) was established by property owners and tenants to contest any possible violation of their rights.[72] While the municipality organized individual meetings with the property owners for expropriation proposals, it never shared the renewal project with inhabitants, arguing that making the projects public would cause land speculation, despite the fact that the municipality was legally bound to publish the projects before implementation. This situation forced FeBayDer to organize protests to obtain the renewal project, and following a lawsuit, the municipality was forced to share the project with FeBayDer in January 2010.[73]

The renewal projects proposed a change in the urban character of the site. In the renewal projects of acclaimed architectural firms, which were, luckily, never implemented, ownership patterns were completely altered through amalgamations of building lots. These amalgamations would both help overcome the property ownership problems (like many historic structures, also in Fener and Balat, historic buildings have multiple owners since ownership is divided between inheritors) and enable the insertion of huge volumes. The complex ownership structure could initially discourage investors, but once the building lots were united through obligatory amalgamations, they could invest more easily. There were nineteen blocks to be designed with 567 building lots, 290 of which had listed historic structures. Amalgamations were proposed in seventeen blocks. As a result, 317 lots (103 of them were listed) were reduced to 103.[74]

In short, the effects of the renewal projects on the urban pattern can be summarized as changes in building lots through amalgamations. These enabled the insertion of bigger masses, changes in functions and changes in street facades through additions, removals and alterations (façadism). However, as the identity of the built environments would be replaced with a new urban pattern, the actual identity of inhabitants would also be replaced with a richer class. The renewal project proposed simply replacing the inhabitants of Fener and Balat with a wealthier community. This replacement is the main criticism directed towards to all renewal projects that came with the recent legislation. After FeBayDer obtained the project and saw the changes proposed, following a series of open meetings with the participation of mainly FeBayDer members, Chamber of Architects and the residents of Fener and Balat, a lawsuit was filed to stop the project on 12 March 2010.

Resistance in Fener and Balat

In the March 2010 lawsuit, the plaintiffs of the case were residents and members of FeBayDer, while the defendants were the Fatih Municipality, the Ministry of Culture and Tourism and the Istanbul Metropolitan Municipality. The subject matter of the case was that (i) the process was contrary to the Constitution's principle of equality, and so the principle of public welfare was ignored in the project, (ii) regarding the organizational scheme of the process, the project was beyond the authority of the Fatih Municipality and Istanbul Metropolitan Municipality in terms of preparation and approval of the renewal project, (iii) the administrative act contradicted the principal decisions of the High Council of Conservation Board (*Kültür ve Tabiat Varlıklarını Koruma Yüksek Kurulu*), (iv) the defendants committed acts leading to 'unfair competition (*haksız rekabet*)' by providing public resources to benefit private companies and hide information from the public, (v) the Renewal Act was against the Constitution, (vi) the process was against international agreements that Turkey had signed (the Convention for the Protection of the Architectural Heritage of Europe published in the Official Gazette on 22 July 1989), and (vi) the reason for renewal on the basis of the Disaster Law did not make sense because the renewal project did not refer to any sort of earthquake preparedness. Furthermore, the plaintiffs requested the cancellation of the Renewal Act, the termination of the Fener Balat Renewal Project and the preparation of an export report.[75]

On 2 June 2011 the request for an expert report had been refused; however, an objection to this decision had been approved as of 18 June 2011 (eighteen months after the placement of the lawsuit). However, this time, the report fee – the fee that plaintiffs were expected to pay since they had requested the expert report – was deemed to be too high (25,000 TL), but this issue was objected to and the report fee was then decreased (15,000 TL). After the preparation of the expert report, the court decided on the cancellation of the Fener Balat Ayvansaray Urban Renewal Project (FBAURP) on 20 June 2012.[76]

On 21 June 2012, the mayor of the Fatih Municipality announced that they would be appealing to the Council of State to oppose this decision.[77] However, the Cabinet of Ministries came to the mayor's rescue by making an 'urgent expropriation decision' (*acele kamulaştırma kararı*) in regard to the project area on 7 October 2012. Following this decision, FeBayDer appealed to the Council of the State on the basis that making an 'urgent expropriation decision' would require an extreme national emergency, like a war or a serious earthquake. Luckily, this frustrating process ended in December 2013 with the Council of State's decision to cancel the urgent expropriation decision. With this cancellation decision, the state-led violation of property rights has been interrupted. However, the whole process shows how the state may operate to form the legal and institutional base of the neoliberal economies' relentless urban projects.

The project proposed new buildings with functions such as shopping malls, boutique hotels, offices, single-room flats, underground car parks etc. Given that the renewal law aims at *Preservation by Renovation and Utilization by Revitalization,* one can understand the hidden meanings behind the words 'renovation' and 'revitalization'. As can be observed in the renewal processes of the above-mentioned historic sites, it can be said that these projects renovate areas through a complete change of urban use with new commercial activities, and revitalize them through the forced displacement of current inhabitants in order to be able to sell the land to wealthier classes.

Conclusion

The scholarly critical understanding of cultural heritage and built environment has shown that historic cities are managed through power dynamics, rather than concrete policies, and that their implementations follow the most updated international standards. Thus, cultural heritage has political underpinnings, and any research conducted on it requires a full investigation of power dynamics.

In contemporary Turkey, the control of the central authority over historic urban areas reached an unprecedented peak via a gradual power concentration process. Even though the early period of the AKP regime launched a decentralization process (following the requirements of EU membership in urban management), since the 2010s this process has been completely abandoned, together with any intention of EU membership. The urban conservation process of this concentration of power operates in a complex set of dynamics, meaning that any researcher who deals with Turkey's contemporary heritage policies needs to attend to the various power struggles, political ambitions, land speculations, media manipulation, gender imbalance and crime networks. The main constant in this complex process is the condition of emergency, which can be either a real condition (as in the case of earthquakes) or manufactured (as in the case of criminalization of inhabitants). For instance, in regard to the Fener and Balat districts, the deprived condition of the physical environment as required by the renewal law was not in place. The problem was the poverty of the inhabitants who were planned to be replaced by a wealthier class.

The strong link between politics and urban conservation is clear; however, this link lies on a very slippery slope in which emergencies function to enact, reproduce and reinforce existing power relations. Yet, the very same link also provides the possibility to disturb these relations from within, as happened in the two heritage sites discussed in this chapter: both of them having been managed via the rhetoric of emergency and wrought by catastrophe and displacement.

Notes

1. In the same article, Harari also argued that the COVID-emergency will force us make chooses between 'totalitarian surveillance and citizen empowerment' and 'nationalist isolation and global solidarity'; see Yuval Noah Harari, 'The World After Coronavirus', *Financial Times,* 20 March 2020, https://www.ft.com/content/19d90308-6858-11ea-a3c9-1fe6fedcca75.

2. A case in point is Naomi Klein—already renowned for her previous work on how conservative governments in the US have manipulated shocking events (wars, terror attacks, natural disasters, etc.) to enable radical free-market policies—who argued during an online webinar that the virus emergency may also function as a wake-up call; see Naomi Klein, *The Shock Doctrine: The Rise of Disaster Capitalism* (New York: Allen Lane, 2007); 'How to Beat Coronavirus Capitalism', 26 March 2020, https://www.youtube.com/watch?v=5lxwLHRKaB0; Naomi Klein, 'Coronavirus Capitalism — And How To Beat It', *The Intercept,* 16 March 2020, https://theintercept.com/2020/03/16/coronavirus-capitalism/. Mike Davis also held an open seminar on the COVID emergency's relation with capitalism, arguing the spread of the virus was an outcome of capitalist structuring of space; see 'Capitalism is the Disease: Mike Davis on the Coronavirus Crisis', 31 March 2020, https://www.youtube.com/watch?v=xOp9G5hoQnM.

3. For instance, in Italy, independent transmission channels organized a national assembly under the name 'open microfone' to confront political problems emerging with regional differences- 'L'informaizone di Blackout, Domenica 5 Aprile: Assemblea Nazionale', accessed 27 April 2020, https://radioblackout.org/2020/04/domenica-5-aprile-assemblea-nazionale/. Similarly, the initiative *Rising Majority,* a US based 2017-born initiative, organized an online live stream event to discuss potential movement-making methods against COVID-capitalism.

A. Davis and N. Klein, 'Movement Building in the Time of the Coronavirus Crisis. A Left Feminist Perspective on 21st Century Racial Capitalism in This Moment', 2020, accessed 27 April 2020, https://therisingmajority.com/events/movement-building/

4   Even though the two İstanbul-based study cases of Bartu Candan and Biray Kolluoğlu (Göktürk, a gated town, and Bezirganbahçe, a public housing project) are non-historic sites, their study outlines the mechanisms of neoliberal urbanism in İstanbul. A. Bartu Candan and Biray Kolluoğlu, 'Emerging Spaces of Neoliberalism: A Gated Town and a Public Housing Project in İstanbul', *New Perspectives on Turkey* 39 (2008): 5–46.

5   On the relationship between neoliberalism and urban environments, see the special issue of *Antipode* 34, no. 3 (Also published as Neil Brenner and Nik Theodore, eds, *Spaces of Neoliberalism: Urban Restructuring in Western Europe and North America* (Oxford: Blackwell, 2002)). Also see Neil Brenner and Nik Theodore, 'Cities and the Geographies of "Actually Existing Neoliberalism"', *Antipode* 34, no. 3 (2002): 349–79. Cf. Jamie Peck and Adam Tickell, 'Neoliberalizing Space', *Antipode* 34, no. 3 (2002): 380–404. Also see David Harvey, *A Brief History of Neoliberalism* (Oxford: Oxford University Press, 2002) and Jamie Peck, *Constructions of Neoliberal Reason* (Oxford: Oxford University Press, 2010).

6   Historic Urban Landscape Approach is recommended by UNESCO as an approach to couple economic development with urban conservation. This approach addresses the conflict between historic preservation and economic development and proposes that the change in urban settings should not be opposed but 'managed' for the favour of urban heritage together with the intangible values of a site. Francesco Bandarin and Rob van Oers, *The Historic Urban Landscape: Managing Heritage in an Urban Century* (Oxford: Wiley-Blackwell, 2012). The Historic Urban Landscape (HUL) approach, which is promoted by the two authors, had been published as an official UNESCO policy recommendation as well. UNESCO, *Recommendation on the Historic Urban Landscape, Including a Glossary of Definitions*, 2011, accessed 27 April 2020, https://whc.unesco.org/en/news/1026.

7   European Commission, *Getting Cultural Heritage Work for Europe*, 2015, accessed 27 April 2020, https://ec.europa.eu/programmes/horizon2020/en/news/getting-cultural-heritage-work-europe. Also see, European Commission, *Towards an Integrated Approach to Cultural Heritage for Europe*, 2014, accessed 27 April 2020, https://ec.europa.eu/assets/eac/culture/library/publications/2014-heritage-communication_en.pdf. UNESCO, *The Hangzhou Declaration Placing*

Culture at the Heart of Sustainable Development Policies, 2013, accessed 27 April 2020, http://www.unesco.org/new/fileadmin/MULTIMEDIA/HQ/CLT/images/FinalHangzhouDeclaration20130517.pdf.

8   Mona Serageldin, 'Preserving the Historic Urban Fabric in a Context of Fast-Paced Change', in *Values and Heritage Conservation,* ed. Erica Avrami, Randall Mason and Marta de la Torre (Los Angeles: The Getty Conservation Institute, 2000), 51–8.

9   Even though the term 'historic urban landscape', considering how UNESCO defines it ('The historic urban landscape is the urban area understood as the result of a historic layering of cultural and natural values and attributes, extending beyond the notion of "historic centre" or "ensemble" to include the broader urban context and its geographical setting'), could be a better term to describe historic areas of Istanbul, in the current heritage literature, this term is associated with an approach (HUL approach) rather than a definition. On how this approach has been adopted and implemented in various parts of the world since its formulation, see Ana Pereira Roders and Francesco Bandarin, eds, *Reshaping Urban Conservation: The Historic Urban Landscape Approach in Action* (Springer, 2019).

10 Tanıl Bora, 'Türk Muhafazakarlığı ve İnşaat Şehveti – Büyük Olsun Bizim Olsun' [Turkish Conservatism and Construction Passion – Bigger is Better], *Birikim* 270 (2011):15–18.

11 Official Gazette. (1956, July 16). *İmar Kanunu*, T.C. Resmi Gazete No. 9359.

12 Cevdat Geray, 'Belediyelerin hızlı kentleşmeye yenik düştüğü dönem (1945-1960) [The period that municipalities got defeated by rapid urbanization (1945-1960)]', in *Türkiye Belediyeciliğinde 60 Yıl Uluslararası Sempozyum, Ankara, 23-24 Kasım 1990* (Ankara: Ankara Büyükşehir Belediyesi, 1990), 217–24.

13 In fact, as early as the 1910s, the condition of *mail-i inhidam* was already defined in the last 1917 decree of *Asar-ı Atika Nizamnameleri*, that are a series of heritage-related decrees promulgated in 1869, 1874, 1884, 1906, and 1917. The 1917 decree regulated the demolition process of historic structures rather than preservation of them. The first preservation council, the 1917-founded the Council for the Preservation of Monuments (*Muhafaza-ı Asar-ı Atika Encümeni*) had functioned as an advisory board to control this demolition process although it was formulated as a preservation council. Cf. Mesut Dinler, *Modernization through Past: Cultural Heritage during the Late-Ottoman and the Early Republican Period in Turkey* (Pisa: Edizioni ETS, 2019), 111–12. Cf. Nur Altınyıldız, 'The Architectural Heritage of Istanbul and the Ideology of Preservation', *Muqarnas* 24 (2007): 286; Emre Madran, 'Cumhuriyet'in İlk

Otuz Yılında (1920-1950) Koruma Alanında Örgütlenmesi', *METU Journal of Faculty of Architecture* 16, no. 1 (1996): 59–97; Pinar Aykaç, 'Archives as Fields of Heritage-Making in Istanbul's Historic Peninsula', *International Journal of Islamic Architecture* 9, no. 2 (2020): 361–87.

14 Emre Sevim, Ibrahim Zivrali and Ü. Nurşah Cabbar, 'A World Heritage Site: Diyarbakır under the Shade of Conflicts', *Proceedings of Tcl 2016 Conference, Infota*, (2016): 503–16. Diren Tas analyses the violent urban restructuring of the historic centre of Diyarbakir aligning the neoliberal policies of Turkey with a deliberate attitude towards Kurdish population and their cities. Diren Tas, 'Urban Transformation as Political And Ideological Intervention In Space: A Case Study In Diyarbakir' (MA diss., Middle East Technical University, 2019).

15 Harvey, *A Brief History*.

16 Brenner and Theodore, 'Cities', 357. Also see Jason Hackworth, *The Neoliberal City: Governance, Ideology, and Development in American Urbanism* (Ithaca: Cornell University Press, 2007); Saskia Sassen, *The Global City: New York, London, Tokyo* (Princeton: Princeton University Press, 1991).

17 İclal Dinçer, 'The Impact of Neoliberal Policies on Historic Urban Space: Areas of Urban Renewal in Istanbul', *International Planning Studies* 16, no. 1 (2011): 43–60. Also see Tolga İslam, 'Outside the Core: Gentrification in Istanbul', in *Gentrification in a Global Context: The New Urban Colonialism*, ed. Rowland Atkinson and Gary Bridge (London: Routledge, 2005), 123–38.

18 Dinçer, 'The Impact'; İslam, 'Outside'; Serap Kayasü and Emine Yetişkul, 'Evolving Legal and Institutional Frameworks of Neoliberal Urban Policies in Turkey', *METU Journal of Faculty of Architecture* 31, no. 2 (2014): 209–22.

19 Ozan Karaman, 'Urban Neoliberalism with Islamic Characteristics', *Urban Studies* 50, no. 16 (2013): 3412–27.

20 Tuna Kuyucu, 'Politics of Urban Regeneration in Turkey: Possibilities and Limits of Municipal Regeneration Initiatives in a Highly Centralized Country', *Urban Geography* 39, no. 8 (2018): 1153.

21 Ibid., 1156–8. The Gezi resistance which was born from the reaction against an urban project has a historical significance not only as a social movement but also in terms of defining the urban heritage strategies of AKP. Can Bilsel, 'The Crisis in Conservation: Istanbul's Gezi Park between Restoration and Resistance', *Journal of the Society of Architectural Historians* 76, no. 2 (2017): 141–5. Also see Umut Özkırımlı, ed., *The Making of a Protest Movement in Turkey: #occupygezi* (New York: Palgrave Macmillan, 2014). The documentary *Turkey on the edge* also focuses on the lives of four actors in urban resistance movements and narrates how AKP's centralized power became more destructive and violent after the

Gezi. Imre Azem, *Turkey on the Edge* (2017). Documentary film. Also see Gül Köksal, 'On Contemporary Urbanization in Turkey, İstanbul: Heinrich Böll Stiftung Turkey', 2020, accessed 27 April 2020, https://tr.boell.org/en/2020/01/28/contemporary-urbanization-turkey.

22 Kuyucu, 'Politics'. Also see Neriman Şahin Güçhan and Esra Kurul, 'A History of Development of Conservation Measures in Turkey: From the Mid-19th Century Until 2004', *METU Journal of Faculty of Architecture* 26, no. 2 (2009): 19–44.

23 Madran, 'Cumhuriyet'in'. Dinler, *Modernization*.

24 Şahin Güçhan and Kurul, 'A History'.

25 Özgün Özçakır, Güliz Bilgin Altınöz, Anna Mignosa, 'Political Economy of Renewal of Heritage Places in Turkey', *METU Journal of Faculty of Architecture* 35, no. 2 (2018): 221–50.

26 Law no. 5226: Law on making changes on the Law on the Protection of Cultural and Natural Assets and some other laws (*Kültür ve Tabiat Varlıklarını Koruma Kanunu ile Çeşitli Kanunlarda Değişiklik Yapılması Hakkında Kanun*). Promulgated on 14 July 2004. This law was a positive breaking point because in introduced *Taşınmaz Kültür Varlıklarının Korunmasına Katkı Payı* (Contribution for the Conservation of Immovable Cultural Entities) as a financial resource for the conservation of publicly owned cultural heritage assets. '*Koruma Uygulama ve Denetim Büroları*' (KUDEB) (Offices of Conservation, Implementation and Supervision) were structured within the body of municipalities. Even today, despite their diminished power, *KUDEBs* are still key actors of urban conservation. And lastly, the law conceptualized all conservation sites as management sites to be 'conserved efficiently, maintained, benefited, developed according to a vision and theme which addresses the cultural and educational needs of society in order to mediate between local and central authorities and NGOs on urban planning and conservation'. Although some definitions are left obscure, as a general framework, this law had predicted the preparation of management plans for conservation sites adopting the policy of UNESCO for World Heritage Sites. Dinçer, 'The Impact'. Şahin Güçhan and Kurul, 'A History'.

27 This law framed all conservation sites as management sites to be 'conserved efficiently, maintained, benefited, developed according to a vision and theme, met with cultural and educational needs of society, in order to mediate between local and central authorities and NGOs on urban planning and conservation.' Although some definitions were left obscure, the law adopted UNESCO policies for World Heritage Sites which requested preparation of management plans for conservation sites. Cf. Dincer, 'The Impact'.

28 Law no. 5366: Law on Preservation by Renovation and Utilization by Revitalization of Deteriorated Immovable Historical and Cultural Properties (*Yıpranan Tarihi ve Kültürel Taşınmaz Varlıkların Yenilenerek Korunması ve Yaşatılarak Kullanılması Hakkında Kanun*). Promulgated on 7 May 2005.

29 (2011), *Istanbul Historic Peninsula Site Management Plan*. It was revised in 2018, accessed 27 April 2020, http://www.alanbaskanligi.gov.tr/tya/samples/magazine/slider.html.

30 The documentary 'Ekumenopolis' unfolds this relation between urban regeneration and economic policies of Turkey in the 2000s. İmre Azem, *Ekümenapolis*. Documentary film (2011).

31 Law No. 5393: Municipalities Law (Belediyeler Kanunu). Promulgated on 13 July 2005.

32 Law No. 6360: The Metropolitan Municipalities Law (*On Dört İlde Büyükşehir Belediyesi ve Yirmi Yedi İlçe Kurulmasi ile Bazi Kanun ve Kanun Hükmünde Kararnamelerde Değişiklik Yapilmasina Dair Kanun*).

33 Law No. 6306: Law on Restructuring Areas under the Risk of Disaster (*Afet Riski Altındaki Alanların Dönüştürülmesi Hakkında Kanun*).

34 Cemar Burak Tansel, 'Reproducing Authoritarian Neoliberalism in Turkey: Urban Governance and State Restructuring in the Shadow of Executive Centralization', *Globalizations* 16, no. 3 (2019): 320–35. Also see Kuyucu, 'Politics'.

35 Özçakır et al., 'Political'.

36 İstanbul Tarihi Alanları Alan Başkanlığı, 'Istanbul Historic Peninsula Site Management Plan: 25', 2018, accessed 27 April 2020, http://www.alanbaskanligi.gov.tr/tya/samples/magazine/slider.html.

37 As mentioned above, with the Law No. 6360, the boundaries of fourteen metropolitan municipalities were enlarged to include district municipalities and the authority of the metropolitan municipalities were reinforced. However, if the area of the potential renewal is not yet under a metropolitan municipal authority, the district municipalities can still propose a renewal site.

38 Özçakır et al., 'Political', 9.

39 Ilke Tekin and Asiye Akgün Gültekin, 'Rebuilding of Beyoğlu-İstiklal Street: A Comparative Analysis of Urban Transformation through Sections Along the Street 2004-2014', *METU Journal of Faculty of Architecture* 34, no. 2 (2017): 153–79.

40 Theodosian Walls are one of the areas enlisted in the UNESCO World Heritage List in 1985. The Sulukule is within the boundaries of the listed area, but it is adjacent.

41 Ülke Evrim Uysal, 'An Urban Social Movement Challenging Urban Regeneration: The Case of Sulukule, Istanbul', *Cities* 29 (2012): 15. Evrim Uysal's reference to

the official webpage of the Fatih Municipality is expired, therefore the quotation is written after Evrim Uysal.

42 Ibid.

43 Güliz Vural, 'Ranzalı Kent: Sulukule', *Nokta*, 25 January 2016, https://kuzeyormanlari.org/2016/02/02/ranzali-kent-sulukule/

44 Hande Akarca and Rifat Doğan, eds, *Tarlabaşı Bir Kent Mücadelesi* (İstanbul: TMMOB Mimarlar Odası İstanbul Büyükkent Şubesi, 2018).

45 For a history of Fener and Balat, Jak Daleon, *Balat ve Çevresi* (İstanbul: Remzi Kitabevi, 1991); Nur Akın, 'Fener', in *Dünden Bugüne İstanbul Ansiklopedisi* (İstanbul: Kültür Bakanlığı & Tarih Vakfı, 1994): 10–12; Nur Akın, 'Balat', in *Dünden Bugüne İstanbul Ansiklopedisi* (İstanbul: Kültür Bakanlığı & Tarih Vakfı, 1994), 279–81.

46 Zeynep Çelik, *The Remaking of İstanbul: Portrait of an Ottoman City in the Nineteenth Century* (London: University of California Press, 1986). On how *Ebniye Nizamnameleri* shaped the urban character of Ankara in the nineteenth century, see Serim Denel, 'Batılılaşma Sürecinde Ebniye Nizamnameleri ve Kentsel Mekânların Değişimine Etkileri Üzerine Bir Deneme', in *IX. Türk Tarih Kongresi* (Ankara: Turk Tarih Kurumu, 1981), 1425–35.

47 Neriman Şahin Güçhan, 'Observations on Earthquake Resistance of Traditional Timber-Framed Houses in Turkey', *Building and Environment* 42 (2007): 840–51.

48 The different urban character of the Fener and Balat districts, according to Tanyeli, is mainly due to this multi-ethnic and multireligious population. According to Tanyeli, despite this diversity, communities had limited interaction and they were 'not totally isolated but still in a closed environment.' Therefore, he argues that it is not possible to write Ottoman urban history without considering ethnicity or religion (or simply diversity of identities). Cf. Uğur Tanyeli, 'İstanbul'da Etnodinsel Çoğulluk ve Osmanlı Mimarlığı (15-19. Yüzyıl): Rumlar, Ermeniler, Türkler', in *Batılılaşan İstanbul'un Rum Mimarları*, ed. Hasan Kuruyazıcı and Eva Şarlak (İstanbul: Zoğrafyon Lisesi Mezunları Derneği, 2010), 60–80.

49 According to Koçu, Balat was a poor and dirty district until second half of 19th century. In fact, even the wealthier Jews preferred to live in Fener. Kocu narrates how sewages would run along the steep streets of Balat and reach the sea creating a sediment at the bottom of the Golden Horn. The situation became so severe that in the 1890s a pier was constructed over piles paled into the water in order to keep the dirt enclosed. Cf. Reşat Ekrem Koçu, *İstanbul Ansiklopedisi* (Istanbul: Koçu Yayınları, 1958). Salt Research is currently in the process of digitizing this vital source on Istanbul's urban history. Also see, Akın, 'Balat'.

50 With the Ottoman Empire's getting hold of the city in 1453, aristocrats of Byzantion (who were already living in Fener) had emigrated. Sultan Mehmet the Conqueror declared 'freedom of religion' (*din serbestisi*) to bring the former owners of the city back to where they belong as a part of a political principle that is to maintain the multicultural character of the city. With the transfer of Patriarchate to Fener, Fener became even more appealing to Roums. Roum Orthodox society became organized under the Patriarchate embracing their Byzantine roots and such an embracement had revealed itself in the architecture of their religious buildings. The Patriarchate has been located to its current place, the Ayios Yeoryios (Saint George) Church in 1601; since then Fener has been internationally important. Before 1601, the Patriarchate was housed in Havariyun Church (where Fatih Mosque stands now) until 1456, in Pammakaristos Church (Fethiye Mosque) between 1456 and 1586, then in Panayia Vahsarai in Fener, in Ayios Demetrios Church until 1597; Cf. Akın, 'Balat'; Zafer Karaca, *İstanbul'da Osmanlı Dönemi Rum Kilisileri* (İstanbul: Yapı Kredi Yayınları, 1995); Sennur Sezer and Adnan Özyalçıner, *Öyküleriyle İstanbul Anıtları-I: Surlardır Kuşatan İstanbul'u* (Istanbul: Evrensel Basım Yayın, 2010).

51 On her social media, Esra Akcan responded to the conversion of the Hagia Sophia from a museum to a mosque showing how the museum historically stood as a meaningful symbolic gesture to heal the pain of the displaced Roums. Her statement can be reached on: Esra Akcan, *Erasing History at the Hagia Sophia*, The Berkley Center for Religion, Peace, and World Affairs, 27 June 2020, https ://berkleycenter.georgetown.edu/responses/erasing-history-at-the-hagia-sophia ?fbclid=IwAR1GdOO7tDLjaJKKW6iDQhnvujHJfSPgou-gyiovfuX0RTsU-1Hsc wGCvCw

52 Cana Bilsel, 'European Side of İstanbul Master Plan, 1937', in *From the Imperial Capital to the Republican Modern City: Henri Prost's Planning of Istanbul (1936-1951)*, ed. Cana Bilsel and Pierre Pinon (İstanbul: Pera Müzesi Yayınları, 2010), 245--60. Murat Gül argues that this was the most controversial decision in Prost's Istanbul Plan. Cf. Murat Gül, *Emergence of Modern Istanbul: Transformation and Modernisation of a City* (London and New York: IB Tauris, 2009).

53 Faik Ökte, *Varlık vergisi faciası* (Istanbul: Nebioğlu Yayınevi, 1951).

54 Asım Uz, 'Bizantoloji Kongresi İçin Hazırlık', *TTOK Belleteni* 161 (1955): 9.

55 Sinan Yıldırmaz, 'Köylüler ve Kentliler: Ellili Yılların Dönüşen Yeni Sosyoekonomik ve Kültürel Coğrafyası', in *Türkiye'nin 1950'li Yılları*, ed. Mete Kaan Kaynar (İstanbul: İletişim Yayınları, 2015), 541–63.

56 Fatih Municipality, E. U., UNESCO WHC, French Institute of Anatolian Studies, *Balat ve Fener Semtlerinin Rehabilitasyonu (İstanbul Tarihi*

Yarımadası), Analiz ve Düzenleme Önerileri (İstanbul, 1998). This was the technical report prepared for *Balat and Fener Districts Rehabilitation Programme* that will be mentioned below. According to the report, as of 1998, %75 of inhabitants were immigrated from Black sea region or East and Southeast Anatolia region, %40 of the population had been living in the neighbourhood for more than 10 years. Monthly income of %70 of population corresponded to poverty level or below. In addition, level of education of public was also low; %64 of them was graduated only from primary school.

57 Nihal Ekin Erkan and Safiye Altıntaş, 'Soylulaştırmanın Gündelik Hayattaki Görünümleri: Balat'ın Mekânsal ve Sosyal Dönüşümü', *Idealkent* 23, no. 9 (2018): 292–335.

58 For a comparative analysis of these three urban projects on the conservation status of the site, see Mesut Dinler, 'Fener ve Balat'ın Dönüşümü Üzerine: Üç Vizyon/Üç Dönem/Üç Ayrı "Koruma" Anlayışı', *Tüba-Ked* 14 (2016): 225–47.

59 Istanbul Büyükşehir Belediyesi, *Amaç Yeşili ve Maviyi Kurtarmak* (Istanbul: İstanbul Büyükşehir Belediyesi, 1988).

60 Çağlar Keyder, 'The Setting', in *Istanbul: Between the Global and the Local*, ed. Çağlar Keyder (Lanham: Rowman and Littlefield Publishers, 1999), 3–10, 13–16.

61 Ibid., 14. Also see Dikmen Bezmez, 'The Politics of Urban Waterfront Regeneration: The Case of Haliç (the Golden Horn), İstanbul', *International Journal of Urban and Regional Research* 32, no. 4 (2009): 815–40.

62 Pierre Pinon, 'Haliç çevresinde sil baştan', *Mimarlık* 26, no. 2 (1988): 70.

63 Fatih Municipality et al., *Balat*.

64 Ibid.

65 United Nations, *Report of the United Nations Conference on Human Settlements* (Habitat II) (Istanbul: United Nations, 1996).

66 On the process of the Balat and Fener Districts Rehabilitation Programme: Burçin Altınsay Özgüner, 'Bir Kentsel Iyileştirme Deneyiminin Içinden: Fener ve Balat Semtleri Rehabilitasyon Programı', in *Kentsel Dönüşümde Politika, Mevzuat, Uygulama: Avrupa Deneyimi, İstanbul Uygulamaları*, ed. Dilek Özedemir (Ankara: Nobel Yayınları, 2010), 369–98. Burçin Altınsay Özgüner, 'Interview with Burçin Altınsay', Interviewer: D. Unsal, in *Cultural Policy and Management (KPY) Yearbook 2011* (Istanbul: Istanbul Bilgi University Press, 2011), 26–33. Evren Aysev Deneç, 'The Re-Production of the Historical Center of İstanbul in 2000s: A Critical Account on Two Projects in Fener – Balat', *METU Journal of Faculty of Architecture* 31, no. 2 (2014): 163–88.

67 Dinler, 'Fener'.

68 Law No. 5366 which came into effect on 7 May 2005. For Fener and Balat, a limited number of building blocks were designated as the renewal area by the Cabinet of Ministries on 3 April 2006 with the decision no. 2006/10299. This decision was published on the Official Gazette on 22 April 2006, Issue: 26147. A second decision designated a larger area which included the above mentioned coastal green band. This second decision was made by the Cabinet of Ministries September 13, 2006 with decision no. 2006/10961. This decision was published on the Official Gazette on 13 October 2006, Issue: 26318.

69 Zeynep Ahunbay, Iclal Dinçer and Cigdem Şahin, eds, *Neoliberal Kent Politikaları ve Fener-Balat-Ayvansaray: Bir Koruma Mücadelesinin Öyküsü* (İstanbul: Türkiye İş Bankası Kültür Yayınları, 2016).

70 Muge Akkar Ercan, *Regeneration, Heritage and Sustainable Communities in Turkey: Challenges, Complexities and Potentials* (Oxon: Routledge, 2019).

71 Eleonora Pasotti, *Resisting Redevelopment: Protest in Aspiring Global Cities* (Cambridge: Cambridge University Press, 2020), 115–22.

72 Hade Turkmen, 'Urban Renewal Projects and Dynamics of Contention in Istanbul: The Cases of Fener-Balat-Ayvansaray and Suleymaniye' (PhD diss., Cardiff University, 2014).

73 Mesut Dinler, 'Impact Assessment of Major Urban Interventions on the Cultural Heritage of Fener and Balat Districts (MA diss., Middle East Technical University, Ankara, 2013).

74 Dinler, 'Fener'.

75 TMMOB, *41. Dönem Çalışma Raporu* (İstanbul: TMMOB, 2012). Also see Çigdem Şahin, 'Fener-Balat Dönüşüm Projesinde Nereden Nereye', *Arkitera 12* (2012), accessed 14 December 2012, http://www.arkitera.com/haber/index/detay/fener-balat-donusum-projesinde-nereden-nereye/11358

76 Expert Report for Lawcase No:2010/465. İstanbul. The expert report (which is a public document) was written by Demet Binan, Adem Erdem Erbaş, and Kemal Çorapçıoğlu. I was lucky enough to assist the preparation of the export report back then while undertaking my academic research as a teaching and research assistant. I would like to underline the role of Prof. Binan in the cancellation of the renewal project because I have personally witnessed how Prof. Binan, the only woman member of the expert committee, strongly advocated the cancellation of the project providing academic arguments. It is also noteworthy that FeBayDer was alarmed when the court announced the members of the expert committee because Prof. Çorapçıoğlu had already had a role in Tarlabasi expert report which approved the renewal project.

77 'Fener-Balat'a da iptal', *Radikal Newspaper 21* (2012).

After the emergency?

Jane Rendell

emergency: the sudden or unexpected occurrence (of a state of things, etc.)[1]

Much discourse around emergency in architecture has, drawing on its theorization by Giorgio Agamben, tended to favour the term 'state of exception.' As Agamben points out, German theory uses the term 'state of exception', whereas Italian and French law favours emergency decrees, and martial laws and emergency powers are referred to in the Anglo-Saxon context. Agamben explains that the difference in terms is related less to the specifics of the situation itself, and more to the cultural location, noting that: 'the state of exception is not a special kind of law (like the law of war); rather, insofar as it is a suspension of the juridical order itself, it defines law's threshold or limit concept.'[2]

As Banu Pekol discusses in her essay here, with reference to the work of Karl Schmitt, a state of exception occurs, when, in response to different kinds of events, the sovereign powers or the state suspend usual legal orders and put in place new measures – 'unconventional rules, institutions' – declared to be for the public good.[3] As Pekol goes on to argue, this phenomenon of the apparently temporary emergency that then becomes permanent has been studied extensively[4] – for Agamben, 'the state of exception has by now become the rule,'[5] and in Michael Hardt and Antonio Negri, 'the state of exception has become permanent and general; the exception has become the rule.'[6]

The essays in this volume explore, with reference to the specific case of Turkey, how when living through times where the state of exception has become the rule, new kinds of normal emerge. One, if not the key, conceptual contribution this book makes then is to look – in great detail through a set of specific studies based in Turkey – at the ways in which the exception and the rule are related. In the introduction, co-editor Eray Çaylı argues that it is important to keep in mind not only how exceptions become rules, but also the more complex relation between emergency and normalcy:

> A major body of scholarship that considers critically the relationship between emergency and normalcy revolves around the notion of exception. This critical scholarship has shown that the relationship between the exception and the rule as modes of governmentality has, throughout modern history, been one of interdependence and entanglement rather than antitheticality.[7]

The focus on how emergency and normalcy are entangled in Turkey in the late 2000s and early 2010s, but specifically after the introduction in mid-2012 of a piece of legislation known popularly as the Disaster Act, is teased out in different contexts, projects and ways throughout the book. This study of what happens to attitudes of normalcy connected to the design and use of architecture and urbanism in a state of emergency is something of great value, not only for scholarship concerned with the Turkish context, but also more broadly for the wider field of architectural and urban studies, and especially today. We all need to learn now, from the intricate manner in which emergency and normalcy are connected, how power is played out through building and material processes, and the ways in which architecture can be used to rethink, resist and reimagine new and old normals in and through emergencies.

Wherever we are, right now in June to July 2020, within the space of just a few months, from the weak and often ineffectual responses generated by populist right-wing governments to the more stringent measures imposed by more authoritarian ones, we have all found ourselves living through some version of the emergency created by the Covid-19 pandemic. But this pandemic emergency is just one symptom of the ongoing ecological emergency, itself the result of centuries of extractivism perpetrated by colonial capitalism. The Extinction Rebellion protests of 2019 organized to highlight the climate emergency have now been joined by Black Lives Matter activists and their allies who demand immediate responses to the injustices of systemic and historical racism. None of these emergencies have ended yet, and are not likely to conclude any time soon; each one has its own particular relation to cause and response, its own unique temporal mode of intensity and duration, and yet they are all interrelated, as responses to the differing symptoms of extractive neoliberal capitalism.

At the start of the outbreak of the coronavirus pandemic, some citizens – including me – were calling for governments to take action, to instigate lockdowns, to put in place states of emergency in order to protect citizens. In the UK, when Covid-19 hit, many academics were on strike at the universities across the country, engaging in activities outside normal academic life, creating a break, an emergency of resistance, to draw attention to the inequalities and precarity of labour conditions caused by the financialization of universities. Reading an 'Open Letter to the Trade Union Movement' from *Labour Transformed* encouraged me to act with comrades to close our picket at the Bartlett School of Architecture, UCL, as an act of social solidarity with the United Kingdom's National Health Service, to help to 'level the peak' of the Covid-19 infection, and create an interruption to the business-as-usual model of operation which was spreading the virus at a rapid rate. So we posted this message from *Labour Transformed* on Instagram and on the outside of our building:

> Staying at home and self-isolating is an act of social solidarity, one that ensures that the burden of ill bodies falling onto the shoulders of our brothers and sisters in the NHS is someway manageable.[8]

So we see here, how a desire to protect citizens from the health risks posed by the potential for the virus to spread due to normal patterns of behaviour led to a call for a break to normalcy and a demand for something different, though we did not envisage a suspension of law as a solution. One of the UK government's former scientific advisers is now making clear that the delay in taking decisive action and installing a 'lockdown', itself a state of emergency, has resulted in the unnecessary loss of at least 25,000 lives,[9] and a year later, in June 2021, at the time of copy-editing this essay, the total death toll has risen to 128,124.[10] And it is important to note that the relaxed and apparently milder positions adopted by populist neoliberal governments, which avoid the kind of 100 per cent lockdown or quarantine associated with states of emergency, have been intended, not to save lives but to appeal to sections of the voting population and to safeguard the economy by removing restrictions on trade, while some of those enforcing strict rules have done so in the public interest to protect vulnerable groups.

On 20 May 2020, during the UK's Covid-19 first 'lockdown', W1A, the BBC political comedy show, aired their special 'zoom' 'Initial Lockdown Meeting', and as this quote makes clear, by then, the manipulation of normals, old and new, had already become a full-fledged aspect of managing the crisis and communicating the government message:

> Welcome to the first ever lockdown meeting of the BBC COVID19 'Bounce Back' Group. I know we've all got used to thinking of ourselves as the 'Way Ahead Group' but in the current circumstances it didn't seem to ring true with the realities of the new normal, whereas the Bounce Back Group seems positive, clear and very much does what it says on the tin . . . but really the remit couldn't be more exciting, to try to imagine what the new normal will look like, and to begin to plot a path towards it, from wherever it is that we are now. . . . What we know of course is that it won't look anything like the old normal, or as I think we can safely call it now, the past, which really frees us up to think creatively.[11]

An emergency is often posed in the present tense, flanked by past and future normals, both of which are ideally envisioned as the same. In the moment of rupture created by the emergency, no normal is present, and this allows us to see the qualities of the normal more clearly, to define what constitutes the normal and the range of nuances of normalcies, and to distinguish between normalcy and emergency more carefully. Yet when immersed in the emergency itself, when nothing is normal anymore, anxieties emerge and many resort to calls for normalcy in order to reduce them: some normalize the emergency itself; others look for normals that remain or can be invented despite the emergency; others even try to locate the normal elsewhere or afterwards, in order to provide a spatial boundary or time limit to the emergency operating in the here and now. At first, during Covid-19 in the UK I noticed how the 'new' normal was pitched in the time ahead of us by those who were set to benefit from a future cast in the same image as the past, but soon there was talk of the present moment, the lockdown itself, as the new normal, and then as normals started to multiply, to appear everywhere, it became harder to locate oneself in time, to see the edge of the emergency and indeed any distinction at all between emergency and normalcy.

normalcy: the usual state or condition

In this book, in the chapter 'The politics of normalcy: Examining the festival on the island of Imbros/Gökçeada', Sevcan Ercan notes how it is important to connect normalcy with a form of hegemony that 'constantly suppresses any deviance from the various conceptions of the sovereign powers regarding the everyday'. She describes how the exception, in this case a festival, 'provides us a way to perceive how normalcy is a construct', and how the

> normalcy of the everyday involves the notion of exception . . . . The politics of normalcy which control the everyday rely upon an awareness of an exceptional element, i.e., normalcy does not make any sense without an understanding of the opposite contained within it (abnormal, exceptional, emergency etc.).[12]

Ercan discusses how 'the festival's reassuring regularity as a planned site of exception reveals how the politics of normalcy operates as a set of mechanisms governing both what counts as normal and what counts as exceptional'. It is not only, she writes, that authorities can engineer situations where exceptions become rules, or that one can try to insert patterns of behaviour that one is comfortable with in order to alleviate stress by making an emergency feel normal, but that certain kinds of emergency – like festivals, like play, like jokes – are required in order to allow the functioning of the normal.

Architectures of Emergency in Turkey tracks the impact of Turkey's state of emergency on architecture and urbanism, specifically through three themes – heritage, displacement and catastrophe – so here I'd like to consider the particular possibilities of each in terms of the interplay between emergency and normalcy.

First, regarding urban heritage and the material visibility of culture, the instigation of an emergency by a state, in this case Turkey, provides an opportunity for artefacts representing the lives of unwanted communities to be removed, and the struggle that emerges is for communities that have been marginalized to seek to hold on what they value. At the same time, emergencies can also provide the chance for a breach in normality, in the operation of an oppressive regime like South African apartheid, for example, and it is through this breach in the status quo that more liberatory practices can break through. With the 'Rhodes Must Fall' movement, originally directed against a statue at the University of Cape Town (UCT) that commemorated Cecil Rhodes, the removal of racist monuments from public space by protesters, created a hiatus, and in this break, came an opportunity to address the racist past in the present, and question given normalities. We can see also how the protests following George Floyd's death, interrupted the state of emergency, which was the Covid-19 lockdown, producing a powerful range of anti-racist activities. Enacted against the normalcy of colonial history, some have involved the removal of statues, as well as the names of slave owners and other colonialists from their revered public positions in UK towns and universities.

Among those who, in the name of history, argue against the removal of such statues and plaques are some who wish to see the anti-racist protesters themselves removed from public space, and traditions of colonialism maintained. Such arguments should not be seen to be on the side of history; history's role as a discipline is to actively and critically engage with what has come before, to see precisely *how* the past enters the present, and how the present acts to refigure the past, not to uncritically preserve what has come before, just because it took place earlier. In this case, it is the emergency of the protests, their very emergent nature, that provides the possibility of disrupting normalcy, revealing it as an ideological construction, and one that can be displaced.

emergent: an unforeseen occurrence, a contingency not specially provided for

The intersection of the Covid-19 and the climate emergencies has been discussed in terms of 'a crisis in a crisis',[13] but also in terms of how the virus is a symptom of the ecological crisis. The climate emergency is such a huge crisis that it has largely been disavowed by governments, to the extent that citizens have had to call, through 'Extinction Rebellion', for example, for governing bodies, such as states, to impose states of emergency in order to rapidly reduce carbon emissions. The response to the climate emergency has varied from a denial of the crisis, to a refusal to trust the science evidencing the human-produced nature of it, to a belief in often-untested future technological fixes, to promises to make inadequate adjustments to carbon emissions to be put in place at some future unspecified date and within a business-as-usual model. In short, the demands of the Extinction Rebellion have often been rejected as impossible, because they oppose the normalcy of neoliberal carbon-fuelled capitalism. And yet we have seen how it has been possible to respond to the dangers posed by a virus with emergency measures, and, as lockdowns were called for, nation by nation, in early 2020 to combat the spread of Covid-19, to install a 'new normal' almost overnight. However, despite all the new measures that have been put in place to combat Covid-19, which may have reduced annual global carbon emissions by around 4 per cent to 7.5 per cent,[14] the call remains strong, to return to the old normal, to restart economies and so push carbon emissions back up.

Secondly, if we now turn to displacement, as the next theme of this book, then we can see how this features in the case of emergencies, not only in terms of the state-produced wars and destruction – often enacted to secure carbon – and the interrelated impacts of climate change on migration but also in the way in which one form of emergency can displace another, from the climate emergency, to Covid-19, to Black Lives Matter. Perhaps partly because of the immediacy of social media and its amplifying affective effects, our attention is held in a constant state of present-ness, waiting for the next emergency to impact, which makes future planning, and even future imagining, almost impossible. As those who have lived through the crises of displacements caused by emergencies – migrants, displaced communities and persecuted minorities, as described in this book – know from experience that raised adrenalin, exhaustion and trauma have serious health impacts.

This is maybe why, in *Staying with the Trouble*, Donna Haraway refers to the ecological crisis as a permanent and urgent crisis, and write of urgency rather than emergency, exploring what it means to 'cultivate the capacity to respond to worldly urgencies with each other'.[15] Engaging with the work of Anna Tsing, who she argues considers 'multispecies extinctions, genocides, immiserations, and exterminations,' Haraway terms these as 'urgencies rather than emergencies because the latter word connotes something approaching apocalypse and its mythologies';[16] rather, her preference is for the different mode of temporality offered by urgencies.

> *urgency: the state, condition, or fact of being urgent; pressing importance; imperativeness*

What seems to be required in these times of urgencies (then) is for counter forces to come together to take forward initiatives, to subvert the order of things, to live with urgency in a way that is neither part of the emergency nor the old (or even new) normal. But as Özyetiş discusses in *Architectures of Emergency in Turkey* in 'Forum in relation to the polis: The case of 1.39 and Turkey', the production of catastrophe out of emergency can produce breakdown, not only to physical, architectural and environmental settings, but also to political discourse, intellectual capacity and emotional sensibility, rendering certain modes of resistance ineffective. This third theme of the book figures catastrophe or destruction then as a way of understanding the relation between emergency and normalcy.

catastrophe: an event producing a subversion of the order or system of things

Özyetiş examines how some kinds of *parrhesia*, and following Foucault's work on this,[17] a speaking truth to power, rely too strongly on logos, or certain modes of life which prioritize intelligence. Instead Özyetiş traces, through the story of Antigone, the important role of bios, which Foucault underscores as vital to a Socratic form of *parrhesia*, as a practice which balances logos and bios. Foucault examines the function of *parrhesia* in terms of the crisis of democratic institutions, and also how *parrhesia* occurs as an activity in human relations, with respect to care of the self, and in relation to others, specifically through three kinds of relations: individual personal, community and public life. Foucault talks of how, in the shift from a political to a Socratic or ethical form of *parrhesia*, the relation between *logos*, truth and courage alters to include *bios*, and to focus on the balance between *bios* and *logos* with respect to truth:

> Here, giving an account of your life, your bios, is also not to give a narrative of the historical events that have taken place in your life, but rather to demonstrate whether you are able to show that there is a relation between the rational discourse, the logos, you are able to use, and the way that you live. Socrates is inquiring into the way that logos gives form to a person's style of life; for he is interested in discovering whether there is a harmonic relation between the two.[18]

Now, this balancing of human life between logos and bios, has been challenged by other philosophers. In *The Use of Bodies,* Agamben identifies what he calls a 'division of life' that separates 'simple life' or zoe from 'politically qualified life' or bios,[19] and he divides the biographical and the political,[20] positioning bare life as the threshold between the two.[21]

> The political power that we are familiar with is instead always ultimately founded on the separation of the sphere of bare life from the context of forms of life.[22]

Agamben's analysis opens up the discussion of life to include not only bios and logos but zoe; however, Rosi Braidotti takes issue with his view of zoe as 'non-life' and argues, instead, from a feminist and ecological perspective, for a version of zoe which includes vitality.[23] Critical race theorist Sylvia Wynter has also challenged the distinction between bios and logos, reframing the human being as a hybrid, as bios and mythoi together.[24] She argues this through her concept of 'human being as praxis', as Katherine McKittrick has noted 'Wynter is suggesting that our cognitive understanding of the world and our selves is *simultaneously* biological and cultural (bios/mythoi).'[25]

Pekol ends her chapter in this book with a section titled, 'Emergency as Normalcy', something she elsewhere describes as acting 'in lieu of' a conclusion. I read this as an unwillingness to perform simple endings, and as a desire to acknowledge what it means to face up to endings. Both normalcy and emergency refuse to end: they offer two different versions of a continuous presence, one endless, the other timeless. As the reality of living in these interlocking emergencies becomes normalized, the past and future disappear from view. How then to engage with beginings and endings?

> *resurgency: that rises, or tends to rise, again; increasing or reviving after a period of little activity, popularity, or occurrence*

Writing this essay during the Covid-19 emergency I have seen the resurgence of 'natural' life even in a time of human death, as well as attempts for forestall transformations. It is this that we need to attend to: the energies released in the interruption of normalities made possible by the emergency. We have to take care of these resurgent powers and the resistance they can offer to the normals of colonial extractivist capitalisms, old and new. Both Braidotti and Wynter engage with life, one affirming zoe as a vital life force, and the other insisting that biology is joined with culture. Haraway, too, argues for the necessity of resurgence in 'mixed-up times', and for what we can do in times of urgency, together:

> In urgent times, many of us are tempted to address trouble in terms of making an imagined future safe, of stopping something from happening that looms in the future, of clearing away the present and the past in order to make futures for coming generations. Staying with the trouble does not require such a relationship to times called the future. In fact, staying with the trouble requires learning to be truly present.[26]

Notes

1 All definitions of terms (in italics) taken from *Oxford English Dictionary*, oed.com.
2 Giorgio Agamben, *State of Exception* (Chicago: University of Chicago Press, 2005), 4.

3   See Carl Schmitt, *Political Theology: Four Chapters on the Concept of Sovereignty* (Chicago: University of Chicago Press, 2005), referred to in Banu Pekol, 'Destabilizing National Heritage: Preserving Turkey's Non-Muslim Architectural Heritage', in *Architectures of Emergency in Turkey: Heritage, Displacement and Catastrophe*, eds. Eray Çaylı et al. (London: I. B. Tauris, 2021).

4   For a discussion of the relevance of Agamben's work for architecture and urbanism and a discussion of his thinking on the 'state of exception' with reference to his oeuvre, see Camillo Boano, *The Ethics of a Potential Urbanism: Critical Encounters between Giorgio Agamben and Architecture* (London: Routledge, 2017).

5   Agamben, *State of Exception*, 9.

6   Michael Hardt and Antonio Negri, *Multitude: War and Democracy in the Age of Empire* (New York: Penguin Press, 2004), 7.

7   Eray Çaylı, 'Architectures of Emergency in Turkey: Heritage, Displacement and Catastrophe', in *Architectures of Emergency in Turkey: Heritage, Displacement and Catastrophe*, eds. Eray Çaylı et al. (London: I. B. Tauris, 2021).

8   'Britain: On the Coronavirus and the social crisis – An open letter to the Trade Union movement from Labour Transformed', Links: International Journal of Socialist Movement, accessed 25 June 2020, http://links.org.au/britain-coronavirus-social-crisis-open-letter-trade-union-movement-labour-transformed.

9   Lizzy Buchan, 'Coronavirus: Lockdown One Week Earlier could have Halved UK's Death Toll, Says Neil Ferguson', *Independent*, 10 June 2020, https://www.independent.co.uk/news/uk/politics/uk-lockdown-coronavirus-death-toll-neil-ferguson-a9559051.html.

10 https://coronavirus.jhu.edu/region/united-kingdom, accessed 10 June 2021.

11 British Comedy Guide, 'W1A: Lockdown Special', accessed 20 May 2020, https://www.comedy.co.uk/tv/w1a/episodes/2020/1/.

12 Sevcan Ercan, 'The Politics of Normalcy: Examining the Festival on the Island of Imbros/Gökçeada', in *Architectures of Emergency in Turkey: Heritage, Displacement and Catastrophe*, eds. Eray Çaylı et al. (London: I. B. Tauris, 2021).

13 Rupert Bickersteth, 'Edward Denison: "Under lockdown people appeared to have a newfound interest in architecture"', *Architects' Journal*, 18 June 2020, https://www.architectsjournal.co.uk/news/culture/data-shows-air-pollution-plunged-during-lockdown-prompting-calls-for-radical-change/10047328.article.

14 Jackson Ryan, 'COVID-19 Lockdowns Caused an "Extreme" Reduction in Carbon Emissions', *cnet*, accessed 10 July 2020, https://www.cnet.com/news/covid-19-lockdowns-caused-an-extreme-reduction-in-carbon-emissions/.

15 Donna Haraway, *Staying with the Trouble: Making Kin in the Chthulucene* (Durham and London: Duke University Press, 2016), 7 and 35.
16 Ibid., 37.
17 See Michel Foucault (ed. J. Pearson), 'Discourse and Truth: The Problematization of Parrhesia: Six Lectures given by Michel Foucault at the University of California at Berkeley, October–November 1983', *Foucault.info*, accessed 4 February 2020, https://foucault.info/parrhesia/. See my discussion of this in relation to institutional critique in Jane Rendell, 'Giving an Account Of Oneself, Architecturally', *Journal of Visual Culture* 15, no. 3 (2016): 334–48.
18 Foucault, 'Discourse and Truth'.
19 Giorgio Agamben, *The Use of Bodies: Homo Sacer, IV, 2*, trans. Adam Kotsko (Stanford: Stanford University Press, [2014] 2015), 203.
20 Ibid., xxi.
21 Ibid., 78.
22 Ibid., 209.
23 Rosi Braidotti, *Transpositions: On Nomadic Ethics* (Cambridge: Polity Press, 2006), 39–42.
24 Sylvia Wynter in Sylvia Wynter and Katherine McKittrick, 'Unparalleled Catastrophe for Our Species? Or, to give Humanness a Different Future: Conversations', in *Sylvia Wynter: On Being Human as Praxis*, ed. Katherine McKittrick (Durham and London: Duke University Press, 2015), 16.
25 Katherine McKittrick, 'Axis, Bold as Love: On Sylvia Wynter, Jimi Hendrix and the Promise of Science', in *Sylvia Wynter: On Being Human as Praxis*, ed. Katherine McKittrick (Durham and London: Duke University Press, 2015), 154.
26 Haraway, *Staying with the Trouble: Making Kin in the Chthulucene*, 1.

Bibliography

'Adli Tıp Kurumu, Tahir Elçi Dosyasını Geri Gönderdi'. *T24*, 6 July 2019. https://t24.com.tr/haber/adli-tip-kurumu-tahir-elci-dosyasini-geri-gonderdi,829411.

'Ankara'da Gökçek döneminde yıkılan cumhuriyet mirası yapılar'. *İleri Haber*. Accessed 23 January 2020. https://ilerihaber.org/icerik/ankarada-gokcek-doneminde-yikilan-cumhuriyet-mirasi-yapilar-78223.html.

'"Ayasofya cami olarak anılsın" talebine soruşturma'. *Birgün*, 6 November 2005. https://www.birgun.net/haber/ayasofya-cami-olarak-anilsin-talebine-sorusturma-24867.

'Ayasofya sahte Atatürk imzasıyla müzeye çevrildi'. *Milliyet*, 24 November 2013. http://www.milliyet.com.tr/gundem/ayasofya-sahte-ataturk-imzasiyla-muzeye-cevrildi-1796961.

'Başbakan'dan Gezi Parkı açıklaması'. *Hürriyet*, 1 June 2013. https://www.sabah.com.tr/gundem/2013/06/01/basbakan-erdogan-konusuyor.

'Convention Concerning the Exchange of Greek and Turkish Populations'. *The American Journal of International Law* 18, no. 2 (April 1924): 84–90. http://www.jstor.org/stable/2212847.

'Cumhurbaşkanı Erdoğan: İstanbul Atatürk Kültür Merkezi bir zafer anıtı olacaktır'. *Anadolu Agency*, 10 February 2019. https://www.cnnturk.com/turkiye/son-dakika-yeni-akmnin-temeli-atiliyor-binali-yildirim-torende-konusuyor.

'Danıştay, Ayasofya'nın ibadete açılması talebini reddetti'. *Hürriyet*, 24 June 2005. http://www.hurriyet.com.tr/gundem/danistay-ayasofyanin-ibadete-acilmasi-talebini-reddetti-329832.

'Dünya Tiyatro Günü'nde suç duyurusu: "AKM'yi kapattınız, işgal ettiniz, talan ettiniz!"', 27 March 2015. https://sendika63.org/2015/03/dunya-tiyatro-gununde-suc-duyurusu-akmyi-kapattiniz-isgal-ettiniz-talan-ettiniz-253994/#more.

'Erdoğan: AKM yıkılacak, Taksim'e cami de yapılacak'. *Radikal*, 02 June 2013. http://www.radikal.com.tr/politika/erdogan-akm-yikilacak-taksime-cami-de-yapilacak-1135947/.

'Erdoğan: Tarihi Eserlerde Ayrımcılık Reddi Mirastır'. *Milliyet*, 2 February 2009. http://www.milliyet.com.tr/siyaset/erdogan-tarihi-eserlerde-ayrimcilik-reddi-mirastir-1057732.

'Ex-PM Davutoglu Ignites Debate on Turkey's Bloodiest Summer in 2015'. *Yerepouni Daily News*, 26 August 2019.

'Olağanüstü Hal Kanunu [State of Emergency Law]'. Accessed 15 December 2019. https://www.mevzuat.gov.tr/MevzuatMetin/1.5.2935.pdf.

'Saraçoğlu Yerleşkesi "Ekonomiye Kazandırmak"(!) Amacıyla Yok Edilemez'. Accessed 24 January 2020. http://www.spo.org.tr/resimler/ekler/826a13a53ad67 67_ek.pdf?tipi=3&turu=X&sube=1.

'Solo pedimos la verdad'. *La Nación*, 10 December 1977.

'Suriyeli Ambalaj Firmasından Gaziantep'e Yatırım'. *Anadolu Agency*, 17 November 2018. https://www.aa.com.tr/tr/ekonomi/suriyeli-ambalaj-firmasindan-gaziantepe-yatirim/1314006.

'Suriyeliler Halep Özlemini Antep Kalesi'yle Gideriyor'. *Hürriyet*, 16 March 2017. https://www.hurriyet.com.tr/suriyeliler-halep-ozlemini-antep-kalesiyle-gi-4039663 9.

'Suriyelilerin İstanbul'a kaydı durduruldu'. *Deutsche Welle*, 6 February 2018. https://www.dw.com/tr/suriyelilerin-istanbula-kayd%C4%B1-durduruldu/a-42465450.

'Türk Medeni Kanunu 1926 [Turkish Civil Code 1926]', no. 639. Accessed 12 January 2019. http://www.mevzuat.gov.tr/MevzuatMetin/5.3.743.pdf

Açıkgöz, Şeyda Güngör. 'Kayseri ve Çevresindeki 19. Yüzyıl Kiliseleri ve Korunmaları İçin Öneriler [19th Century Churches in Kayseri and its Environs and Suggestions for their Preservation]'. PhD diss., Istanbul Technical University, Istanbul, 2007.

Ackerman, Bruce. 'The Emergency Constitution'. *Yale Law Journal* 113, no. 8 (2004): 1030.

Agamben, Giorgio. *Homo Sacer: Sovereign Power and Bare Life*. Stanford: Stanford University Press, 1998.

Agamben, Giorgio. *State of Exception*. Translated by Kevin Attell, Chicago: The University of Chicago Press, 2005.

Agamben, Giorgio. *The Use of Bodies: Homo Sacer, IV, 2*. Translated by Adam Kotsko. Stanford: Stanford University Press, [2014] 2015.

Ahunbay, Zeynep, İclal Dinçer and Çiğdem Şahin, eds. *Neoliberal Kent Politikaları ve Fener-Balat-Ayvansaray: Bir Koruma Mücadelesinin Öyküsü*. İstanbul: Türkiye İş Bankası Kültür Yayınları, 2016.

Akar, Rıdvan and Hülya Demir. *İstanbul'un Son Sürgünleri: 1964'te Rumların Sınırdışı Edilmeleri* [*The Last Exiles of Istanbul: The Expatriation of Rums in 1964*]. İstanbul: Doğan Kitap, 2014.

Akarca, Hande and Rıfat Doğan, eds. *Tarlabaşı Bir Kent Mücadelesi*. İstanbul: TMMOB Mimarlar Odası İstanbul Büyükkent Şubesi, 2018.

Akay, Zafer. 'İstanbul'un Cumhuriyet Dönemi Simgesi: AKM'. *Mimarlık Dergisi* 392 (2016). Accessed 23 January 2020. http://www.mimarlikdergisi.com/index.cfm?sayfa=mimarlik&DergiSayi=406&RecID=4050.

Akçam, Taner. *The Young Turks' Crime against Humanity: The Armenian Genocide and Ethnic Cleansing in the Ottoman Empire*. Princeton: Princeton University Press, 2012.

Akçam, Taner and Ümit Kurt. *Kanunların Ruhu: Emval-i Metruke Kanunlarında Soykırımın İzini Sürmek* [*The Spirit of the Laws: The Plunder of Wealth in the Armenian Genocide*]. Istanbul: İletişim Yayınları, 2012.

Akcan, Esra. *Architecture in Translation: Germany, Turkey, and the Modern House*. Durham: Duke University Press, 2012.

Akcan, Esra. 'How Does Architecture Heal? The AKM as Palimpsest and Ghost'. *South Atlantic Quarterly* 118, no. 1 (2019): 81–94.

Akdemir, Nevra. 'Üç Büyük Göç Dalgası ve Gaziantep'in Mekânsal Sürekli Yeniden İnşası' [Three Main Migration Waves and Gaziantep's Continuous Spatial Reproduction]. In *The Migration Conference 2017: Programme and Abstracts Book–*, edited by Fethiye Tilbe, Elif Iskender and Ibrahim Sirkeci, 209–10. London: Transnational Press, 2017.

Akgönül, Samim. *Azınlık: Türk Bağlamında Azınlık Kavramına Çapraz Bakışlar* [*Minority: Views on the Concept of Minority in the Turkish Context*]. Istanbul: Bgst Press, 2011.

Akgönül, Samim. *Türkiye Rumları: Ulus-Devlet Çağında Küreselleşme Cağına Bir Azınlığın Yok Oluşu* [*The Greeks of Turkey: The Process of Eliminating a Minority during the Era of Nation-states*]. Istanbul: İletişim Yayınları, 2016.

Akın, Nur. 'Balat'. In *Dünden Bugüne İstanbul Ansiklopedisi*, 279–81. İstanbul: Kültür Bakanlığı & Tarih Vakfı, 1994.

Akın, Nur. 'Fener'. In *Dünden Bugüne İstanbul Ansiklopedisi*, 10–12. İstanbul: Kültür Bakanlığı & Tarih Vakfı, 1994.

Akkar Ercan, Müge. *Regeneration, Heritage and Sustainable Communities in Turkey: Challenges, Complexities and Potentials*. Oxon: Routledge, 2019.

Alcan, Toros. 'Millet-i Hakime ve Millet-i Sadıka [The Dominant Nation and the Loyal Nation]'. In *Yok Hükmünde: Müslüman Olmayan Cemaatlerin Tüzel Kişilik ve Temsil Sorunu* [*Declared Null and Void: Legal Entity and Representation Problem of Non-Muslim Communities*], edited by Rober Koptaş and Bülent Usta. Istanbul: Aras Yayınları, 2016.

Alessandri, Emiliano. 'Democratization and Europeanization in Turkey after the September 12 Referendum'. *Insight Turkey* 12, no. 4 (2010): 23–30.

Altaras, Nesi. 'Varagavank Manastırı Mehmet Çoban'a Emanet' [Varagavank Monastery Is Entrusted to Mehmet Çoban]. Accessed 4 April 2020. http://www.agos.com.tr/tr/yazi/22814/varagavank-manastiri-mehmet-cobana-emanet

Altınsay Özgüner, Burçin. 'Bir kentsel iyileştirme deneyiminin içinden: Fener ve Balat Semtleri Rehabilitasyon Programı'. In *Kentsel Dönüşümde Politika, Mevzuat,*

Uygulama: Avrupa Deneyimi, İstanbul Uygulamaları, edited by Dilek Özedemir, 369–98. Ankara: Nobel Yayınları, 2010.

Altınsay Özgüner, Burçin. 'Interview with Burçin Altınsay' (Interviewer: D. Unsal). In *Cultural Policy and Management (KPY) Yearbook 2011*, 26–33. Istanbul: Istanbul Bilgi University Press, 2011.

Altınyıldız, Nur. 'The Architectural Heritage of Istanbul and the Ideology of Preservation'. *Muqarnas* 24 (2007): 281–306.

Angell, Elizabeth. 'Assembling Disaster: Earthquakes and Urban Politics in Istanbul'. *City* 18, no. 6 (2014): 667–78.

Argentine Forensic Anthropology Team. 'The Argentine Experience'. Accessed 11 December 2019. https://www.eaaf.org/.

Argentine Forensic Anthropology Team. 'Following Antigone: Forensic Anthropology and Human Rights Investigations'. Filmed 2002. https://video.alexanderstreet.com/watch/following-antigone-forensic-anthropology-and-human-rights-investigations.

Arslan, Serhat, Derya Aydın, Hakan Sandal and Güllistan Yarkın. *Sur'da Yıkımın İki Yüzü: Kentsel Dönüşüm ve Abluka*. Diyarbakır: Zan Foundation, 2016.

Ashworth, Gregory. 'The Conserved European City as Cultural Symbol: The Meaning of the Text'. In *Modern Europe: Place, Culture, Identity*, edited by B. Graham, 261–86. London: Arnold, 1998.

Ashworth, Gregory J., Brian Graham and John E. Tunbridge. *Pluralising Pasts: Heritage, Identity and Place in Multicultural Societies*. London: Pluto Press, 2007.

Atasoy, Yıldız. 'Repossession, Re-informalization and Dispossession: The "Muddy Terrain" of Land Commodification in Turkey'. *Journal of Agrarian Change* 17, no. 4 (2017): 657–79.

Aykaç, Pinar. 'Archives as Fields of Heritage-Making in Istanbul's Historic Peninsula'. *International Journal of Islamic Architecture* 9, no. 2 (2020): 361–87.

Aykaç, Pınar. 'Contesting the Byzantine Past: Four Hagia Sophias as Ideological Battlegrounds of Architectural Conservation in Turkey'. *Heritage & Society* 11, no. 2 (2018): 151–78.

Aykaç, Pınar. 'Musealisation As An Urban Process: The Transformation Of The Sultanahmet District In Istanbul's Historic Peninsula'. PhD diss., University College London, 2017.

Aysev Deneç, Evren. 'The Re-Production of the Historical Center of İstanbul in 2000s: A Critical Account on Two Projects in Fener – Balat'. *METU Journal of Faculty of Architecture* 31, no. 2 (2014): 163–88.

Azem, Imre. *Turkey on the Edge*. 2017. Documentary film.

Babül, Elif. 'Belonging to Imbros: Citizenship and Sovereignty in the Turkish Republic'. Master diss., Boğaziçi University, 2003.

Baer, Marc David. *Sultanic Saviors and Tolerant Turks: Writing Ottoman Jewish History, Denying the Armenian Genocide*. Bloomington: Indiana University Press, 2020.

Balta, Evangelia. *Nüfus Mübadelesi* [*The Population Exchange*]. Istanbul: Inkılap Yayınları, 2015.

Bandarin, Francesco and Rob van Oers. *The Historic Urban Landscape: Managing Heritage in An Urban Century*. Oxford: Wiley-Blackwell, 2012.

Bartu Candan, Ayfer and Biray Kolluoğlu. 'Emerging Spaces of Neoliberalism: A Gated Town and a Public Housing Project in İstanbul'. *New Perspectives on Turkey* 39 (2008): 5–46.

Başbakanlık Osmanlı Arşivi: Cumhuriyet Arşivleri [The Ottoman Archives of the Prime Minister's Office: Republic Archives]. Decision no: 1039, file no:135-7, 3.29.10, 18 March 1925.

Batuman, Bülent. '"Early Republican Ankara": Struggle over Historical Representation and the Politics of Urban Historiography'. *Journal of Urban History* 37, no. 5 (2011): 661–79.

Batuman, Bülent. '"Everywhere Is Taksim": The Politics of Public Space from Nation-Building to Neoliberal Islamism and Beyond'. *Journal of Urban History* 41, no. 5 (2015): 881–907.

Batuman, Bülent. *New Islamist Architecture and Urbanism: Negotiating Nation and Islam through Built Environment in Turkey*. London: Routledge, 2017.

Bauder, Harald. 'Why We Should Use the Term Illegalized Immigrant'. *RCIS Research Brief* (2013): 1–7. https://www.ryerson.ca/content/dam/centre-for-immigration-and-settlement/RCIS/publications/researchbriefs/2013_1_Bauder_Harald_Why_We_Should_Use_The_Term_Illegalized_Immigrant.pdf

Baykan, Aysegul and Tali Hatuka. 'Politics and Culture in the Making of Public Space: Taksim Square, 1 May 1977, Istanbul'. *Planning Perspectives* 25, no. 1 (2010): 49–68.

Bayraktar, Nuray. 'Ankara Kent Merkezinde Bir Mücadele Alanı: Saraçoğlu Mahallesi'. *Betonart* 56 (2018): 42–7.

Bayram, Öztürk. *Gökçeada: Yeşilin ve Mavinin Özgür Dünyası* [*Gökçeada: The World of Blue and Green*]. Gökçeada: Gökçeada Belediyesi, 2002.

Bertolin, Chiara. *Preservation of Cultural Heritage and Resources Threatened by Climate Change*. Basel: MDPI, 2019.

Beşikçi, İsmail. *Devletlerarası Sömürge Kürdistan*. Istanbul: Alan Yayınları, 1991.

Bezci, Egemen and Güven Gürkan Öztan. 'Anatomy of the Turkish Emergency State: A Continuous Reflection of Turkish Raison d'état between 1980 and 2002'. *Middle East Critique* 25, no. 2 (2016): 163–79.

Bezmez, Dikmen. 'The Politics of Urban Waterfront Regeneration: The Case of Haliç (the Golden Horn), İstanbul'. *International Journal of Urban and Regional Research* 32, no. 4 (2009): 815–40.

Bhabha, Homi K. *The Location of Culture*. London: Routledge: 2004.

Bickersteth, Rupert. 'Edward Denison: "Under lockdown people appeared to have a newfound interest in architecture"'. *Architects' Journal*, 18 June 2020. https://www.architectsjournal.co.uk/news/culture/data-shows-air-pollution-plunged-during-lockdown-prompting-calls-for-radical-change/10047328.article.

Bilsel, Can. 'The Crisis in Conservation: Istanbul's Gezi Park between Restoration and Resistance'. *Journal of the Society of Architectural Historians* 76, no. 2 (2017): 141–5.

Bilsel, Cana. 'European Side of İstanbul Master Plan, 1937'. In *From the Imperial Capital to the Republican Modern City: Henri Prost's Planning of Istanbul (1936–1951)*, edited by Cana Bilsel and Pierre Pinon. İstanbul: Pera Müzesi Yayınları, 2010.

Biner, Zerrin Özlem. 'Precarious Solidarities: "Poisonous Knowledge" and the Academics for Peace in Times of Authoritarianism'. *Social Anthropology* 27, no. S2 (2019): 15–32.

Biner, Zerrin Özlem. *States of Dispossession: Violence and Precarious Coexistence in Southeast Turkey*. Philadelphia: University of Pennsylvania Press, 2020.

Bloxham, Donald. *The Great Game of Genocide: Imperialism, Nationalism, and the Destruction of the Ottoman Armenians*. New York: Oxford University Press, 2005.

Boano, Camillo. *The Ethics of a Potential Urbanism: Critical Encounters Between Giorgio Agamben and Architecture*. New York: Routledge, 2017.

Bora, Tanil. 'Türk Muhafazakarlığı ve İnşaat Şehveti – Büyük Olsun Bizim Olsun' [Turkish Conservatism and Construction Passion – Bigger is Better]. *Birikim* 270 (2011): 15–18.

Braidotti, Rosi. *Transpositions: On Nomadic Ethics*. Cambridge: Polity Press, 2006.

Brenner, Neil and Nik Theodore, eds. *Spaces of Neoliberalism: Urban Restructuring in Western Europe and North America*. Oxford: Blackwell, 2002.

Brickley, Megan B. and Roxana Ferllini. *Forensic Anthropology: Case Studies from Europe*. Springfield: Charles C. Thomas, 2007.

'Britain: On the Coronavirus and the social crisis – An open letter to the Trade Union movement from Labour Transformed'. *Links: International Journal of Socialist Movement*. Accessed 25 June 2020. http://links.org.au/britain-coronavirus-social-crisis-open-letter-trade-union-movement-labour-transformed.

British Comedy Guide. 'W1A: Lockdown Special'. Accessed 20 May 2020. https://www.comedy.co.uk/tv/w1a/episodes/2020/1/.

Buchan, Lizzy. 'Coronavirus: Lockdown One Week Earlier Could Have Halved UK's Death Toll, Says Neil Ferguson'. *Independent*, 10 June 2020. https://www.independent.co.uk/news/uk/politics/uk-lockdown-coronavirus-death-toll-neil-ferguson-a9559051.html.

Butler, Judith. *Antigone's Claim: Kinship between Life and Death*. New York: Columbia University Press, 2000.
Butler, Judith. *Precarious Life: The Powers of Mourning and Violence*. London: Verso, 2004.
Çalışkan, Olgu, ed. *Conflict, Planning and Design*. Ankara: METU Faculty of Architecture Press, 2018.
Çapan, Melike. '1964'ün 54. Yılında İmroz'dan Gökçeada'ya; Rum Tanıklar Anlatıyor: Kıbrıs'ta Ne Olsa Ceremesini Gökçeada Çekti'. *T24*, 6 September 2014. https://t2 4.com.tr/haber/1964un-54-yilinda-imrozdan-gokceadaya-rum-taniklar-anlatiyor -kibrista-ne-olsa-ceremesini-gokceada-cekti,604197.
Carr, Gillian and Keir Reeves, eds. *Heritage and Memory of War: Responses from Small Islands*. Routledge: New York, 2015. Kindle.
Çaylı, Eray. 'Bear Witness: Embedded Coverage of Turkey's Urban Warfare and the Demarcation of Sovereignty against a Dynamic Exterior'. *Theory & Event* 19, no. 1 supplement (2016), muse.jhu.edu/article/610225.
Çaylı, Eray. 'Democracy Under Construction, Construction as Regime: Design, Time and Imaginaries of Publicness in Mid-2010s Turkey'. In *Design, and Democracy: New Critical Perspectives*, edited by Michael Erlhoff and Maziar Rezai, 135–48. Basel: Birkhäuser, 2020.
Çaylı, Eray. 'Inheriting Dispossession, Mobilizing Vulnerability: Heritage amid Protest in Contemporary Turkey'. *International Journal of Islamic Architecture* 5, no. 2 (2016): 359–78.
Çaylı, Eray. '"Make it too public and the riot police will arrive": Turkey's Construction Boom as Opportunity and Publicness as Medium of Subversion'. *Archfondas* 4 (2015). http://www.archfondas.lt/leidiniu/node/175.
Çaylı, Eray. 'Making Violence Public: Spatializing (Counter)publicness through the 1993 Sivas Arson Attack, Turkey'. *International Journal of Urban and Regional Research* 43, no. 6 (2019): 1106–22.
Çaylı, Eray. *Victims of Commemoration: The Architecture and Violence of Confronting the Past in Turkey*. Syracuse: Syracuse University Press, 2021 (forthcoming).
Çelik, Zeynep. *The Remaking of İstanbul: Portrait of an Ottoman City in the Nineteenth Century*. London: University of California Press, 1986.
Cephanecigil, V. Gül. 'Preliminary Remarks on the Late Ottoman Churches in Aintab'. *ITU A|Z* 12, no. 2 (July 2015): 131–43.
Chanter, Tina. *Whose Antigone?: The Tragic Marginalization of Slavery*. Albany: State University of New York Press, 2011.
Chanter, Tina and Sean D. Kirkland, eds. *The Returns of Antigone: Interdisciplinary Essays*. Albany: State University of New York Press, 2014.

Cittaslow. 'Gökçeada'. Accessed 17 June 2018. http://www.cittaslow.org/network/gokceada.

Çızakca, Murat. *A History of Philanthrophic Foundations: The Islamic World from the Seventh Century to the Present*. İstanbul: Boğaziçi University Press, 2000.

Çolak, Yılmaz. 'Ottomanism vs. Kemalism: Collective memory and cultural pluralism in 1990s Turkey'. *Middle Eastern Studies* 42, no. 4 (2006): 587–602.

Çoruhlu, Yakup Emre and Osman Demir. 'Trabzon Ayasofya Camii'nin "Mülkiyet Hakkı" Üzerine Bir İnceleme'. *Vakıflar Dergisi* 42 (2014): 89–98.

Cosgrove, Denis Edmund. 'Should We Take It All So Seriously? Culture, Conservation and Meaning in the Contemporary World'. In *Durability and Change: The Practice, Responsibility and Cost of Sustaining Cultural Heritage*, edited by Wolfgang E. Krumbein, Peter Brimblecombe, Denis Edmund Cosgrove and Sarah Staniforth, 259–66. London: Wiley and Sons, 1994.

Court of Cassation Legal General Assembly 8.5.1974, case no: 1971/2-820. Decision no: 1974/505. *Yargıtay Dergisi* [*Journal of Court of Cassation Decisions*], August 1975.

Daleon, Jak. *Balat ve Çevresi*. İstanbul: Remzi Kitabevi, 1991.

Davis, Lennard J. *Enforcing Normalcy: Disability, Deafness, and the Body*. London and New York: Verso, 1995.

Derrida, Jacques. *Of Hospitality*. Stanford: Stanford University Press, 2000.

DeSilvey, Caitlin and Rodney Harrison. 'Anticipating Loss: Rethinking Endangerment in Heritage Futures'. *International Journal of Heritage Studies* 26, no. 1 (2020): 1–7.

Diken, Bülent and Carsten BaggeLaustsen. *The Culture of Exception: Sociology Facing the Camp*. London: Routledge, 2005.

Dinçer, İclal. 'The Impact of Neoliberal Policies on Historic Urban Space: Areas of Urban Renewal in Istanbul'. *International Planning Studies* 16, no. 1 (2011): 43–60.

Dinler, Mesut. 'Fener ve Balat'ın Dönüşümü Üzerine: Üç Vizyon/ Üç Dönem/ Üç Ayrı "Koruma" Anlayışı'. *Tüba-Ked* 14 (2016): 225–47.

Dinler, Mesut. 'Impact Assessment of Major Urban Interventions on the Cultural Heritage of Fener and Balat Districts'. MA diss., Middle East Technical University, 2013.

Dinler, Mesut. *Modernization through Past: Cultural Heritage during the Late-Ottoman and the Early Republican Period in Turkey*. Pisa: Edizioni ETS, 2019.

Directorate General of Human Rights and Legal Affairs. *ECRI Report on Turkey*. Strasbourg: Council of Europe, 2011.

Doğan, Evinç and Aleksandra Stupar. 'The Limits of Growth: A Case Study of Three Mega-Projects in Istanbul'. *Cities* 60, part A (2017): 281–8.

Doretti, Mercedes and Jennifer Burell. 'Forensic Anthropology in Peace Support Operations'. In *International and Comparative Criminal Law Series*, Volume 28, edited by Roberta Arnold, 179–95. Brill: Nijhoff, 2008. https://doi.org/10.1163/ej.9789004165106.i-442.71.

Dorroll, Courtney Michelle. 'The Spatial Politics of Turkey's Justice and Development Party (AK Party): On Erdoğanian Neo-Ottomanism'. PhD diss., University of Arizona, 2015.

Dostoğlu, Neslihan, Evren Enginöz, Serhat Kut and Erhan Karakoç, eds. *Architecture in Emergency: Rethinking the Refugee Crisis*. Istanbul: Istanbul Kültür University Press, 2016.

Ek, Richard. 'Giorgio Agamben and the Spatialities of the Camp: An Introduction'. *Geografiska Annaler Series B: Human Geography* 88, no. 4 (2006): 363–86.

Ekin Erkan, Nihal and Safiye Altıntaş. 'Soylulaştırmanın Gündelik Hayattaki Görünümleri: Balat'ın Mekânsal ve Sosyal Dönüşümü'. *idealkent* 23, no. 9 (2018): 292–335.

Ercan, Sevcan. 'Finding the Island of Imbros: A Spatial History of Displacement and Emplacement'. PhD diss., University College London, 2020.

Erol, Demet and Kaan Sakaklı. 'Saraçoğlu Mahallesi'nin Değerinin Değişimi'. In *Gazi Üniversitesi Şehir ve Bölge Planlama Bölümü 30. Kuruluş Yılı Anısına Seksen Sonrasi Mekan ve Planlama*, edited by Aysu Uğurlar et al., 385–400. Ankara: Gazi Üniversitesi, 2016.

Esposito, Adèle and Inès Gaulis. *The Cultural Heritages of Asia and Europe: Global Challenges and Local Initiatives*. Leiden and Amsterdam: International Institute for Asian Studies and the Asia-Europe Foundation, 2010.

European Parliament, EU-Turkey Statement, 2016. https://ec.europa.eu/home-affairs/sites/homeaffairs/files/what-we-do/policies/european-agendamigration/proposal-implementation package/docs/20160420/report_implementation_eu-turkey_agreement_nr_01_en.pdf.

Evin, Mehveş. 'Terörle Böyle mi Mücadele Edilecek?'. *Diken*, 4 April 2016. http://www.diken.com.tr/terorle-boyle-mi-mucadele-edilecek/.

Fatih Municipality, E.U., UNESCO WHC, French Institute of Anatolian Studies. *Balat ve Fener Semtlerinin Rehabilitasyonu (İstanbul Tarihi Yarımadası), Analiz ve Düzenleme Önerileri*. İstanbul, 1998.

Feldman, Leonard C. *Citizens without Shelter: Homelessness, Democracy, and Political Exclusion*. Ithaca: Cornell University Press, 2018.

Ferejohn, John and Pasquale Pasquino. 'The Law of Exception: A Typology of Emergency Powers'. *International Journal of Constitutional Law* 2, no. 2 (2004): 210–39.

Forensic Architecture. 'CGI Crime Scene Reconstruction Opens New Leads in Kurdish Activist Killing'. *Opendemocracy*, 8 February 2019. https://www.opendemocracy.net/en/cgi-crime-scene-reconstruction-opens-new-leads-in-tahir-elci-killing/.

Forensic Architecture. 'Report: Investigation of the Audio-visual Material Included in the Case File of the Killing of Tahir Elçi on 28 November 2015'. 13 December 2018. https://content.forensic-architecture.org/wp-content/uploads/2019/03/FA-TE-Report_12_English_public.pdf.

Forensic Architecture. 'Under the Radar'. Accessed 11 December 2019. https://forensic-architecture.org/programme/exhibitions/under-the-radar.

Foucault, Michel. *The Courage of the Truth (The Government of Self and Others II): Lectures at the Collège de France 1983–1984*, edited by Frédéric Gros. Translated by Graham Burchell. Basingstoke: Palgrave Macmillan, 2011.

Foucault, Michel. (edited by J. Pearson). 'Discourse and Truth: the Problematization of Parrhesia: Six Lectures given by Michel Foucault at the University of California at Berkeley, October–November 1983'. Foucault.info. Accessed 4 February 2020. https://foucault.info/parrhesia/.

Foucault, Michel. *Fearless Speech*, edited by Joseph Pearson. Los Angeles: Semiotext(e), 2001.

Foucault, Michel. *The Government of Self and Others I: Lectures at the Collège de France 1982–1983*, edited by Frédéric Gros. Translated by Graham Burchell. Basingstoke: Palgrave Macmillan, 2010.

Foucault, Michel. *Power/Knowledge: Selected Interviews and Other Writings, 1972–77*. New York: Pantheon, 1980.

Foucault, Michel. *Society Must Be Defended*. London: Penguin, 2003.

Foucault, Michel. *Society Must be Defended: Lectures at the Collège de France, 1975–1976*. London: Penguin, 2004.

Gambetti, Zeynep. 'Decolonizing Diyarbakir: Culture, Identity and the Struggle to Appropriate Urban Space'. In *Comparing Cities: The Middle East and South Asia*, edited by Kamran Asdar Ali and Martina Rieker, 5–127. Karachi: Oxford University Press, 2009.

Gambetti, Zeynep and Joost Jongerden. 'The Spatial (Re)production of the Kurdish Issue: Multiple and Contradicting Trajectories—Introduction'. *Journal of Balkan and Near Eastern Studies* 13, no. 4 (2011): 375–88.

Gaunt, David. *Katliamlar, Direniş, Koruyucular: I. Dünya Savaşı Sırasında Doğu Anadolu'da Müslüman-Hristiyan İlişkileri* [*Massacres, Resistance, Protectors: Muslim-Christian Relations in Eastern Anatolia during World War I*]. Istanbul: Belge Yayınları, 2007.

Geray, Cevdat. 'Belediyelerin hızlı kentleşmeye yenik düştüğü dönem (1945–1960)' [The period that municipalities got defeated by rapid urbanization (1945–1960)]. In *Türkiye Belediyeciliğinde 60 Yıl Uluslararası Sempozyum, Ankara, 23–24 Kasım 1990*, 217–24. Ankara: Ankara Büyükşehir Belediyesi, 1990.

Gökaçtı, Mehmet Ali. *Nüfus Mübadelesi* [*The Population Exchange*]. Istanbul: Iletisim Yayınları, 2004.

Gökarıksel, Saygun and Z. Umut Türem. 'The Banality of Exception? Law and Politics in "Post-Coup" Turkey'. *The South Atlantic Quarterly* 118, no. 1 (2019): 175–87.

Gölbaşı, Edip. '1895–96 Katliamları: Doğu Vilayetlerinde Cemaatler Arası Şiddet İklimi ve Ermeni Karşıtlığı [The Massacres of 1895–96: The Climate of Intercommunal Violence and Anti-Armenianism in the Eastern Provinces]'. In *1915: Siyaset, Tehcir ve Soykırım [Politics, Relocation and Genocide]*, edited by Oktay Özel and Fikret Adanır. Istanbul: Tarih Vakfı Yurt Yayınları, 2015.

Gölbaşı, Edip. 'The Official Conceptualization of the anti-Armenian Riots of 1895–1897: Bureaucratic Terminology, Official Ottoman Narrative, and Discourses of Revolutionary Provocation'. *Études Arméniennes Contemporaines* 10 (2017): 33–63.

Gregory, Derek. *The Colonial Present: Afghanistan, Palestine, Iraq*. Oxford: Blackwell, 2004.

Gross, Andreas. 'Gökçeada (Imbros) and Bozcaada (Tenedos): Preserving the Bicultural Character of the Two Turkish islands as a Model for Co-operation between Turkey and Greece in the Interest of the People Concerned'. *Committee on Legal Affairs and Human Rights*. Parliamentary Assembly 2008. Accessed 15 February 2018. http://assembly.coe.int/nw/xml/XRef/Xref-DocDetails-EN.asp?fileid=12011.

Gül, Murat. *Emergence of Modern Istanbul: Transformation and Modernisation of a City*. London and New York: I.B. Tauris, 2009.

Günay, Z., T. K. Koramaz and A. Ş. Özüekren. 'From Squatter Upgrading to Large-Scale Renewal Programmes: Housing Renewal in Turkey'. In *Renewing Europe's Housing*, edited by R. Turkington and C. Watson, 215–44. Bristol: Policy Press, 2014.

Güneydoğu Anadolu Bölgesi Belediyeler Birliği [South-east Anatolia Union of Municipalities]. 'Nusaybin Sokağa Çıkma ve Sonrası Durum ile İlgili Bilgilendirme Notu [Southeastern Anatolia Region Union of Municipalities, Information Note on Nusaybin Curfew and After]'. 2016. Accessed 11 December 2019. http://hakikatadalethafiza.org/kaynak/nusaybin-sokaga-cikma-yasagi-ve-sonrasi-durum-ile-ilgili-bilgilendirme-notu.

Güsten, Susanne. *A Farewell to Tur Abdin*. Istanbul: Istanbul Policy Center, 2016.

Güzel, Özlem. 'The Last Round in Restructuring the City: Urban Regeneration Becomes a State Policy of Disaster Prevention in Turkey'. *Cities* 50 (2016): 40–53.

Gwinn, Nancy E. and Johanna G. Wellheiser. *Preparing for the Worst, Planning for the Best: Protecting our Cultural Heritage from Disaster: Proceedings of a special IFLA conference held in Berlin in July 2003*. München: K. G. Saur, 2005.

Hackworth, Jason. *The Neoliberal City: Governance, Ideology, and Development in American Urbanism*. Ithaca: Cornell University Press, 2007.

Hall, Stuart. 'Whose Heritage? Un-Settling "The Heritage", Re-imagining the Post-Nation'. In *The Politics of Heritage, The Legacies of 'Race'*, edited by Jo Littler, 21–31. New York: Routledge, 2005.

Haraway, Donna. *Staying with the Trouble: Making Kin in the Chthulucene*. Durham and London: Duke University Press, 2016.

Hardt, Michael and Antonio Negri. *Multitude: War and Democracy in the Age of Empire*. New York: Penguin Press, 2004.

Harrison, Rodney. *Heritage: Critical Approaches*. London: Routledge, 2013.

Harrison, Rodney. 'Heritage Ontologies: Understanding Heritage as Future-Making Practices'. *Heritage Futures / Utopian Currents*, 4 June 2019. https://sites.grenadine.co/sites/patrimoine/en/ACHS2016/items/733.

Harrison, Rodney. 'Heritage as Social Action'. In *Understanding Heritage in Practice*, edited by Susie West, 240–76. Manchester: Manchester University Press, 2010.

Hart, Laurie Kain. *Time, Religion, and Social Experience in Rural Greece*. Lanham: Rowman & Littlefield, 1992.

Harvey, David. *A Brief History of Neoliberalism*. Oxford: Oxford University Press, 2002.

Harvey, David C. 'Heritage Pasts and Heritage Presents: Temporality, Meaning and the Scope of Heritage Studies'. *International Journal of Heritage Studies* 7, no. 4 (2001): 319–38.

Heyman, Philip. *Terrorism, Freedom, and Security: Winning without War*. Cambridge, MA, and London: The MIT Press, 2003.

Houston, Donna. 'Crisis Is Where We Live: Environmental Justice for the Anthropocene'. *Globalizations* 10, no. 3 (2013): 439–50.

Human Rights Watch. 'Time for Justice: Ending Impunity for Killings and Disappearances in 1990s Turkey'. 3 September 2012. https://www.hrw.org/report/2012/09/03/time-justice/ending-impunity-killings-and-disappearances-1990s-turkey.

Huyssen, Andreas. *Present Pasts: Urban Palimpsests and the Politics of Memory*. Stanford: Stanford University Press, 2003.

İçduygu, Ahmet. 'Syrian Refugees in Turkey: The Long Road Ahead'. *Transatlantic Council on Migration: Migration Policy Institute*, 2015. Accessed 09 April 2020. www.migrationpolicy.org/transatlantic.

İHD. 'Kayıpları Unutmadık'. 2003. Accessed 11 December 2019. http://www.ihd.org.tr/wp-content/uploads/2007/11/kayiplari_unutmadik.pdf.

Ilıcak, Şükrü and Jonathan Varjabedian. *My Dear Son Garabed, I Read Your Letter, I Cried, I Laughed*. Istanbul: Histor Press, 2018.

Imvrians on the Net. 'Σύλλογος Ιμβρίων [The Imbrian Syllogos]'. Accessed 20 March 2019. http://www.imvrosisland.org/imvros.php?catid=2.

İnalcık, Halil. 'Istanbul: An Islamic City'. *Journal of Islamic Studies* 1 (1990): 1–23.

İnce, Ayça. 'Converted Spaces, Converted Meanings: Looking at New Cultural Spaces in Istanbul through a Cultural Policy Lens'. In *Turkish Cultural Policies in a Global World*, edited by M. Girard, J. Polo and C. Scalbert-Yücel, 105–25. Cam: Springer International Publishing, 2018.

International Crisis Group. 'Türkiye'deki PKK Çatışmasını Yönetmek: Nusaybin Örneği' [Governing PKK Conflict in Turkey: The Case of Nusaybin]. 2017. Accessed 11 December 2019. https://d2071andvip0wj.cloudfront.net/243-man aging-turkeys-pkk-conflict-turkish.pdf.

İslam, Tolga. 'Current Urban Discourse, Urban Transformation and Gentrification in Istanbul'. *Architectural Design* 80, no. 1 (2010): 58–63.

İslam, Tolga. 'Outside the Core: Gentrification in Istanbul'. In *Gentrification in a Global Context: The New Urban Colonialism*, edited by Rowland Atkinson and Gary Bridge, 123–38. London: Routledge, 2005.

Istanbul Chamber of Architects. 'Basına ve Kamuoyuna: Atatürk Kültür Merkezi 9 yıldır kapalı!'. 28 June 2017. http://www.mimarist.org/basina-ve-kamuoyuna-a taturk-kultur-merkezi-9-yildir-kapali/.

İstanbul Tarihi Alanları Alan Başkanlığı. *Istanbul Historic Peninsula Site Management Plan, 2018*. Accessed 27 April 2020. http://www.alanbaskanligi.gov.tr/tya/samples/magazine/slider.html.

Jongerden, Joost. 'Conquering the State and Subordinating Society under AKP Rule: A Kurdish Perspective on the Development of a New Autocracy in Turkey'. *Journal of Balkan and Near Eastern Studies* 21, no. 3 (2019): 260–73.

Jongerden, Joost. 'Crafting Space, Making People: The Spatial Design of Nation in Modern Turkey'. *European Journal of Turkish Studies* 10 (2009). http://journals.openedition.org/ejts/4014.

Jongerden, Joost. *The Settlement Issue in Turkey and the Kurds: An Analysis of Spatial Policies, Modernity and War*. Leiden: Brill, 2007.

Jongerden, Joost. 'Under (Re)Construction: The State, the Production of Identity, and the Countryside in the Kurdistan Region in Turkey'. In *After Civil War: Division, Reconstruction, and Reconciliation in Contemporary Europe*, edited by Bill Kissane, 150–87. Philadelphia: University of Pennsylvania Press, 2014.

Kant, Immanuel. *Perpetual Peace: A Philosophical Essay*. Translated by M. C. Smith. New York: Macmillan, 2001 [1795].

Kaplanoğlu, Raif. 'Bursa Kiliseleri' [Churches of Bursa]. *Bursa Araştırmaları Dergisi* [Journal of Bursa Studies] 30, no. 8 (2010): 10–25.

Karaca, Zafer. *İstanbul'da Osmanlı Dönemi Rum Kiliseleri*. İstanbul: Yapı Kredi Yayınları, 1995.

Karaman, Ozan. 'Urban Neoliberalism with Islamic Characteristics'. *Urban Studies* 50, no. 16 (2013): 3412–27.

Karas, Meliton. 'İmroz'da Dini Hayat ve Kiliseler [The Religion and Churches on Imbros]'. In *İmroz Rumları: Gökçeada Üzerine [Rums of Imbros]*, edited by Feryal Tansuğ, 50–79. İstanbul: Heyamola, 2013.

Kavuncu, Ömer Faruk. *Suriyelilerin Sosyal Uyumunda Sivil Toplumun Rolü*. Gaziantep: BEKAM, 2018.

Kaya, Deniz İkiz and Mehmet Çalhan. 'Impediment or Resource? Contextualisation of the Shared Built Heritage in Turkey'. In *Cultural Contestation: Palgrave Studies in Cultural Heritage and Conflict*, edited by Jeroen Rodenberg and Pieter Wagenaar, 81–103. Cham: Palgrave Macmillan, 2018.

Kaya, Önder. 'İzmir Sinagogları [Synagogues of İzmir]'. *Şalom*, 4 January 2017. http://www.salom.com.tr/arsiv/haber-101636-Izmir_sinagoglari.html.

Kayasü, Serap and Emine Yetişkul. 'Evolving Legal and Institutional Frameworks of Neoliberal Urban Policies in Turkey'. *METU Journal of Faculty of Architecture* 31, no. 2 (2014): 209–22.

Keenan, Thomas and Eyal Weizman. *Mengele's Skull: The Advent of a Forensic Aesthetics*. Berlin: Sternberg Press, 2012.

Kevorkian, Raymond. *The Armenian Genocide: A Complete History*. London: I.B. Tauris, 2011.

Keyder, Çağlar. 'Imperial, National, and Global Istanbul: Three Istanbul 'Moments' from the Nineteenth to Twenty-First Centuries'. In *Istanbul: Living with Difference in a Global City*, edited by N. Fisher-Onar, S. C. Pearce and E. F. Keyman, 25–37. New Brunswick: Rutgers University Press, 2018.

Keyder, Çağlar. 'The Setting'. In *Istanbul: Between the Global and the Local*, edited by Çağlar Keyder, 3–31. Lanham: Rowman and Littlefield Publishers, 1999.

Kindingen, Evangelia and Mark Schmitt, eds. *The Intersections of Whiteness*. Oxon and New York: Routledge, 2019.

Köksal, Gül. *On Contemporary Urbanization in Turkey*. İstanbul: Heinrich Böll Stiftung Turkey, 2020. https://tr.boell.org/en/2020/01/28/contemporary-urbanization-turkey.

Kouymjian, Dickran. 'The Destruction of Armenian Historical Monuments as a Continuation of the Turkish Policy of Genocide'. In *A Crime of Silence: The Armenian Genocide*, edited by Gerard Libaridian, 173–85. London: Zed Books, 1985.

Kurgan, Laura. 'Residues: ICTY Courtroom No.1 and the Architecture of Justice'. In *Alphabet City 7: Social Insecurity*, edited by Cornelius Heesters and Len Guether, 112–29. Toronto: House of Anansi. 2001.

Kurt, Ümit. 'Birinci Cihan Harbi Sonrası Ermeni Mallarının İadesi Cebel-i Bereket Örneği [Return of Armenian Goods After WWI: The Cebel-i Bereket Example]'. In *Yok Edilen Medeniyet: Geç Osmanlı ve Erken Cumhuriyet Dönemlerinde*

Gayrimüslim Varlığı [*A Civilization Destroyed: Non-Muslim Presence in the Late Ottoman and Early Republican Periods*], edited by Ararat Şekeryan and Nvart Taşçı, 202–14. Istanbul: Aras Yayınları, 2017.

Kurt, Ümit. 'The Plunder of Wealth through Abandoned Properties Laws in the Armenian Genocide'. *Genocide Studies International* 10, no. 1 (Spring 2016): 38.

Kuruyazıcı, Hasan and Eva Şarlak. *Batılılaşan İstanbul'un Rum Mimarları*, 60–80. İstanbul: Zoğrafyon Lisesi Mezunları Derneği, 2010.

Kuymulu, Mehmet Barış. 'Reclaiming the Right to the City: Reflections on the Urban Uprisings in Turkey'. *City* 17, no. 3 (2013): 274–8.

Kuyucu, Tuna. 'Politics of Urban Regeneration in Turkey: Possibilities and Limits of Municipal Regeneration Initiatives in a Highly Centralized Country'. *Urban Geography* 39, no. 8 (2018): 1152–76.

Kuyucu, Tuna and Didem Danış. 'Similar Processes, Divergent Outcomes: A Comparative Analysis of Urban Redevelopment Projects in Three Turkish Cities'. *Urban Affairs Review* 51, no. 3 (2015): 381–413.

Lefebvre, Henri. *The Critiques of Everyday Life*. London and New York: Verso, [1961] 2005. Kindle.

Levi, Ayner. *Türkiye Cumhuriyeti'nde Yahudiler* [*Jews in the Turkish Republic*]. Istanbul: İletişim Yayınları, 2010.

Lewis, Stephen. 'Gezi Park/Taksim Square: A Change of Banners on the Atatürk Cultural Center + A Few Words on the Iconography of Public Space'. 24 June 2013. https://bubkes.org/2013/06/24/gezi-parktaksim-square-ataturk-cultural-center-during-and-after-occupation-plus-a-word-on-the-iconography-of-public-space/.

Lowenthal, David. *The Past Is a Foreign Country*. Cambridge: Cambridge University Press, 1999.

Luxmoore, Jonathan. 'Swiss Scholars Want Famous Church Returned Before Turkey Joins EU'. *Catholic News Service*, 25 September 2005. http://www.orthodoxytoday.org/articles5/LuxmooreHagiaSophia.php.

Madran, Emre. 'Cumhuriyet'in İlk Otuz Yılında (1920-1950) Koruma Alanında Örgütlenmesi'. *METU Journal of Faculty of Architecture* 16, no. 1 (1996): 59–97.

Malkki, Liisa H. 'Refugees and Exile: From "Refugee Studies" to the National Order of Things'. *Annual Review of Anthropology*, no. 24 (1995): 495–523. www.annualreviews.org.

Mannaert, Celia. 'New Issues in Refugee Research, Irregular Migration and Asylum in Turkey'. Working Paper No. 89 for Evaluation and Policy Analysis Unit, United Nations High Commissioner for Refugees. 2013. Accessed 9 April 2020. https://www.unhcr.org/3ebf5c054.pdf.

McKittrick, Katherine. 'Axis, Bold as Love: On Sylvia Wynter, Jimi Hendrix and the Promise of Science'. In *Sylvia Wynter: On Being Human as Praxis*, edited by

Katherine McKittrick, 142–63. Durham and London: Duke University Press, 2015.

Mitchell, Timothy. *Rule of Experts: Egypt, Techno-Politics, Modernity*. Berkeley and Los Angeles; London: University of California Press, 2002.

Mülteciler (Refugees). 'Türkiyedeki Suriyeli Sayısı'. 2019. Accessed 9 April 2020. https ://multeciler.org.tr/turkiyedeki-suriyeli-sayisi/.

Nichols, Theo, Nadir Sugur and Serap Sugur. 'Muhacir Bulgarian Workers in Turkey: Their Relation to Management and Fellow Workers in the Formal Employment Sector'. *Middle Eastern Studies* 39, no. 2 (2003): 37–54. https://www.jstor.org/stable /4284291.

Nora, Pierre. 'Between Memory and History: Les Lieux de Mémoire'. *Representations* 26, Special Issue: Memory and Counter-Memory (1989): 7–24.

Official Newspaper. 'Law No. 5393; Municipality Law'. *Resmi Gazete*, n. 25874, 3 May 2005. http://www.resmigazete.gov.tr/eskiler/2005/07/20050713-6.htm.

Official Newspaper. 'Law No. 6458: Law on Foreigners and International Protection'. *Resmi Gazete*, no. 28615, 11 April 2013.

Official Newspaper. 'The Settlement Law' [İskan Kanunu]. Law No. 2510, 14 June 1934. *Resmi Gazete*, no. 2733, 21 June 1934. http://www.resmigazete.gov.tr/arsiv /2733.pdf.

Official Newspaper. 'Türkiye'ye İltica Eden veya Başka Bir Ülkeye İltica Etmek Üzere Türkiyeden İkamet İzni Talep Eden Münferit Yabancılarile Topluca Sığınma Amacıyla Sınırlarımıza Gelen Yabancılara ve Olabilecek Nüfus Hareketlerine Uygulanacak Usul ve Esaslar Hakkında Yönetmelik'. *Resmi Gazete*, no. 22127, 30 November 1994. http://www.multeci.org.tr/wp-content/uploads/2016/12/1994 -Yonetmeligi.pdf.

Oltermann, Philip and Constanze Letsch. 'Turkey Recalls Ambassador after German MPs' Armenian Genocide Note'. *The Guardian*, 2 June 2016. Accessed 26 January 2019. https://www.theguardian.com/world/2016/jun/02/germany-braces-for-turki sh-backlash-as-it-votes-to-recognise-armenian-genocide.

Onaran, Nevzat. *Cumhuriyet'te Ermeni ve Rum Mallarının Türkleştirilmesi: Emval-i Metrukenin Tasfiyesi-I (1914–1919) [Turkification of Armenian and Greek Commodities in the Republic: Liquidation of the Abandoned Property (1914–1919)]*. Istanbul: Evrensel Yayınevi, 2013.

Öncü, Ayşe. 'The Politics of İstanbul's Ottoman Heritage in the Era of Globalism: Refractions through the Prism of a Theme Park'. In *Cities of the South: Citizenship and Exclusion in the 21st Century*, edited by B. Mermier, F. Drieskens and H. Wimmen, 233–64. Beirut: Saqi Books, 2007.

Öner, Suna Gülfer Ihlamur. 'İnsani Boyutlarıyla Suriye Krizi'. *Ortadoğu Analiz Dergisi* 61, no. 6 (2014): 42–5.

Örs, İlay Romain. *İstanbullu Rumlar ve 1964 Sürgünleri* [*Rums of Istanbul and the 1964 Exiles*]. Istanbul: Iletisim Yayınları, 2019.

Ötüken, Yıldız, Aynur Durukan, Hakkı Acun and Sacit Pekak. *Türkiye'de Vakıf Abideler ve Eski Eserler IV* [*Foundation Monuments and Historic Buildings in Turkey*]. Ankara: Vakıflar Genel Müdürlüğü Yayınları, 1986.

Oxford English Dictionary. Oxford University Press, 2020. oed.com.

Özçakır, Özgün, Güliz Bilgin Altınöz and Anna Mignosa. 'Political Economy of Renewal of Heritage Places in Turkey'. *METU Journal of Faculty of Architecture* 23, no. 2 (2018): 221–50.

Özkan Eren, Miray and Özlem Özçevik. 'Institutionalization of Disaster Risk Discourse in Reproducing Urban Space in Istanbul'. *ITU A|Z* 12, no. 1 (2015): 221–42.

Özkırımlı, Umut, ed. *The Making of a Protest Movement in Turkey: #occupygezi*. New York: Palgrave Macmillan, 2014.

Özkut, Gizem Tuğba and Jülide Aşçı. 'Long-Lasting State of Emergency: Use of (In)securities for Consolidation of Power in Turkey'. *Democracy and Security* 16, no. 3 (2020): 189–209.

Öztemiz, Mutay. *II. Abdulhamit'ten Günümüze Süryaniler* [*Syriacs from Abdülhamit II to Today*]. Istanbul: Ayrıntı Yayınları, 2012.

Parliament Papers. 'Treaty Series no. 16: Treaty of Peace with Turkey, and Other Instruments Signed at Lausanne on July 24, 1923, Together with Agreements between Greece and Turkey Signed on January 30, 1923, and Subsidiary Documents Forming Part of the Turkish Peace Settlement'. Accessed 21 June 2016. http://parlipapers.chadwyck.co.uk/fullrec/fullrec.do?id=1923-026125&DurUrl=Yes.

'Parliamentary Inquiry for Investigation of "Ceylanpınar"'. *Bianet*, 6 March 2018.

Pasotti, Eleonora. *Resisting Redevelopment: Protest in Aspiring Global Cities*. Cambridge: Cambridge University Press, 2020.

Pearson, Lionel. 'Party Politics and Free Speech in Democratic Athens'. *Greece & Rome* 7, no. 19 (1937): 41–50.

Peck, Jamie. *Constructions of Neoliberal Reason*. Oxford: Oxford University Press, 2010.

Peck, Jamie and Adam Tickell. 'Neoliberalizing Space'. *Antipode* 34, no. 3 (2002): 380–404.

Pekol, Banu, ed. *Kayseri Adana İzmir Elazığ Niğde Bursa: Assessment Reports of Cultural Heritage*. Istanbul: Anadolu Kültür, 2018.

Penpecioğlu, Mehmet. 'Urban Development Projects and the Construction of Neo-Liberal Urban Hegemony: The Case of Izmir'. *METU Journal of the Faculty of Architecture* 30, no. 1 (2013): 165–90.

Pereira Roders, Ana and Francesco Bandarin, eds. *Reshaping Urban Conservation: The Historic Urban Landscape Approach in Action*. Springer, 2019.

Pınarcıoğlu, Melih and Oğuz Işık. 'Not Only Helpless but also Hopeless: Changing Dynamics of Urban Poverty in Turkey, the Case of Sultanbeyli, Istanbul'. *European Planning Studies* 16, no. 10 (2008): 1353–70.

Povinelli, Elizabeth. *Economies of Abandonment: Social Belonging and Endurance in Late Liberalism*. Durham: Duke University Press, 2011.

'President Erdoğan: Turkey will Continue Open Door Policy for Syrian Refugees'. *Daily Sabah*, 13 March 2016. https://www.dailysabah.com/politics/2016/03/13/president-erdogan-turkey-will-continue-open-door-policy-for-syrian-refugees.

Prost, Henri. *Taksim Amenagement Des Terrains de la Caserne*, File no: 40 Hrt_Gec_002057. Atatürk Library Archives.

Pye, Elizabeth. *Caring for the Past: Issues in Conservation for Archaeology and Museums*. London: James & James, 2000.

Rendell, Jane. 'Giving An Account Of Oneself, Architecturally'. *Journal of Visual Culture* 15, no. 3 (2016): 334–48.

Rico, Trinidad. 'Heritage at Risk: The Authority and Autonomy of a Dominant Preservation Framework'. In *Heritage Keywords: Rhetoric and Redescription in Cultural Heritage*, edited by K. L. Samuels and T. Rico, 146–62. Boulder: University Press of Colorado, 2015.

Riegl, Alois. 'The Modern Cult of Monuments: Its Character and Its Origins'. *Oppositions* 25 (1951): 21–51.

Ryan, Jackson. 'COVID-19 Lockdowns Caused an "Extreme" Reduction in Carbon Emissions'. *Cnet*. Accessed 10 July 2020, https://www.cnet.com/news/covid-19-lockdowns-caused-an-extreme-reduction-in-carbon-emissions/.

Şahin, Çigdem. 'Fener-Balat Dönüşüm Projesinde Nereden Nereye'. *Arkitera* 12 (2012). Accessed 14 December 2012. http://www.arkitera.com/haber/index/detay/fener-balat-donusum-projesinde-nereden-nereye/11358.

Şahin Güçhan, Neriman and Esra Kurul. 'A History of Development of Conservation Measures in Turkey: From the Mid-19th Century Until 2004'. *METU Journal of Faculty of Architecture* 26, no. 2 (2009): 19–44.

Salama, M. Cohen. *Tumbas Anónimas: Informe sobre la identificación de restos de víctimas de la represión ilegal*. Buenos Aires: Catálogos Editora, 1992.

Sarı, Gökhan. *Ermeni Meselesi Işığında Süryaniler [Syriacs in Light of the Armenian Matter]*. Ankara: Barış Platin, 2013.

Say, Yaşar Ozan. 'Celebrating the Saints in Imbros: The Politics of Ritual and Belonging in Turkey'. PhD diss., Indiana University, 2013.

Saygı, Erol. *Gökçeada/Imbros/Ἴμβρος*. İzmir: Erol Saygı, 2010.

Schmidli, W. Michael. 'Institutionalizing Human Rights in U.S. Foreign Policy: U.S.-Argentine Relations, 1976-1980'. *Diplomatic History* 35, no. 2 (2011): 351–77.

Schmitt, Carl. *Political Theology: Four Chapters on the Concept of Sovereignty*. Translated by George D. Schwab. Cambridge, MA: MIT Press, 1985.

Schmitt, Carl. *Political Theology: Four Chapters on the Concept of Sovereignty.* Chicago: University of Chicago Press, 2005.

Schuppli, Susan. 'Entering Evidence: Cross-examining the Court Records of the ICTY'. In *Forensis: The Architecture of the Public Truth*, edited by Forensic Architecture, 279–316. Berlin: Sternberg Press, 2014.

Sennett, Richard. *The Fall of Public Man.* London: Faber and Faber, 1986.

Serageldin, Mona. 'Preserving the Historic Urban Fabric in a Context of Fast-Paced Change'. In *Values and Heritage Conservation*, edited by Erica Avrami, Randall Mason and Marta de la Torre, 51–8. Los Angeles: The Getty Conservation Institute, 2000.

Sevim, Emre, Ibrahim Zivrali and Nurşah Ü. Cabbar. 'A World Heritage Site: Diyarbakır under the Shade of Conflicts'. *Proceedings of Tcl 2016 Conference, Infota* (2016): 503–16. http://tcl.infota.org/proceedings/articles/Proceedings_TCL2016.pdf

Shaw, Stanford J. *The Jews of the Ottoman Empire and the Turkish Republic.* New York: New York University Press, 1991.

Simmel, Georg. 'The Bridge and the Door'. In *Rethinking Architecture: A Reader in Cultural Theory*, edited by N. Leach, 64–8. London: Routledge, 1997,

Smith, Laurajane. 'Discussion'. In *Heritage Regimes and The State*, edited by R. F. Bendix, A. Eggert and A. Peselmann, 389–95. Göttingen: Universitätsverlag Göttingen, 2013.

Smith, Laurajane, Margaret Wetherell and Gary Campbell, eds. *Emotion, Affective Practices, and the Past in the Present.* London: Routledge, 2018.

Smith, Laurajane. *Uses of Heritage.* London: Routledge, 2006.

Sofsky, Wolfgang. *The Order of Terror: The Concentration Camp.* Princeton: Princeton University Press, 1997.

Sophocles. *The Theban Plays: Oedipus the Tyrant, Oedipus at Colonus, Antigone.* Translated by Peter J. Ahrensdorf and Thomas L. Pangle. Ithaca: Cornell University Press, 2014.

Spencer, Douglas. *The Architecture of Neoliberalism: How Contemporary Architecture Became an Instrument of Control and Compliance.* London: Bloomsbury, 2016.

Stoler, Ann. *Imperial Durabilities in Modern Times.* Durham: Duke University Press, 2016.

Stovel, Herb. *Risk Preparedness: A Management Manual for World Cultural Heritage.* Rome: ICCROM, 1998.

Tahir Elçi Vakfı. 'Savcılık Adli Tıp'tan yeni rapor istedi'. Published 3 April 2019. http://www.tahirelcivakfi.org/savcilik-adli-tip-tan-yeni-rapor-istedi/.

Tahir Elçi Vakfı. 'Vakfımızdan Suç Duyurusu'. Published 23 September 2019. http://www.tahirelcivakfi.org/vakfimizdan-suc-duyurusu/.

Tansel, Cemar Burak. 'Reproducing Authoritarian Neoliberalism in Turkey: Urban Governance and State Restructuring in the Shadow of Executive Centralization'. *Globalizations* 16, no. 3 (2019): 320–35.

Tas, Diren. 'Urban Transformation as Political and Ideological Intervention in Space: A Case Study in Diyarbakir'. MA diss., Middle East Technical University, Ankara, 2019.

Tekin, Ilke, Asiye Akgün Gültekin. 'Rebuilding of Beyoğlu-İstiklal Street: A Comparative Analysis of Urban Transformation through Sections Along the Street 2004-2014'. *METU Journal of Faculty of Architecture* 34, no. 2 (2017): 153-79.

TIHV. 'Cizre Field Report, 31 March 2016'. Accessed 11 December 2019. http://en.tihv.org.tr/wp-content/uploads/2017/10/Cizre-Field-Report.pdf.

TMMOB Diyarbakir Provincial Coordination Board. *2015-2016: TMMOB Destroyed Cities Report*. Ankara: Union of Chambers of Turkish Engineers and Architects, 2017.

Tozer, Henry Fanshawe. *Turkish Armenia*. London: Longmans Green and Co., 1881.

Tsimouris, Giorgos. 'Pilgrimages to Gökçeada (Imvros), a Greco-Turkish Contested Place: Religious Tourism or a Way to Reclaim the Homeland'. In *Pilgrimage, Politics and Place-Making in Eastern Europe: Crossing the Borders*, edited by John Eade and Mario Katic, chapter 3. Surrey and Burlington: Ashgate, 2014. Kindle.

Tsimouris, Giorgos. 'Reconstructing "Home" among the "Enemy": The Greeks of Gökçeada (Imvros) after Lausanne'. *Balkanologie: Revue d'études pluridisciplinaires* 5, nos 1-2 (2001): 1-15. http://journals.openedition.org/balkanologie/727.

Tuğal, Cihan. 'Urban Symbolic Violence Re-Made: Religion, Politics and Spatial Struggles in İstanbul'. *International Journal of Urban and Regional Research* 45, no. 1 (2021): 154-63.

Tumarkin, Maria. *Traumascapes: The Power and Fate of Places Transformed by Tragedy*. Victoria: Melbourne University Press, 2005.

'Türkiye İnsan Hakları Vakfı'. *2003 Türkiye İnsan Hakları Raporu*. Ankara: Buluş, 2004.

Türkiye İstatistik Kurumu [Turkish Statistical Institute]. 'Çanakkale İmroz İlçelere göre Şehir ve Köy Nüfusları [City and Village Populations of Çanakkale Imbros]'. 1965 Genel Nüfus Sayımı Veri Tabanı [Database of 1965 General Census of Population]. Accessed 21 March 2019. http://rapory.tuik.gov.tr/21-03-2019-17:25:44-11512968171252922092697253647.html?

'Türkiye'nin Başında İki Bela Var'. *Milliyet*, 7 October 1984. http://gazetearsivi.milliyet.com.tr/Arsiv/1984/10/07.

Türkmen, Hade. 'Urban Renewal Projects and Dynamics of Contention in Istanbul: The Cases of Fener-Balat-Ayvansaray and Suleymaniye'. PhD diss., Cardiff University, 2014.

Türkün, Asuman. 'Urban Regeneration and Hegemonic Power Relationships'. *International Planning Studies* 16, no. 1 (2011): 61-72.

Turner, Joe, 'Internal Colonisation: The Intimate Circulations of Empire, Race and Liberal Government'. *European Journal of International Relations* 24, no. 4 (2018): 765–90.

Üngör, Uğur Ü. and Mehmet Polatel. *Confiscation and Destruction: The Young Turk Seizure of Armenian Property*. New York: Continuum, 2011.

UNHCR. 'Syria Regional Refugee Response: Turkey, Operational Portal Refugee Response, 2019'. Accessed 09 April 2020. https://data2.unhcr.org/en/situations/syria/location/113.

UNHCR. 'Türkiye'deki Suriyeli Mülteciler için Sıkça Sorulan Sorular, İkamet ve Hareketlilik Bölümü'. Accessed 9 April 2020. https://data2.unhcr.org/en/documents/download/59167.

United Nations. *Report of the United Nations Conference on Human Settlements* (Habitat II). Istanbul: United Nations, 1996.

Ünsal, Özlem. 'Inner City Regeneration and the Politics of Resistance in Istanbul: A Comparative Analysis of Sulukule and Tarlabaşı'. PhD diss., City University London, 2013.

US Embassy to Secretary of State Vance. 'Videla's Visit: Videla's Position on the Eve of His U.S. Visit'. *ADP*, 2 September 1977.

Uysal, Ülke Evrim. 'An Urban Social Movement Challenging Urban Regeneration: The case of Sulukule, Istanbul'. *Cities* 29, no. 1 (2012): 12–22.

Varjabedian, Jonathan. 'Efkere: Surp Garabed Monastery'. Accessed 30 October 2018. http://efkere.com/places-of-worship/surp-garabed-monastery/.

Viñas, Salvador Muñoz. *Contemporary Theory of Conservation*. Amsterdam: Elsevier Butterworth Heinemann, 2005.

'We will Continue our "open door" Policy for Syrians'. *Anadolu Agency*, 3 April 2013. https://www.aa.com.tr/en/turkey/we-will-continue-our-open-door-policy-for-syrians/258882.

Weber, Cynthia. *Queer International Relations: Sovereignty, Sexuality and the Will to Knowledge*. Oxford: Oxford University Press, 2015.

Weizman, Eyal. *Forensic Architecture: Violence at the Threshold of Detectability*. New York: Zone Books, 2017.

Wynter, Sylvia and Katherine McKittrick. 'Unparalleled Catastrophe for our Species? Or, to give Humanness a Different Future: Conversations'. In *Sylvia Wynter: On Being Human as Praxis*, edited by Katherine McKittrick, 9–89. Durham and London: Duke University Press, 2015.

Yackley, Ayla Jean. 'Court ruling Converting Turkish Museum to Mosque could Set Precedent for Hagia Sophia'. *The Art Newspaper*, 3 December 2019. https://www.theartnewspaper.com/news/court-ruling-converting-turkish-museum-to-mosque-could-set-precedent-for-hagia-sophia.

Yonucu, Deniz. 'The Absent Present Law: An Ethnographic Study of Legal Violence in Turkey'. *Social & Legal Studies* 27, no. 6 (2018): 716–33.

Yonucu, Deniz. 'Urban Vigilantism: A Study of Anti-Terror Law, Politics and Policing in Istanbul'. *International Journal of Urban and Regional Research* 42, no. 3 (2018): 408–22.

Yücel, Tahsin, ed. *Rum Olmak Rum Kalmak* [*Being Rum Remaining Rum*]. İstanbul: İstos Yayınları, 2016.

Zafiriadis, Aleksandros. *Η Ιστορία της Εκκλησίας Ίμβρου* [*The History of the Imbros Church*]. Athens: 1938.

Zeiderman, Austin, Sobia Ahmad Kaker, Jonathan David Silver and Astrid Wood. 'Uncertainty and Urban Life'. *Public Culture* 27, no. 2 (2015): 281–304.

Zencirci, Gizem. 'Civil Society's History: New Constructions of Ottoman Heritage by the Justice and Development Party in Turkey'. *European Journal of Turkish Studies* (2014). http://ejts.revues.org/5076.

Index

Agamben, Giorgio   2, 3, 23, 46, 139, 189, 196
agora   13, 14, 90, 91, 93, 97
AKP (Justice and Development Party)   6, 21, 24, 26, 31, 35, 100, 161–3, 165, 174, 178
aletheia   96
amalgamation   151, 176
Amed (Kurdish for Diyarbakır)   5, 13, 69–73, 75–7, 79, 81, 83–5
Antigone   95–9, 103, 104, 196
anti-minority   138, 143
architectural heritage   43, 46, 47, 55, 57, 61, 62, 160, 177
Armenian   5, 25, 43, 45, 47, 51–4, 56–60, 62, 75, 82
asylum seeker   116
Atatürk Cultural Centre   12, 21, 22, 29, 30
authorized heritage discourse   22, 23, 34, 35

Balat   15, 16, 159, 160, 167–78
biopolitics   2, 3

camp   3, 115, 117, 118, 121, 123–6, 132, 133
catastrophe (including disaster)   2, 6, 12–14, 179, 193, 195, 196
central authority   165, 174, 178
citizenship   113–16, 118, 119, 121, 144, 146
cityzenship (hemşehri)   126, 128, 132
civilizational   73
  civilizationalism (including civilizationalist)   74, 77, 80
colonialism   71, 73, 80, 194
  colonization (including internal colonization)   13, 71–4, 83–5
construction   xiii, 2, 4, 8, 11, 13, 21, 29–31, 33, 44, 69, 70, 75, 81, 83, 93, 101, 106, 120, 145, 147, 160, 161, 165, 167, 169, 172, 194
  construction boom   2, 6, 8, 75

container   122–6
contested heritage   56
counterinsurgency   74
Creon   96–8, 103, 104
cultural heritage   xiii, 29–32, 35, 45, 50, 57, 101, 163, 174, 178

democracy   1, 4, 6, 13, 61, 90, 91, 97
democratization   4, 6, 75
development (including redevelopment), xiii   1, 4, 7, 8, 10, 11, 76, 79, 80, 83, 141, 160, 161, 163, 164, 171, 172
developmentalism (including developmentalist)   74, 77, 80, 84, 85
diaspora   15, 44, 46, 137, 138, 144, 145, 148, 149, 153
disaster (catastrophe)   4, 10, 11, 13, 16, 61, 70, 71, 75, 93, 121
  Disaster Act   4, 8, 9, 11–13, 15, 16, 32, 35, 70, 79, 80, 84, 85, 190
  Disaster Law   161, 164, 177
  disaster risk   8, 32–5, 164
displacement   xiii, 2, 6, 10–12, 14–16, 84, 132, 140, 142, 144, 145, 147–50, 152, 164, 165, 170, 175, 178, 179, 193, 195
Diyarbakır (Turkish for Amed)   5, 13, 69, 76–8, 82, 83, 101–3, 105, 106, 161

Early Republican Architecture   31
emergency   xi, 1–6, 10–16, 21–5, 28, 31–6, 43, 44, 46, 47, 60–2, 69–75, 83, 85, 93, 99, 101, 114–17, 119, 127, 131, 137–41, 153, 159–62, 164, 166, 167, 177–9, 189–95, 197
  emergency rule   2, 5, 10, 11, 13, 71, 84
emplacement   144–7
environment   1, 2, 6, 11, 15, 26, 28, 32, 34, 70, 75, 83, 85, 100, 164, 165, 178
EU membership   162, 178
everyday life   15, 16, 142, 143, 147, 153

evidence   4, 16, 23, 45, 94, 102–4, 106, 132, 150
exception (including state of exception)   2, 3, 36, 46, 61, 117, 139, 140, 142, 152, 153, 189, 190, 193
expropriation   33, 70, 77, 82, 145, 172, 175, 177

Fatih Municipality   166, 173–7
FeBayDer   175–7
Fener   15, 16, 159, 160, 167–78
festival   15, 137, 138, 140, 142–5, 148–53, 192, 193
Foreigners and International Protection Law   113, 114, 119, 131
forensic   91–5, 102, 104, 105
  Forensic Architecture   102, 104, 105
forum   13, 14, 89, 93–5, 104, 105, 195
Foucault, Michel   xi, 89, 93, 97, 98, 104, 196

gecekondu (Turkish for informal/squatter housing)   76, 77
genocide   7, 47, 52, 54, 58, 62
ghost   117, 118
Gökçeada   5, 14, 15, 137, 146, 192
governance   4, 26, 74, 83, 161, 165
guest   14, 53, 115–19, 121, 123, 124, 126, 127, 131, 132

Haemon   98, 103, 104
Hagia Sophia   25–8
  Hagia Sophia Mosque   25
  Hagia Sophia Museum   12, 22, 27
heritage   xiii, 2, 6, 10–12, 15, 16, 21–5, 27–35, 43–7, 50, 55–8, 61, 62, 70, 76, 80, 83–5, 101, 127, 139, 160–3, 165, 167, 173–5, 177–9, 193
  heritage-making   21, 23–5, 34–6
  heritage protection   11, 84
hospitality   113, 115–18, 121–9, 131–3
  unconditional hospitality   118
  universal hospitality   116, 117, 121, 127, 128, 131, 132
host   14, 113, 116–19, 121, 123, 126, 127, 131–3
hostage   117, 118, 121, 132
hostility   56, 115, 117, 118, 131
human rights   3, 83, 89, 91, 93–5, 101, 105, 114, 116, 118

Imbrian   144, 145, 148–53
Imbros   5, 14, 15, 137–53
infrastructure   70, 122, 125, 131, 145, 147, 170, 172
island   14, 15, 25, 59, 126, 137–40, 142–53
İznik   27, 28

junta   89, 91, 94, 99

Kurdish   5, 6, 9, 10, 13, 59, 69, 70, 72, 78–81, 83, 99–101, 121, 161, 162
Kurdistan   5–7, 69–72, 75, 79, 81, 84

law   3, 23, 27, 28, 30, 32, 43, 49, 52, 59, 72, 80, 90, 92, 96–9, 101, 104, 114, 116–19, 121, 126, 128, 131, 132, 146, 161, 163–5, 174, 177–9, 189, 191
local authorities   78, 101, 142, 149, 161, 163, 165

Mesopotamia   75
Metropolitan Municipality   26, 69, 76, 77, 164–6, 176, 177
migration   7, 14, 55, 113–19, 121, 127, 129, 131–3, 146, 170–2, 195
minorities (including minority)   6, 12, 15, 49, 59, 137, 138, 140, 143, 145, 171, 195
Municipalities Bank   32

nation state   7, 12, 14, 15, 25, 31, 46, 114–19, 121, 132, 139, 146
neoliberal   3, 10, 33, 160, 162, 172, 178, 190, 191, 194
  neoliberalism   xiii, 162, 165, 174
  neoliberal state   161, 162
Neo-Ottomanist (including Neo-Ottomanist heritage policies)   12, 21, 22, 24, 25, 27, 28, 31–5
non-Muslim   6, 7, 12, 13, 15, 43–7, 49, 54, 55, 57–62, 71, 84, 171
normal   15, 61, 126, 137–41, 150, 153, 159, 163, 189, 191–5
  normalcy   2, 4, 11, 13, 15, 16, 43, 46, 60, 61, 69–73, 75, 83, 85, 137–43, 148–50, 152, 153, 190–5, 197

Oedipus   95, 96, 98
official practices of heritage   22–5

Orthodox Christian 148, 150, 151
Ottoman 6, 17, 21, 25–30, 35, 49, 52, 54, 59, 72, 75, 120, 139, 169, 170, 172

Panagia 145, 148, 150–3
panigyri 148, 151, 152
parrhesia 13, 89–91, 93, 94, 97, 99, 103, 104, 196
parrhesiastes 89–91, 94, 95, 98, 103, 104
Pious foundations 26–8
polis 13, 14, 89–91, 93, 94, 96, 97, 101, 105, 195
Povinelli, Elizabeth 74
preservation 34, 46, 76, 80, 84, 160, 162, 163, 167, 178

reconstruction 21, 32, 80, 164
refugee 9, 10, 12, 14, 72, 84, 113, 119, 131, 167
renewal 6, 15, 16, 30, 33, 59, 76, 163–5, 174, 177, 178
   Renewal Act 163, 165, 174, 177
   renewal project 30, 31, 77, 165, 167, 172, 174–7
   renewal site 165–8, 174
representation 13, 45, 103, 114, 117, 125, 127, 128, 131–3, 141, 149, 160
risk (including disaster risk) 8, 24, 32–4, 43, 44, 46, 47, 51, 53, 55, 60–2, 75, 90, 132, 161, 164, 165, 191
   risky area (including disaster risk area) 33, 35, 78–80, 82
Rum (including Roum) 15, 43, 49–51, 56, 57, 59, 137, 138, 140, 142–8, 151, 170, 171

Saraçoğlu Quarter 12, 22, 31–5
secular 26, 28, 35, 144, 151
Settlement Law 146
solidarity 14, 115, 127, 131–3, 159, 160, 191

squatting/squatter housing (including *gecekondu*) 59, 76, 77
Syriac 43, 47, 52, 57, 59
Syria War (including Syrian migrants/refugees) 9, 12, 119, 121, 127, 167

Tahir Elçi 83, 101, 102, 105, 106
temporality 8, 9, 34, 73, 195
tent 122–5
threshold 118, 123, 124, 126, 189, 196
TOKİ (Turkey's centrally governed Housing Development Administration) 7, 33, 76–8, 81, 164, 165, 167
Trabzon 27, 28
tragedy 95, 96, 103
truth 13, 14, 89–99, 103–5

uncertainty 12, 14, 22–5, 27–9, 31, 32, 34, 35, 44, 61, 114–16, 118, 124, 127, 131–3
UNESCO 101, 173
   UNESCO World Heritage Site 70, 161, 163, 173
urban xi, xiii, 6–14, 16, 21, 22, 25, 30–3, 72, 75, 76, 78, 80, 83, 84, 100, 119, 125, 132, 159–65, 167–72, 175, 176, 178, 190, 193
   urban conservation 163, 178, 179
   urban renewal 16, 31, 76, 77, 164, 167, 172, 174, 177
   urban transformation 8, 75, 76, 79, 81, 82, 164, 169
   urban warfare 10, 12, 13, 16, 100

violence xiii, 1, 4, 6, 7, 9, 13, 14, 60, 71, 75, 100, 101, 104, 113, 127, 132, 171

war xiii, 7, 9, 13, 14, 29, 43, 70, 79, 81, 91–4, 100, 119–21, 127, 139, 177, 189

www.ingramcontent.com/pod-product-compliance
Lightning Source LLC
Chambersburg PA
CBHW062215300426
44115CB00012BA/2071